The Miracle of
DUNKIRK

The Miracle of
DUNKIRK

Walter Lord

ALLEN LANE

ALLEN LANE
Penguin Books Ltd
536 King's Road
London SW10 0UH

First published in the U.S.A. by The Viking Press 1982
First published in Great Britain by Allen Lane 1983

ISBN 0 7139 1211 1

Leaflet on page 75 courtesy
Imperial War Museum.

Drawing of the eastern mole on page 136
courtesy Lieutenant Robin Bill.

Maps by Paul J. Pugliese.

Set in Videocomp Baskerville
Printed in the United States of America

FOR EDDIE RESOR

Contents

Maps

Foreword

There seemed to be no escape. On May 24, 1940, some 400,000 Allied troops lay pinned against the coast of Flanders near the French port of Dunkirk. Hitler's advancing tanks were only ten miles away. There was virtually nothing in between.

Yet the trapped army was saved. By June 4—just eleven days later—over 338,000 men had been evacuated safely to England in one of the great rescues of all time. It was a crucial turning point in World War II.

"So long as the English tongue survives," proclaimed the *New York Times*, "the word Dunkerque will be spoken with reverence." Hyperbole, perhaps, but certainly the word—the event—has lived on. To the British, Dunkirk symbolizes a generosity of spirit, a willingness to sacrifice for the common good. To Americans, it has come to mean *Mrs. Miniver*, little ships, *The Snow Goose*, escape by sea. To the French, it suggests bitter defeat; to the Germans, opportunity forever lost.

There's an element of truth in all these images, but they fail to go to the heart of the matter. It is customary to look upon Dunkirk as a series of days. Actually, it should be regarded as a series of crises. Each crisis was solved, only to be replaced by another, with the pattern repeated again and again. It was the collective refusal of men to be discouraged by this relentless sequence that is important.

Seen in this light, Dunkirk remains, above all, a stirring reminder of man's ability to rise to the occasion, to improvise, to overcome obstacles. It is, in short, a lasting monument to the unquenchable resilience of the human spirit.

The Miracle of
DUNKIRK

1

The Closing Trap

Every man had his own special moment when he first knew that something was wrong. For RAF Group Captain R.C.M. Collard, it was the evening of May 14, 1940, in the market town of Vervins in northeastern France.

Five days had passed since "the balloon went up," as the British liked to refer to the sudden German assault in the west. The situation was obscure, and Collard had come down from British General Headquarters in Arras to confer with the staff of General André-Georges Corap, whose French Ninth Army was holding the River Meuse to the south.

Such meetings were perfectly normal between the two Allies, but there was nothing normal about the scene tonight. Corap's headquarters had simply vanished. No sign of the General or his staff. Only two exhausted French officers were in the building, crouched over a hurricane lamp . . . waiting, they said, to be captured.

Sapper E. N. Grimmer's moment of awareness came as the 216th Field Company, Royal Engineers, tramped across the French countryside, presumably toward the front. Then he noticed a bridge being prepared for demolition. "When you're advancing," he mused, "you don't blow bridges." Lance Corporal

E. S. Wright had a ruder awakening: he had gone to Arras to collect his wireless unit's weekly mail. A motorcycle with sidecar whizzed past, and Wright did a classic double take. He suddenly realized the motorcycle was German.

For Winston Churchill, the new British Prime Minister, the moment was 7:30 a.m., May 15, as he lay sleeping in his quarters at Admiralty House, London. The bedside phone rang; it was French Premier Paul Reynaud. "We have been defeated," Reynaud blurted in English.

A non-plussed silence, as Churchill tried to collect himself.

"We are beaten"; Reynaud went on, "we have lost the battle."

"Surely it can't have happened so soon?" Churchill finally managed to say.

"The front is broken near Sedan; they are pouring through in great numbers with tanks and armored cars."

Churchill did his best to soothe the man—reminded him of the dark days in 1918 when all turned out well in the end—but Reynaud remained distraught. He ended as he had begun: "We are defeated; we have lost the battle."

The crisis was so grave—and so little could be grasped over the phone—that on the 16th Churchill flew to Paris to see things for himself. At the Quai d'Orsay he found "utter dejection" on every face; in the garden elderly clerks were already burning the files.

It seemed incredible. Since 1918 the French Army had been generally regarded as the finest in the world. With the rearmament of Germany under Adolf Hitler, there was obviously a new military power in Europe, but still, her leaders were untested and her weapons smacked of gimmickry. When the Third Reich swallowed one Central European country after another, this was attributed to bluff and bluster. When war finally did break out in 1939 and Poland fell in three weeks, this was written off as something that could happen to Poles—but not to the West. When Denmark and Norway went in April 1940, this seemed just an underhanded trick; it could be rectified later.

Then after eight months of quiet—"the phony war"—on the 10th of May, Hitler suddenly struck at Holland, Belgium, and Luxembourg. Convinced that the attack was a replay of 1914, the Supreme Allied Commander, General Maurice Gamelin, rushed his northern armies—including the British Expeditionary Force—to the rescue.

But Gamelin had miscalculated. It was not 1914 all over again. Instead of a great sweep through Flanders, the main German thrust was farther south, through the "impenetrable" Ardennes Forest. This was said to be poor tank country, and the French hadn't even bothered to extend the supposedly impenetrable Maginot Line to cover it.

Another miscalculation. While General Colonel Fedor von Bock's Army Group B tied up the Allies in Belgium, General Colonel Gerd von Rundstedt's Army Group A came crashing through the Ardennes. Spearheaded by 1,806 tanks and supported by 325 Stuka dive bombers, Rundstedt's columns stormed across the River Meuse and now were knifing through the French countryside.

General Corap's Ninth Army was the luckless force that took the brunt. Composed mainly of second-class troops, it quickly collapsed. Here and there die-hard units tried to make a stand, only to discover that their antitank guns were worthless. One junior officer ended up at the Le Mans railroad station, where he committed suicide after penning a postcard to Premier Reynaud: "I am killing myself, Mr. President, to let you know that all my men were brave, but one cannot send men to fight tanks with rifles."

It was the same story with part of General Charles Huntziger's Second Army at Sedan, fifty miles farther south. As the German tanks approached, the men of the 71st Division turned their helmets around—a rallying sign of the Communists—and bolted for the rear.

Three brigades of French tanks tried to stem the tide, but never had a chance. One brigade ran out of gas; another was caught de-training in a railroad yard; the third was sprinkled in small packets along the front, where it was gobbled up piecemeal.

Now the panzers were in the clear—nothing to stop them. Shortly after 7:00 a.m., May 20, two divisions of General Heinz Guderian's crack XIX Corps began rolling west from Péronne. By 10:00 they were clanking through the town of Albert, where

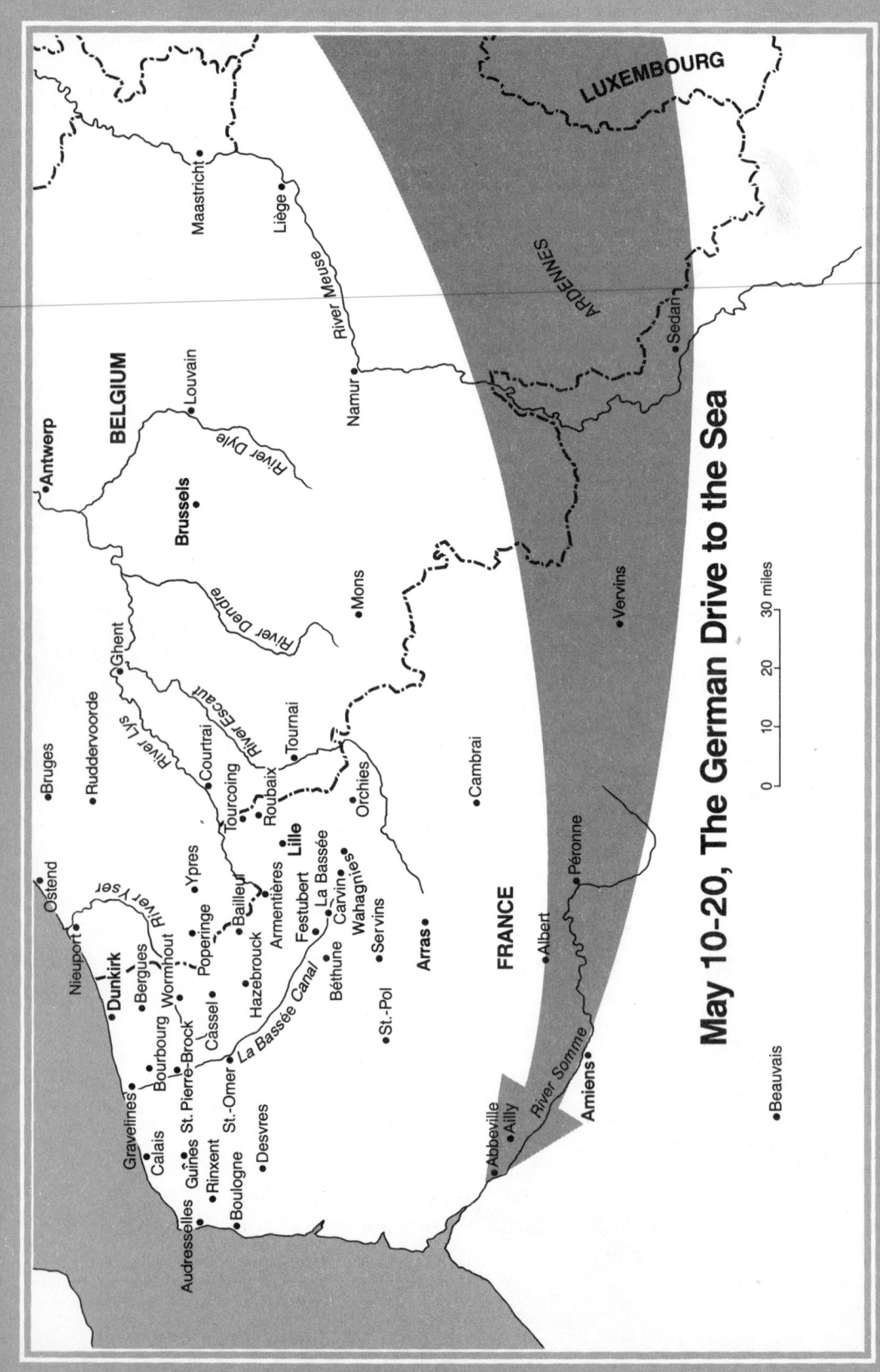

May 10-20, The German Drive to the Sea

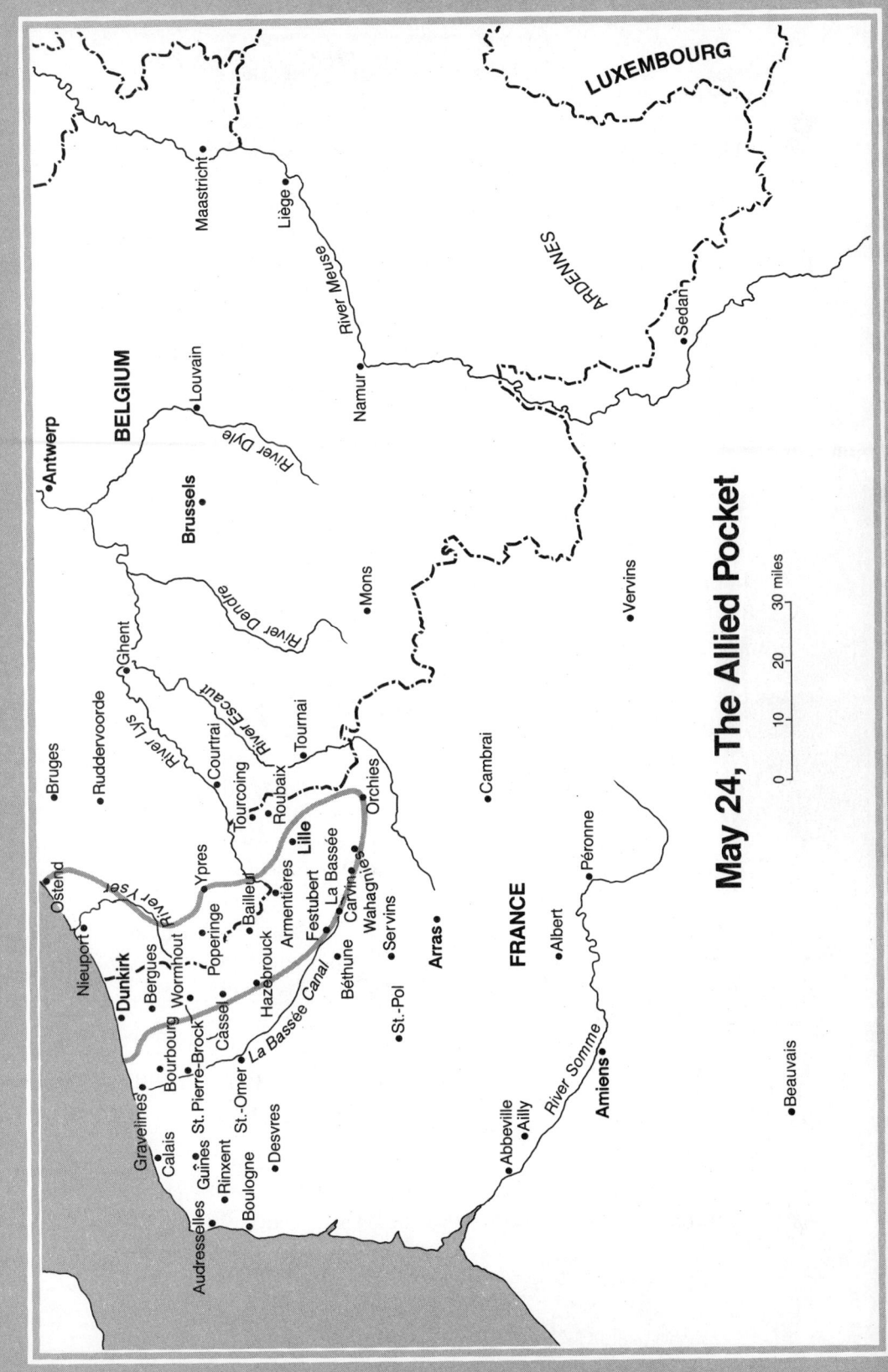

May 24, The Allied Pocket

a party of untrained English Territorials tried to hold them with a barricade of cardboard boxes.... 11:00, they reached Hédauville, where they captured a British battery equipped with only training shells ... noon, the 1st Panzer Division had Amiens, where Guderian took a moment to savor the towers of the lovely cathedral.

The 2nd Panzer Division rolled on. By 4:00 p.m. they had Beauquesne, where they captured a depot containing the BEF's entire supply of maps. And finally, at 9:10, they reached Abbeville and then the sea. In one massive stroke they had come 40 miles in fourteen hours, cutting the Allied forces in two. The BEF, two French armies, and all the Belgians—nearly a million men—were now sealed in Flanders, pinned against the sea, ready for plucking.

Deep in Belgium the British front-line troops had no way of knowing what had happened on their flank or to the rear. They only knew that they were successfully holding the Germans facing them on the River Dyle. On May 14 (the day Rundstedt routed Corap), Lance Bombardier Noel Watkin of the Royal Artillery heard rumors of a great Allied victory. That night he had nothing but good news for the diary he surreptitiously kept:

> Enemy retreat 6½ miles. Very little doing till the evening. We fire on S.O.S. lines and prevent the Huns crossing the River Dyle. Many Germans are killed and taken prisoner. 27,000 Germans killed (official).

Next day was different. As the French collapsed to the south, the Germans surged into the gap. Soon shells were unaccountably pouring into the British flank. That evening a bewildered Noel Watkin could only write:

> What a day! We are due to retreat at 10:30 p.m., and as we do, we get heavy shellfire, and we thank God we are all safe. . . . Except for the shock I am o.k.

Most of the BEF were equally mystified by the sudden change in fortune. Throughout the 16th and 17th, the troops began to pull back all along the line; more and more guns were shifted to face south and southwest. On the 18th, when the 2nd Essex was ordered to man the La Bassée Canal, facing *south*, the battalion commander Major Wilson was incredulous—wasn't the enemy supposed to be to the east? "I can't understand it, sir," agreed Captain Long Price, just back from brigade headquarters, "but those are our orders."

One man who could understand it very well was the architect of these stop-gap measures: General the Viscount Gort, Commander-in-Chief of the British Expeditionary Force. A big burly man of 53, Lord Gort was no strategist—he was happy to follow the French lead on such matters—but he had certain soldierly virtues that came in handy at a time like this. He was a great fighter—had won the Victoria Cross storming the Hindenburg Line in 1918—and he was completely unflappable.

General Alphonse-Joseph Georges, his French superior, might be in tears by now, but never Gort. He methodically turned to the job of protecting his exposed flank and pulling his army back. His trained combat divisions were tied up fighting the Germans to the east. To meet the new threat to the south and the west, he improvised a series of scratch forces, composed of miscellaneous units borrowed from here and there. Gort appointed his intelligence chief, Major-General Noel Mason-MacFarlane, as the commander of one of these groups, appropriately called MACFORCE. Mason-MacFarlane was an able leader, but the main effect of his assignment was to raise havoc with the intelligence set-up at GHQ in Arras. That didn't seem to bother Gort; always the fighting man, he had little use for staff officers anyway.

Meanwhile, using a timetable worked out by the French, on the evening of May 16 he began pulling his front-line troops back from the Dyle. The new line was to be the River Escaut,* 60 miles to the rear, the retreat to be carried out in three stages.

Crack units like the 2nd Coldstream Guards carried out their orders meticulously—generations of tradition saw to that. For others, these instructions—so precise on paper—didn't neces-

---

*This book uses the geographical names that were most common at the time. Today the River Escaut is generally known as the Scheldt; the town of La Panne has become De Panne.

sarily work out in fact. Dispatch riders carrying the orders couldn't always find the right headquarters. Some regiments started late. Others lost their way in the dark. Others made the wrong turn. Others ran into hopeless traffic jams. Still others never got the orders at all.

The 32nd Field Regiment, Royal Artillery, was hurrying toward the Dyle, unaware of any retreat, when word came to take position in a field some miles short of the river. Gunner R. Shattock was told to take one of the unit's trucks and get some rations. This he did, but by the time he got back, the whole regiment had vanished. After a night of worry, he set out for the main road, hoping to find at least a trace of somebody he knew.

He was immediately swamped by a wave of running men. "Come on, get going," they shouted; "the Jerries have broken through, and it's every man for himself." They swarmed over the truck, piling on the roof, the hood, the fenders.

Shattock headed west, flowing with the tide. At first he made good mileage, but gradually the drive became a nightmare. Stuka dive bombers poured out of a dazzling sun. They had let the British columns advance deep into Belgium without interference, but the trip back was different. With toy whistles attached to both planes and bombs (the Germans called them the "trumpets of Jericho"), they screeched down in an orgy of killing and terror. Pulling out of their dives, they flew along the roads at car-top height, strafing for good measure.

The hot, still air filled with black smoke and the smell of burning rubber; the traffic slowed to a crawl. Weeping refugees swarmed among the dazed troops. Discarded hand-carts, bicycles, baby carriages, burnt-out family cars lay cluttered along the roadside.

Finally the traffic stopped altogether. Shattock's passengers, seeing they could make better time on foot, abandoned him, and soon he sat alone in his stalled truck. He climbed onto the roof, but could see no way out. Traffic had piled up behind as well as ahead, and deep ditches on either side of the road ruled out any cross-country escape. He was simply glued in place on this blazing hot, smoky May afternoon. He had never felt so alone and helpless. Before, there had always been someone to give orders. Here, there was no one.

Actually, he could not have been very far from his own regiment, which had disappeared so mysteriously the previous day. They had pulled out when a battery observer, sent up a telegraph pole, reported "a lot of soldiers with coal scuttles on their heads a couple of fields away."

To Lance Bombardier H. E. Gentry, it was the chariot race in *Ben-Hur* all over again. The regiment hooked up their guns . . . roared out of the meadow . . . and swung wildly onto the main road, heading back the way they had come.

It was dark by the time they stopped briefly to fire off all their ammunition—at extreme range and at no particular target, it seemed. Then on again into the night. Gentry hadn't the remotest idea where they were going; it was just a case of follow the leader.

Midnight, they stopped again. It was raining now, and the exhausted men huddled around a low-burning fire, munching stew and trading stories of the hell they had been through.

Dawn, the rain stopped, and they were off again into another beautiful day. A German Fieseler Storch observation plane appeared, flying low, hovering over them, clearly unafraid of any interference. The men of the 32nd understood: they hadn't seen a sign of the RAF since the campaign began. From past experience, they also knew that rifles were useless. In exasperation Gentry blazed away anyhow, but he knew that the real time to worry was when the Storch *left*.

When it finally did veer off, a dozen bombers appeared from the right. The 32nd came to a jolting stop at the edge of a village, and the shout went up, "Disperse—take cover!" Gentry ran into a farmyard, deep in mud and slime; he dived into a hayrick as the planes began unloading. Bedlam, capped by one particularly awesome *swoosh*, and the ground shook like jelly. Then the silence of a cemetery.

Gentry crept out. There, stuck in the slime a few feet away, was a huge unexploded bomb. It was about the size of a household refrigerator, shaped like a cigar, with its tail fins sticking up. A large pig slowly waddled across the barnyard and began licking it.

On again. To Gentry, the 32nd seemed to be going around in circles. They always seemed to be lost, with no set idea where they were supposed to be or where they were going. Occasionally they would stop, fire off a few rounds (he never knew the target), and then, on their way again. His mind drifted back to last winter in Lille, where he and his friends would go to their favorite café and sing "Run Rabbit Run." Now, he ruefully thought, We are the rabbits and are we running!

At the River Dendre the 32nd once again got ready to go into action. Traffic was particularly bad here—few crossings and everyone trying to get over. Gentry noticed a number of motorcycles with sidecars moving into a field on the left. The soldiers in the sidecars jumped out and began spraying the 32nd with machine guns.

Jerry had arrived. The British gunners scrambled into action, firing over open sights, and for five minutes it was a rousing brawl. Finally they drove the motorcyclists off, but there was no time to celebrate: a squadron of German fighters swooped down from out of the sun and began strafing the road.

As if this wasn't enough, word spread of a new peril. Enemy troops masquerading as refugees were said to be infiltrating the lines. From now on, the orders ran, all women were to be challenged by rifle. What next? wondered Lance Bombardier Gentry; Germans in drag!

Fear of Fifth Columnists spread like an epidemic. Everyone had his favorite story of German paratroopers dressed as priests and nuns. The men of one Royal Signals maintenance unit told how two "monks" visited their quarters just before a heavy bombing attack. Others warned of enemy agents, disguised as Military Police, deliberately misdirecting convoys. There were countless tales of talented "farmers" who cut signs in corn and wheat fields pointing to choice targets. Usually the device was an arrow; sometimes a heart; and in one instance the III Corps fig leaf emblem.

The Signals unit attached to II Corps headquarters had been warned that the Germans were dropping spies dressed as nuns, clergy, and students, so they were especially on their guard as they pulled off the main road for a little rest one dark night during the retreat. Dawn was just breaking when they were awakened by the sentry's shouts. He reported a figure trailing a parachute lurking among some trees. After two challenges got no response, the section sergeant ordered the sentry and Signalman E. A. Salisbury to open fire. The figure crumpled, and the two men ran up to see what they had hit. It turned out to be a civilian in a gray velvet suit, clutching not a parachute but an ordinary white blanket. He had died instantly and carried no identification.

The sergeant muttered something about one less Boche in the world, and the unit was soon on the road again. It was only later that Salisbury learned the truth: an insane asylum at Louvain had just released all its inmates, and one of them was the man he had shot. The incident left Salisbury heartsick, and forty years later he still worried about it.

There were, of course, cases of real Fifth Column activity. Both the 1st Coldstream and the 2nd Gloucesters, for instance, were harassed by sniper fire. But for the most part the "nuns" were really nuns, and the priests were genuine clerics whose odd behavior could be explained by pure fright. Usually the Military Police who misdirected traffic were equally genuine— just a little mixed up in their work.

Yet who could know this at the time? Everyone was suspicious of everyone else, and Bombardier Arthur May found that life could be deadly dangerous for a straggler. He and two mates had been separated from their howitzer battery. They heard it had pulled back to the Belgian town of Tournai on the Escaut, and now they were trying to catch up with it. As they drove the company truck along various back roads, they were stopped and interrogated again and again by the British rear guard, all of whom seemed to have itchy trigger-fingers.

Finally they did reach Tournai, but their troubles weren't over. A sergeant and two privates, bayonets fixed, made them destroy their truck. Then they were escorted across the last remaining bridge over the Escaut, put in the charge of three more tough-talking riflemen, and marched to a farmhouse on the edge of town. Here they were split up and put through still another interrogation.

Cleared at last, the three men searched two more hours before they finally found their battery. Nobody wanted to tell them anything, and the few directions they pried loose were intentionally misleading. May found it hard to believe that all these unfriendly chaps were his own comrades-in-arms.

But it was so; and more than that, these grim, suspicious rear-guard units were all that stood between the confused mass of retreating troops and the advancing Germans. Some, like the Coldstream and the Grenadiers, were Guards regiments of legendary discipline. Others, like the 5th Northamptons and the 2nd Hampshires, were less famous but no less professional. The standard routine was to dig in behind some canal or river, usually overnight, hold off the German advance during the day with artillery and machine guns, then pull back to the next canal or river and repeat the formula.

They were as efficient as machines, but no machines could be so tired. Digging, fighting, falling back; day after day there was never time to sleep. The 1st East Surreys finally invented a way to doze a little on the march. By linking arms, two outside men could walk a man between them as he slept. From time to time they'd switch places with one another.

When Lieutenant James M. Langley of the 2nd Coldstream was put in charge of the bridge across the Escaut at Pecq, the Company commander, Major Angus McCorquodale, ordered a sergeant to stand by and shoot Langley if he ever tried to sit or lie down. Langley's job was to blow the bridge when the Germans arrived, and McCorquodale explained to him, "The moment you sit or lie down, you will go to sleep, and *that* you are not going to do."

The enemy advance was often no more than ten or fifteen minutes away, but by May 23 most of the troops somehow got back to the French frontier, the starting point of their optimistic plunge into Belgium only two weeks earlier. The first emotion was relief, but close behind came shame. They all remembered the cheers, the flowers, the wine that had greeted them; now they dreaded the reproachful stares as they scrambled back through the rubble of each burned-out town.

With the 1st East Surrey's return to France, 2nd Lieutenant R. C. Taylor was ordered to go to Lille to pick up some stores. Lille lay far to the rear of the battalion's position, and Taylor expected to find the assignment a peaceful change from the hell he had been through in Belgium. To his amazement, the farther back he drove, the heavier grew the sound of battle. It finally dawned on him that the Germans lay not only to the east of the BEF, but to the south and west as well. They were practically surrounded.

The scratch forces that General Gort had thrown together to cover his exposed flank and rear were desperately hanging on. South of Arras, the inexperienced 23rd Division faced General Major Erwin Rommel's tanks without a single antitank gun. At Saint Pol a mobile bath unit struggled to hold off the 6th Panzer Division. At Steenbecque the 9th Royal Northumberland Fusiliers grimly bided their time. A scantily trained Territorial battalion, they had been building an airfield near Lille when "the balloon went up." Now they were part of an improvised defense unit called POLFORCE. They had no instructions, only knew that their commanding officer had vanished.

At this point Captain Tufton Beamish, the only regular army officer in the battalion, assumed command. Somehow he rallied the men, dug them into good positions, placed his guns well, and managed to hold off the Germans for 48 important hours.

Things were usually not that tidy. Private Bill Stratton, serving in a troop-carrying unit, felt he was aimlessly driving all over northeastern France. One evening the lorries were parked in a tree-lined field just outside the town of Saint-Omer. Suddenly some excited Frenchmen came pouring down the road shouting "*Les Boches! Les Boches!*" A hastily dispatched patrol returned with the disquieting news that German tanks were approaching, about ten minutes away.

The men stood to, armed only with a few Boyes antitank rifles. This weapon did little against tanks but had such a kick it was said to have dislocated the shoulder of the inventor. Orders were not to fire until the word was given.

Anxious moments, then the unmistakable rumble of engines and treads. Louder and louder, until—unbelievably—*there they were*, a column of tanks and motorized infantry clanking along the road right by the field where Stratton crouched. The trees apparently screened the lorries, for the tanks took no notice of them, and the British never attracted attention by opening fire. Finally they were gone; the rumbling died away; and the troop-carrier commander began studying his map, searching for some route back that might avoid another such heart-stopping experience.

It was so easy to be cut off, lost—or forgotten. Sapper Joe Coles belonged to an engineering company that normally serviced concrete mixers but was now stuffed into MACFORCE east of Arras. They had no rations or water and were trying to milk some cows when Coles was posted off with a sergeant to repair a pumping station near the town of Orchies.

By the following evening the two men had the pumps going again and decided to go into Orchies, since they still had no rations, nor even a blanket. The place turned out to be a ghost town—citizens, defending garrison, everybody had vanished.

They did find a supply depot of the Navy, Army and Air Force Institute. British servicemen always regarded NAAFI as the ministering angel for all their needs, but even in his wildest dreams Coles never imagined anything like this. Here, too, all the staff was gone, but the shelves were packed with every conceivable delicacy.

A stretcher was found and loaded with cigarettes, whisky, gin, and two deck chairs. Back at the pumping station, Coles and the sergeant mixed themselves a couple of generous drinks and settled down in the deck chairs for their best sleep in days.

Next morning, still no orders; still no traffic on the roads. It was now clear that they had been left behind and forgotten. Later in the day they spotted four French soldiers wandering around the farm next door. The poilus had lost their unit too, and on the strength of this bond, Coles dipped into his NAAFI hoard and gave them a 50-pack of cigarettes. Overwhelmed, they reciprocated with a small cooked chicken. For Coles and the sergeant it was their first meal in days, and although they didn't know it yet, it would also be their last in France.

At the moment they thought only about getting away from the pumping station. The disappearance of everybody could only mean they were in no-man's-land. By agreement, Coles went down to the main road and began waiting on the off-chance that some rear-guard vehicle might happen by. It was a long shot, but it paid off when a lone British Tommy on a motorcycle came boiling along. Coles flagged him down, and the Tommy promised to get help from a nearby engineering unit, also lost and forgotten. Within twenty minutes a truck swerved into the pumping station yard, scooped up Coles and his companion, and sped north toward relative safety and the hope, at least, of better communications.

The communications breakdown was worst in the west—an

inevitable result of slapping together those makeshift defense units—but the problem was acute everywhere. From the start of the war the French high command had rejected wireless. Anybody could pick signals out of the air, the argument ran. The telephone was secure. This meant stringing miles and miles of cable, and often depending on overloaded civilian circuits—but at least the Boches wouldn't be listening.

Lord Gort cheerfully went along. Once again, the French were the masters of war; they had studied it all out, and if they said the telephone was best, the BEF would comply. Besides, the French had 90 divisions; he had only ten.

Then May, and the test of battle itself. Some telephone lines were quickly chewed up by Rundstedt's tanks. Others were inadvertently cut by Allied units moving here and there. Other breaks occurred as various headquarters moved about. Gort's Command Post alone shifted seven times in ten days. The exhausted signalmen couldn't possibly string lines fast enough.

After May 17 Gort no longer had any direct link with Belgian headquarters on his left, with French First Army on his right, or with his immediate superior General Georges to the rear. Nor were orders getting through to most of his own commanders down the line. At Arras his acting Operations Officer, Lieutenant-Colonel the Viscount Bridgeman, soon decided it was hopeless to rely on GHQ. Living on a diet of chocolate and whisky, he simply did what he thought was best.

The only reliable way to communicate was by personal visit or by using dispatch riders on motorcycle. Driving through the countryside, the jaunty commander of 3rd Division, Major-General Bernard Montgomery, would jam a message on the end of his walking stick and hold it out the car window. Here it would be plucked off by his bodyguard, Sergeant Arthur Elkin, riding up on a motorcycle.

Elkin would then scoot off to find the addressee. But it was a tricky business, driving along strange roads looking for units constantly on the move. Once he rode up to three soldiers sitting on a curb, hoping to get some directions. As he approached, one of the soldiers put on his helmet, and Elkin realized just in time that they were German.

To Gort, the communications breakdown was one more item

in a growing catalogue of complaints against the French. Gamelin was a forlorn cipher. General Georges seemed in a daze. General Gaston Billotte, commanding the French First Army Group, was meant to coordinate but didn't. Gort had received no written instructions from him since the campaign began.

The French troops along the coast and to the south seemed totally demoralized. Their horse-drawn artillery and transport cluttered the roads, causing huge traffic jams and angry exchanges. More than one confrontation was settled at pistol-point. Perhaps because he had gone along with the French so loyally for so long, Gort was now doubly disillusioned.

It's hard to say when the idea of evacuation dawned on him, but the moment may well have come around midnight, May 18. This was when General Billotte finally paid his first visit to Gort's Command Post, currently in Wahagnies, a small French town south of Lille. Normally a big, bluff, hearty man, Billotte seemed weary and deflated as he unfolded a map showing the latest French estimate of the situation. Nine panzer divisions had been identified sweeping west toward Amiens and Abbeville—with no French units blocking their way.

Billotte talked about taking countermeasures, but it was easy to see that his heart was not in it, and he left his hosts convinced that French resistance was collapsing. Since the enemy now blocked any retreat to the west or south, it appeared that the only alternative was to head north for the English Channel.

At 6:00 a.m., May 19, six of Gort's senior officers met to begin planning the retreat. It turned out that the Deputy Chief of Staff, Brigadier Sir Oliver Leese, had already been doing some thinking; he had roughed out a scheme for the entire BEF to form a hollow square and move en masse to Dunkirk, the nearest French port.

But this assumed that the army was already surrounded, and it hadn't come to that. What was needed was a general pulling back, and as a first step GHQ at Arras closed down, with part of the staff going to Boulogne on the coast and the rest to Hazebrouck, 33 miles closer to the sea. For the moment the Command Post would remain at Wahagnies.

At 11:30 the Chief of Staff, Lieutenant-General H. R. Pownall, telephoned the War Office in London and broke the news to the Director of Military Operations and Plans, Major-General R. H. Dewing. If the French could not stabilize the front south of the BEF, Pownall warned, Gort had decided to pull back toward Dunkirk.

In London it was a serenely beautiful Sunday, and the elegant Secretary for War, Anthony Eden, was about to join Foreign Secretary Lord Halifax for a quiet lunch, when he received an urgent call to see General Sir Edmund Ironside, Chief of the Imperial General Staff. Ironside, a hulking, heavy-footed man (inevitably nicknamed "Tiny"), was appalled by Gort's proposed move to Dunkirk. It would be a trap, he declared.

Ironside's consternation was evident when at 1:15 p.m. a new call came in from Pownall. Dewing, again on the London end of the line, suggested that Gort was too gloomy, that the French might not be as badly off as he feared. In any case, why not head for Boulogne or Calais, where air cover would be better, instead of Dunkirk? "It's a case of the hare and the tortoise," Pownall answered dryly, "and a very simple calculation will show that the hare would win the race."

Dewing now put forward Ironside's pet solution: the BEF should turn around and fight its way south to the Somme. It was a theory that totally overlooked the fact that most of the British Army was locked in combat with the German forces to the east and couldn't possibly disengage, but Pownall didn't belabor the point. Instead he soothingly reassured Dewing—again and again—that the Dunkirk move was "merely a project in the mind of the C-in-C" . . . that it was just an idea mentioned only to keep London informed of Headquarters' thinking . . . that any decision depended on whether the French could restore their front. Since he was already on record as saying that the French were "melting away," London was understandably not mollified.

· Dewing took another tack: Did Pownall realize that evacuation through Dunkirk was impossible and that maintaining any force there was bound to be precarious? Yes, Pownall answered, he knew that, but heading south would be fatal. The conversation ended with Pownall feeling that Dewing was "singularly stupid and unhelpful," and with the War Office convinced that Gort was about to bottle himself up.

Ironside urged that the War Cabinet be convened at once. Messages went out recalling Churchill and Chamberlain, who had each gone off for a quiet Sunday in the country, and at 4:30 p.m. the Cabinet assembled in what Churchill liked to call "the fish room" of the Admiralty—a chamber festooned with carved dolphins leaping playfully around.

Churchill agreed with Ironside completely: the only hope was to drive south and rejoin the French on the Somme. The others present fell in line. They decided that Ironside should personally go to Gort—this very night—and hand him the War Cabinet's instructions.

At 9:00 p.m. Ironside caught a special train at Victoria Station. . . . At 2:00 a.m. on the 20th he was in Boulogne . . . and at 6:00 he came barging into Gort's Command Post at Wahagnies. With the War Cabinet's order backing him up, he told Gort that his only chance was to turn the army around and head south for Amiens. If Gort agreed, he'd issue the necessary orders at once.

But Gort didn't agree. For some moments, he silently pondered the matter, then explained that the BEF was too tightly locked in combat with the Germans to the east. It simply couldn't turn around and go the other way. If he tried, the enemy would immediately pounce on his rear and tear him to bits.

Then, asked Ironside, would Gort at least spare his two reserve divisions for a push south which might link up with a French force pushing north? Gort thought this might be possible, but first they must coordinate the effort with General Billotte, the overall commander for the area.

Taking Pownall in tow, Ironside now rushed down to French headquarters at Lens. He found Billotte with General Blanchard of the French First Army—both in a state of near collapse. Trembling and shouting at each other, neither had any plans at all. It was too much for the volcanic Ironside. Seizing Billotte by the buttons on his tunic, he literally tried to shake some spirit into the man.

Ultimately it was agreed that some French light mechanized units would join Gort's two reserve divisions in an attack tomorrow south of Arras. They would then meet up with other French forces pushing north. A command change at the very highest level should help: the placid Gamelin had finally been replaced by General Maxime Weygand. He was 73, but said to be full of fire and spirit.

Ironside now returned to London, convinced that once the two forces joined, the way would finally be opened for the BEF to turn around and head south—still his pet solution for everything. Gort remained unconvinced, but he was a good soldier and would try.

At 2:00 p.m., May 21, a scratch force under Major-General H. E. Franklyn began moving south from Arras. If all went well, he should meet the French troops heading north in a couple of days at Cambrai. But all didn't go well. Most of the infantry that Franklyn had on paper were tied up elsewhere. Instead of two divisions he had only two battalions. His 76 tanks were worn out and began to break down. The French support on his left was a day late. The new French armies supposedly moving up from the Somme never materialized. The Germans were tougher than expected. By the end of the day Franklyn's attack had petered out.

This was no surprise to General Gort. He had never had any faith in a drive south. Midafternoon, even before Franklyn ran into trouble, Gort was giving his corps commanders a gloomy picture of the overall situation. Franklyn's attack was brushed off as "a desperate remedy in an attempt to put heart in the French."

Meanwhile, at another meeting of staff officers, Lieutenant-General Sir Douglas Brownrigg, Gort's Adjutant-General, ordered rear GHQ to move from Boulogne to Dunkirk; medical personnel, transport troops, construction battalions, and other "useless mouths" were to head there at once. Later, at still another meeting, a set of neat, precise instructions was issued for the evacuation of these troops: "As vehicles arrive at various evacuation ports, drivers and lorries must be kept, and local transport staffs will have to make arrangements for parking. . . ."

But neither Gort nor anyone from his staff attended the most important conference held this hectic afternoon. The new Supreme Commander General Weygand had flown up from Paris and was now at Ypres, explaining his plan to the commanders of the trapped armies, including Leopold III, King of the Belgians. But Gort couldn't be located. He had once again shifted his Command Post—this time to Prémesques, just west of Lille—and by the time he and Pownall arrived at Ypres, it was too late. Weygand had gone home.

This meant that Gort had to learn about Weygand's plan sec- ondhand from Billotte, which was fortunate, since the British were to play a crucial role. The BEF was to spearhead still an- other drive south, linking up with a new French army group driving north. If the French and Belgians could take over part of his line, Gort agreed to contribute three divisions—but not before May 26.

He agreed, but that didn't make him a true believer. Once back in Prémesques, Pownall immediately summoned the acting Operations Officer, Lieutenant-Colonel Bridgeman. The pur- pose, it turned out, was not to get Bridgeman working on the drive south. Rather, he was to draw up a plan for retiring north . . . for withdrawing the whole BEF to the coast for evacuation.

Bridgeman worked on it all night. Starting with the premise that an evacuation could take place anywhere between Calais and Ostend, he had to find the stretch of coast that could most easily be reached and defended by the three corps that made up the BEF. Which had the best roads leading to it? Which had the best port facilities? Which offered the best chance for air cover? Which had the best terrain for defense? Were there canals that could be used to protect the flanks? Towns that could serve as strong-points? Dykes that could be opened to flood the land and stop those German tanks?

Poring over his maps, he gradually decided that the best bet was the 27-mile stretch of coast between Dunkirk and the Bel- gian town of Ostend. By the morning of May 22 he had covered every detail he could think of. Each corps was allocated the routes it would use, the stretch of coast it would hold.

This same morning Winston Churchill again flew to Paris, hoping to get a clearer picture of the military situation. Rey- naud met him at the airport and whisked him to *Grand Quartier Général* at Vincennes, where the oriental rugs and Moroccan sentries lent an air of unreality that reminded Churchill's mili- tary adviser, General Sir Hastings Ismay, of a scene from *Beau Geste*.

Here the Prime Minister met for the first time Maxime Weygand. Like everyone else, Churchill was impressed by the new
commander's energy and bounce (like an India rubber ball, Ismay decided). Best of all, his military thinking seemed to parallel Churchill's own. As he understood it, the Weygand Plan in
its latest refinement called for eight divisions from the BEF and
the French First Army, with the Belgian cavalry on the right, to
strike southwest the very next day. This force would "join
hands" with the new French army group driving north from
Amiens. That evening Churchill wired Gort his enthusiastic approval.

"The man's mad," was Pownall's reaction when the wire
reached Gort's Command Post next morning, the 23rd. The
military situation was worse than ever: in the west, Rundstedt's
Army Group A was closing in on Boulogne, Calais, and Arras;
to the east, Bock's Army Group B was pushing the lines back to
the French frontier. Churchill, Ironside—all of them—clearly
had no conception of the actual situation. Eight divisions
couldn't possibly disengage . . . the French First Army was a
shambles . . . the Belgian cavalry was nonexistent—or seemed
so.

Worse, Billotte had just been killed in a traffic accident, and
he was the only man with firsthand knowledge of Weygand's
plans. His successor, General Blanchard, seemed a hopeless
pedant, lacking any drive or power of command. With all coordination gone, troops from three different countries couldn't
conceivably be thrown into battle on a few hours' notice.

London and Paris dreamed on. After the meeting with
Churchill, Weygand issued a stirring "Operation Order No. 1."
In it he called on the northern armies to keep the Germans
from reaching the sea—ignoring the fact that they were already
there. On May 24 he announced that a newly formed French
Seventh Army was advancing north and had already retaken
Péronne, Albert, and Amiens. It was all imaginary.

Churchill too lived in a world of fantasy. On the 24th he fired
a barrage of questions at General Ismay. Why couldn't the British troops isolated at Calais simply knife through the German
lines and join Gort? Or why didn't Gort join *them*? Why were
British tanks no match for German guns, but British guns no

match for German tanks? The Prime Minister remained sold on the Weygand Plan, and a wire from Eden urged Gort to cooperate.

The General was doing his best. The attack south—his part of the Weygand Plan—was still on, although the BEF contribution had been cut from three to two divisions. The German pressure in the east left no other course. As an extra precaution, Colonel Bridgeman had also been told to bring his evacuation plan up to date, and the Colonel produced a "second edition" on the morning of the 24th. Finally, Gort asked London to send over the Vice-Chief of the Imperial General Staff, Lieutenant-General Sir John Dill. Until April, Dill had been Gort's I Corps Commander. He was more likely to understand. If he could see for himself how bad things were, he might take back a little sanity to London.

"There is no blinking at the seriousness of situation in Northern Area," Dill reported an hour and ten minutes after his arrival on the morning of May 25. His wire went on to describe the latest German advances. He assured London that the Allied drive south was still on, but added, "In above circumstances, attack referred to above cannot be important affair."

At this point General Blanchard appeared. In a rare moment of optimism he said the French could contribute two or three divisions and 200 tanks to the drive. Dill returned to London in a hopeful mood—he had more faith than Gort in French figures.

This was the last good news of the day. Starting around 7:00 a.m., reports began coming in from the east that the Belgian line was cracking just where it joined the British near Courtrai. If this happened, Bock's Army Group B would soon link up with Rundstedt's Army Group A to the west, and the BEF would be completely cut off from the sea.

There were no Belgian reserves. If anyone were to stop the Germans, it would have to be the British. Yet they too were spread dangerously thin. When Lieutenant-General Alan Brooke, commanding the endangered sector, appealed to headquarters, the most that Gort could spare was a brigade.

Not enough. The news grew worse. The usually reliable 12th Lancers reported that the enemy had punched through the Belgian line on the River Lys. A liaison officer from the 4th Division said that the Belgians on his front had stopped fighting completely; they were just sitting around in cafés.

By 5:00 p.m. Gort had heard enough. He retired alone to his office in Prémesques to ponder the most important decision of his professional career. All he had left were the two divisions he had promised for the attack south tomorrow. If he sent them north to plug the gap in the Belgian line, he would be ignoring his orders; he would be reneging on his understanding with Blanchard; he would be junking not only the Weygand Plan but the thinking of Churchill, Ironside, and all the rest; he would be committing the BEF to a course that could only lead to the coast and a risky evacuation.

On the other hand, if he sent these two divisions south as promised, he would be cut off from the coast and completely encircled. His only chance then would be a last-minute rescue by the French south of the Somme, and he had no faith in that.

His decision: send the troops north. At 6:00 p.m. he canceled the attack south and issued new orders: one of the divisions would join Brooke immediately; the other would follow shortly. Considering Gort's utter lack of faith in the French, it was a decision that should have required perhaps less than the hour it took. The explanation lay in Gort's character. Obedience, duty, loyalty to the team were the mainsprings of his life. To go off on his own this way was an awesome venture.

If anything were needed to steel his resolve, it came in the form of a leather wallet stuffed with papers and a small boot-jack, which had been found in a German staff car shot up by a British patrol. Brooke brought the wallet with him when he arrived at the Command Post for a conference shortly after Gort made his big decision. While he and Gort conferred, the intelligence staff examined the documents in the wallet. These included plans for a major attack at Ypres—confirming the wisdom of Gort's decision to call off the drive south and shift the troops north.

There was only one worry. Could the papers be a "plant"? No, Brooke decided, the bootjack meant they were genuine. Not even Hitler's brightest intelligence agents would have thought of that touch. Far more likely, the wallet belonged to some real staff officer whose boots were too tight.

Gort's decision might not have been so difficult had he

known that London was also going through some soul searching. Dill had returned, and his assessment finally convinced the War Office that Gort's plight was truly desperate. Reports from liaison officers indicated that the French along the Somme couldn't possibly help; the new armies were just beginning to assemble. Later that evening the three service ministers and their chiefs of staff met, and at 4:10 a.m., May 26, War Secretary Eden telegraphed Gort that he now faced a situation in which the safety of the BEF must come first.

> In such conditions only course open to you may be to fight your way back to west where all beaches and ports east of Gravelines will be used for embarkation. Navy would provide fleet of ships and small boats and RAF would give full support. . . . Prime Minister is seeing M. Reynaud tomorrow afternoon when whole situation will be clarified, including attitude of French to the possible move. In meantime it is obvious that you should not discuss the possibility of the move with French or Belgians.

Gort didn't need to be told. When he received Eden's telegram he had just returned from a morning meeting with General Blanchard. There he reviewed his decision to cancel the attack south; he won French approval for a joint withdrawal north; he worked out with Blanchard the lines of retreat, a timetable, a new defense line along the River Lys—but never said a word about evacuation. In fact, as Blanchard saw things, there would be no further retreat. The Lys would be a new defense line covering Dunkirk, giving the Allies a permanent foothold in Flanders.

For Gort, Dunkirk was no foothold; it was a springboard for getting the BEF home. His views were confirmed by a new wire from Eden that arrived late in the afternoon. It declared that there was "no course open to you but to fall back upon the coast. . . . You are now authorized to operate towards the coast forthwith in conjunction with French and Belgian armies."

So evacuation it was to be, but now a new question arose: *Could* they evacuate? By May 26 the BEF and the French First

Army were squeezed into a long, narrow corridor running inland from the sea—60 miles deep and only 15 to 25 miles wide. Most of the British were concentrated around Lille, 43 miles from Dunkirk; the French were still farther south.

On the eastern side of the corridor the trapped Allied forces faced Bock's massive Army Group B; on the western side they faced the tanks and motorized divisions of Rundstedt's Army Group A. His panzers had reached Bourbourg, only ten miles west of Dunkirk. It seemed almost a mathematical certainty that the Germans would get there first.

"Nothing but a miracle can save the BEF now," General Brooke noted in his diary as the pocket took shape on May 23.

"We shall have lost practically all our trained soldiers by the next few days—unless a miracle appears to help us," General Ironside wrote on the 25th.

"I must not conceal from you," Gort wired Anthony Eden on the 26th, "that a great part of the BEF and its equipment will inevitably be lost even in the best circumstances."

Winston Churchill thought that only 20,000 or 30,000 men might be rescued. But the Prime Minister also had a streak of pugnacious optimism. In happier days he and Eden had once met at Cannes and won at roulette by playing No. 17. Now, as the War Cabinet met on one particularly grim occasion, he suddenly turned to Eden and observed, "About time No. 17 turned up, isn't it?"

2

No. 17 Turns Up

The men of the 1st and 2nd Panzer Divisions would have been the first to agree with the British estimates—only a miracle could save the BEF. They had reached Abbeville so quickly that the bewildered French civilians in the villages along the way thought that these blond, dusty warriors must be Dutch or English. So quickly that OKW, the German high command, hadn't planned what to do next—head south for the Seine and Paris, or north for the Allied armies trapped in Flanders.

North was the decision. At 8:00 a.m., May 22, OKW flashed the code words, "*Abmarsch Nord.*" The tanks and motorized infantry of Gerd von Rundstedt's Army Group A were once again on the march.

The 1st and 2nd Panzer Divisions, soon to be joined by the 10th, formed the left wing of the advance. Together, they made up General Heinz Guderian's XIX Corps, and their mission was in keeping with Guderian's reputation as Germany's greatest expert in tank warfare. They were to seize the Channel ports, sealing off any chance of Allied escape. The 2nd Panzer would head for Boulogne; the 10th for Calais; and the 1st for Dunkirk—farthest away but the busiest and most important of the three ports. On this first day they covered 40 miles.

At 10:50 a.m. on the 23rd General Lieutenant Friedrich Kirchner's 1st Division tanks started out from the old fortified town of Desvres. Dunkirk lay 38 miles to the northeast. The way things were going, they should be there tomorrow, or the next day.

By noon the tanks were in Rinxent—33 miles to go. At 1:15 they reached Guînes—only 25 more miles. Around 6:00 they rumbled into Les Attaques—now the distance was down to 20 miles.

Here they had to cross the Calais–Saint-Omer canal, and anticipating that the Allies had blown the bridge, General Kirchner ordered up a company of engineers. They weren't needed. Someone had forgotten, and the bridge was still intact. The tanks rolled across . . . and on into the Flanders evening, now bearing east.

At 8:00 p.m. Kirchner's advance units reached the Aa Canal—at its mouth, only twelve miles from Dunkirk. The Aa formed a crucial part of the "Canal Line" the British were trying to set up to guard their right flank, but few troops had yet arrived. Around midnight the 1st Panzer stormed across, establishing a bridgehead at Saint Pierre-Brouck. By the morning of the 24th three more bridgeheads were in hand, and one battle group had pushed on to the outskirts of Bourbourg—just ten miles from Dunkirk.

Spirits were sky-high. Prisoners poured in, and the spoils of war piled up. An elated entry in the division's war diary observed, "It's easier to take prisoners and booty than to get rid of them!"

Higher up there was less elation. The Panzer Group commander General Ewald von Kleist fretted about tank losses—there was no chance for maintenance, and he estimated that he was down to 50% of his strength. The Fourth Army commander General Colonel Guenther Hans von Kluge felt that the tanks were getting too far ahead of their supporting troops. Everybody was worried about the thin, exposed flanks; and the faster and further they marched, the more exposed they became. The British sortie from Arras had been repulsed, but it caused a scare.

No one could understand why the Allies didn't keep attacking these flanks. To commanders brought up on World War I—

where successes were measured in yards rather than scores of miles—it was incomprehensible. Adolf Hitler and Winston Churchill had very little in common, but in this respect they were as one. Neither appreciated the paralyzing effect of the new tactics developed by Guderian and his disciples.

It was the same at army group and army levels. At 4:40 p.m. on the 23rd, as the 1st Panzer Division rolled unchecked toward Dunkirk, the Fourth Army commander General von Kluge phoned General von Rundstedt at Army Group A headquarters in Charleville. Kluge, an old-school artilleryman, voiced his fears that the tanks had gotten too far ahead; "the troops would welcome an opportunity to close up tomorrow." Rundstedt agreed, and the word was passed down the line. The panzers would halt on the 24th, but no one regarded the pause as more than a temporary measure—a chance to catch their breath.

From a mobile headquarters train, hidden in a forest near the Franco-German border, General Field Marshal Hermann Göring also followed the dash of the panzers with mounting concern. But his worries had little to do with exposed flanks or mechanical breakdowns. Göring, an exceptionally vainglorious man, was Commander-in-Chief of the Luftwaffe, and he was worried that these dramatic tactics were robbing his air force of its proper share in the coming victory.

On the afternoon of May 23 he was working at a big oak table that had been set up beside his train, when an aide arrived with the latest reports on the panzers' exploits. It looked as though Dunkirk and the whole coast might be taken in a couple of days. Slamming his fist on the table, Göring bellowed, "This is a wonderful opportunity for the Luftwaffe! I must speak to the Fuehrer at once. Get me a line!"

A call was immediately put through to Hitler at his forest headquarters near the village of Münstereifel in northwestern Germany. Göring poured out his case: This was the moment to turn the Luftwaffe loose. If the Fuehrer would order the army to stand back and give him room, he guaranteed his planes would wipe out the enemy alone. . . . It would be a cheap victory, and the credit would go to the air arm, associated with the new Reich of National Socialism, rather than to the army generals and old-line Prussian aristocrats.

"There goes Göring, shooting off his big mouth again," remarked General Major Alfred Jodl, Chief of Operations at OKW, who was one of several staff officers hovering around Hitler during the call.

Actually, Göring knew his man very well. He struck all the right chords. And his arguments found Hitler in a most receptive mood. For days the Fuehrer had been growing ever more nervous about the safety of his armor. At OKW, Generals Keitel and Jodl had been warning him that Flanders was not good tank country, and there was always the haunting memory of 1914, when the French, apparently beaten, staged "the miracle of the Marne."

The shadow of World War I hung over him in another way too: France was the real enemy; Paris the real target. The great French city had dangled just out of reach for four years last time—it must not happen again. Faced with the choice of using his tanks to throw nine shattered British divisions into the sea, or saving them for 65 fresh French divisions blocking the road to Paris and the south, who wouldn't go for Göring's easy way out?

In this state of mind, Hitler flew down to Charleville the following morning, May 24, to consult with General von Rundstedt. It was a most satisfying meeting. The conservative Rundstedt explained he had stopped the panzers so the rest could catch up, and went on to suggest the next steps to take. The infantry should continue attacking east of Arras, but the panzers should hold fast on the Aa Canal Line. Here they could simply gather in the BEF as it was driven back by Army Group B, pushing from the other side of the pocket.

It was a plan that fitted Hitler's own thinking exactly. He immediately approved, emphasizing that the tanks must be saved for future operations. In addition, he observed, any further narrowing of the pocket would only interfere with Göring's bombers—a consideration that would have amazed the Stuka pilots, who prided themselves on their precision bombing.

At 12:41 p.m. new orders went out, backed by the Fuehrer's own authority. They not only confirmed Rundstedt's "halt order" of the previous day; they made it more explicit. The General had not specified any particular line to stop on, and some panzer commanders were already sneaking forward a few extra miles. Hitler corrected this oversight by spelling out exactly where the tanks were to hold:

> the forces advancing to the northwest of Arras are not to go beyond the general line Lens–Béthune–Aire–St.-Omer–Gravelines. On the west wing, all mobile units are to close up and let the enemy throw himself against the above-mentioned favorable defensive line.

"We were utterly speechless," Heinz Guderian later declared, recalling the effect the halt order had on his tank commanders and crews. By now four panzer and two motorized infantry divisions had arrived at the Aa ... six bridgeheads had been planted on the other side ... the advanced patrols were meeting little opposition ... just over the horizon lay Dunkirk. Colonel Wilhelm Ritter von Thoma, a staff officer attached to one of the most forward units, could even make out the massive square belfry of the Church of Saint Eloi. Why stop now?

General Colonel Walther von Brauchitsch, Chief of OKH—the Army's high command—wondered about the same thing. He didn't even hear of the order till midafternoon. It seemed an incredible step, and even more incredible to take it without consulting the Army's top command. Summoned to Hitler's headquarters that evening, he was prepared to argue his case.

He never had a chance. He got a chewing out instead. Hitler had learned that Brauchitsch had ordered the Fourth Army to be transferred from Army Group A to Army Group B, to put the final phase of the battle under one field command. The Fuehrer felt this was a mistake and was outraged that Brauchitsch had done it without consulting him first.

Ranting at the unfortunate General, he canceled the transfer and reconfirmed the halt order. At 8:20 p.m. Brauchitsch returned to OKH angry and humiliated. His Chief of Staff General Franz Halder was in an even worse mood. For the first time in anybody's memory he was nearly an hour late for the OKH evening conference, and the intelligence officer Colonel Liss had never seen him in such a rage. He broke the news of the halt order, storming, "The General Staff is not guilty!"

Nor was he ready to take it lying down. After the meeting, when he had cooled off a little, he recruited his operations officer Colonel von Greiffenberg, and the two of them tried to figure out some way to get around the order. They mustn't be too obvious, but the OKH—the normal source of all army orders—did at least give them a pipeline. Shortly after midnight they had their scheme ready: OKH issued new instructions supplementing the halt order and *permitting* (but not ordering) Army Group A to advance beyond the Canal Line. Under the normal chain of command, Rundstedt would pass the order on to Fourth Army, which would pass it on to Guderian's XIX Corps, and "Fast Heinz" would get the hint.

But the normal chain of command didn't function. The cautious Rundstedt didn't pass along the new orders, pointing out that Hitler had delegated to him the decision on how operations were to be conducted, and he still didn't think it was safe to lift the halt order. Besides, said Rundstedt, there wasn't time to alert the Luftwaffe to adjust its morning targets.

Rundstedt was, of course, under OKH, and in the annals of the German Army it was unheard of for an army group commander to ignore an OKH order, but here both Halder's and Brauchitsch's hands were tied. Their only recourse was to run to Hitler, and everyone knew how *he* felt.

Nevertheless, on the morning of May 25 the two Generals went back to the Fuehrer for one more try. Prolonging the halt order, Brauchitsch argued, meant nothing less than risking certain victory. As the campaign had been planned, Army Group A was the hammer and B the anvil; now the hammer was being stopped in midair. Then Halder added his bit. Playing on the Fuehrer's sense of history, he showed how OKH's original plan would lead to "a little Cannae."

Hitler would have none of it. The tanks must be saved for the future, and in the course of the discussion a new factor arose: he didn't want the climax of the campaign to be fought on Flemish soil. He hoped to encourage a separatist movement there, and too much destruction wrought by the German war machine might be bad politics. The best way to avoid this was for Army Group B to push the British back into France.

As Brauchitsch and Halder sulked back to OKH empty-handed, others were trying to achieve the same goal by pulling strings. General von Kleist had initially favored the halt order, but no longer. During the morning of the 25th he called his good friend General Major Wolfram von Richthofen, commanding Fliegerkorps VIII, who called *his* good friend General Major Hans Jeschonnek, Göring's Chief of Staff. Could he get Göring to ask Hitler to lift the halt order? Jeschonnek wasn't about to touch such a hot potato, and the effort fell through.

During the day separate appeals were made by the Fourth Army commander, General von Kluge, by General Albert Kesselring of the 2nd Air Fleet, even by General von Bock, commanding Army Group B—all turned down cold.

By the evening of the 25th there were doubts even at OKW, normally a faithful echo of the Fuehrer's voice. Colonel Lieutenant Bernard von Lossberg, a young staff officer, buttonholed General Jodl and reminded him of the old German military maxim, Never let up on a defeated enemy. Jodl mildly brushed aside the advice, explaining, "The war is won; all that is left is to finish it. It's not worth sacrificing a single tank, if we can do it more cheaply by using the Luftwaffe."

Lossberg had no better luck with the Chief of OKW, General Keitel, whom he found outside headquarters, sitting on a grassy bank enjoying a cigar. Keitel said he found it easy to agree with the halt order. He knew Flanders from World War I days: the ground was marshy and tanks could easily get stuck. Let Göring do the job alone.

By the 26th even Rundstedt had doubts about the order. The Luftwaffe hadn't lived up to Göring's promises, and Bock's Army Group B, advancing from the east, was bogged down. More behind-the-scenes telephone calls followed: Colonel Lieutenant von Tresckow, Army Group A operations staff, phoned his close friend Colonel Schmundt, Hitler's chief adjutant, and urged that something be done to get the tanks moving again.

The first break came around noon. OKW phoned Halder that the Fuehrer would now allow the panzers and motorized infantry to move within artillery range of Dunkirk "in order to cut off, from the land side, the continuous flow of shipping (evacuations and arrivals)."

Another order followed at 1:30, lifting the halt order completely. At OKH fresh objectives were set, new orders cut and transmitted by 3:30. Army Group A couldn't raise Fourth Army headquarters either by radio or telephone; so at 4:15 a special courier plane carried the good news to General von Kluge: Guderian's tanks could roll again.

The panzer crews were alerted; fuel tanks topped off; ammunition loaded; and the columns reassembled. All this took sixteen more hours, and it wasn't until the predawn hours of May 27 that XIX Corps finally resumed its advance.

For the Wehrmacht, three full days had been lost. For Churchill, the roulette player, No. 17 had at last come up—a lucky and totally unexpected windfall. Whether the British would be able to profit by this stroke of good fortune would largely depend on how General Gort used the time.

Curiously, neither Gort nor any of his staff attached much significance to the halt order, although it was broadcast in clear and picked up by British eavesdroppers. General Pownall was briefly elated ("Can this be the turn of the tide?" he asked his diary), but he soon turned his mind to other things. There was much to worry about: Boulogne had probably fallen; Calais was cut off; the Belgians were crumbling; Weygand and London were still clamoring for a counterattack; the list was endless.

The situation along the Canal Line was particularly desperate. By May 22 the reliable 6th Green Howards were helping the French hold Gravelines, but to the south there was practically nothing. Only 10,000 men covered a 50-mile front, and these were mostly the cooks, drivers, and company clerks who made up the various scratch units Gort had pulled together.

There was one consolation. As the eastern wall of the corridor was pushed back by Bock's massed infantry, it became easier to shift troops to bolster the west. On the evening of the 23rd Gort began transferring three of his seven eastern divisions.

When the 2nd Division moved on the night of May 24–25, the 2nd Dorsets were trucked westward for 25 miles to Festubert, a sleepy village near the La Bassée Canal. All was quiet as 2nd Lieutenant I.F.R. Ramsay's C Company settled into their billets. The old lady who lived next door even dropped by to see how the boys were getting along. It was rumored that the battalion had been withdrawn for a rest.

To their left and right other 2nd Division units were digging in. They too found everything quiet, although the 1st Cameron Highlanders uneasily noted a concentration of enemy tanks and transport building up across the canal. To the north, the 44th and 48th Divisions also moved in; while the French 60th Division took over the area around the coast. Here and there additional corps and headquarter units, some spare artillerymen, a Belgian machine-gun company, a few French tanks fattened up the defense.

Even so, there weren't enough troops to man the whole Canal Line. Gort hoped to minimize the shortage by concentrating his men in towns and villages just east of the canal. These strong-points—or "stops" as he called them—were to hold up the German tanks as long as possible.

On the evening of May 25 the 2nd Gloucesters arrived in Cassel, conspicuous because it sat on the only hill for miles around. It was a good position, but 2nd Lieutenant Julian Fane still felt badly as he turned the local people out of their houses and began punching holes in the walls for his guns. Life began looking up again when a foraging party brought back a case of Moët & Chandon, ten bottles of brandy, and assorted liqueurs.

By the afternoon of May 26—about the time Hitler finally lifted the halt order—tough, seasoned troops held all the key towns on the western side of the escape corridor. On the eastern side two fresh divisions, switched from the canceled counterattack south, joined the four already in place; while all the way south, the French First Army blocked the enemy advance at Lille.

Within this long, narrow passageway the rest of the trapped forces—over 150,000 troops—swarmed north toward the coast. There were no longer separate retreats from the east and from the west. The two streams merged into one swirling, turbulent river of men.

And all the while the Stukas continued their assault. "Stand up to them. Shoot at them with a Bren gun from the shoulder. Take them like a high pheasant. . . ." The advice came from Brigadier Beckwith-Smith, a throwback to the glory days of the

Empire. But even those who understood what he was talking about found it hard to grasp the analogy. The Stukas had an implacable ferocity all their own.

No target seemed too small. Corporal Bob Hadnett, a dispatch rider with the 48th Division, was riding his motorcycle along an exposed stretch of road when a single Stuka spotted him. Machine guns blazing, it made two passes, but missed both times as Hadnett weaved wildly from side to side on the road. Still after him, the Stuka climbed, peeled off, and dived straight at him. Again it missed, and this time the pilot misjudged his dive. He tried to pull out too late and plunged into the road just ahead, exploding in a ball of fire. Hadnett turned off the road into a field, smoked a cigarette, and carried on.

Most of the men showed less nonchalance. The drivers of the 2nd Ordnance Field Park felt compelled to run for cover when attacked, but their officer felt that only attracted attention. "The next time one of you bastards runs," he promised, "I will shoot him down." After that the men lay flat, but Lance Corporal Reginald Lockerby discovered a new kind of fear. As the machine-gun bullets whacked into the earth around him, he felt an almost irresistible urge to draw his legs up under his body. He was always sure they would be cut off.

Numbed by the Stuka attacks, exhausted from lack of sleep, the men lost all sense of time and place. The days merged with one another. The towns ceased to have any identity of their own. Poperinge was remembered for its tangle of trolley wires; Armentières for the cats that howled all night. Carvin was the place where 60 convent girls, killed by a bomb, lay in neat rows in the moonlight. Tournai was the spot where the traveling circus got hit—a nightmare of wounded elephants and four plunging white horses dragging an unconscious girl rider.

Few of the men knew where they were going. Private Bill Warner, headquarters clerk in the 60th Heavy Anti-Aircraft Regiment, lost his unit in the dark, and had absolutely no destination in mind. He just wandered along, following the crowd, doing what everybody else did. Private Bob Stephens, 2nd Searchlight Battalion, was one of seven men in a lorry that somehow got separated from the rest of the battalion. They simply drove along without the vaguest idea where they were heading. Trying to find which way to go, they would occasionally get out and examine tire tracks in the dust, like Indian fighters in the old West.

Often the "brass" was almost as uninformed. Major Charles Richardson, Deputy Assistant Quartermaster General, 4th Division, gradually became aware that they were moving toward the coast, but evacuation never occurred to him. He vaguely thought that a bridgehead might be established somewhere, letting the Allies keep a foothold on the Continent.

There was no such thinking at General Gort's headquarters in Prémesques. When Colonel Bridgeman, the acting Operations Officer, reported for duty early on the morning of May 26, General Pownall told him that evacuation was definite.

This was no surprise to Bridgeman. He had been developing his evacuation plan off and on for five days in the little operations office he shared with Colonel Philip Gregson-Ellis. The rest of his time he concentrated on shoring up the western wall of the corridor, while Gregson-Ellis took care of the east. In spare moments they would argue over who had the worst job: Gregson-Ellis, with the Belgians collapsing, or Bridgeman, with virtually no idea where his troops were or what they were good for.

But today would be no office day. With communications so bad, Bridgeman decided to tour the western sector personally to get a better idea of what needed to be done. It was a long day, which included a visit to Bastion 32, the reinforced concrete bunker that served as French headquarters at Dunkirk. Here he met General Marie B. A. Fagalde, commanding the French troops along the Aa Canal. He had once been military attaché in London and spoke good English. It was a promising start: the Allies could at least communicate.

Near Bergues, a walled medieval town five miles south of Dunkirk, Bridgeman took a break for lunch. Climbing to the top of an artificial mound—the only rise in the area—he sat alone with his driver, munching his rations and contemplating the problem of defending this flat countryside. The south seemed the best tank country—fewer canals to cross—and he decided that the panzers would probably come that way. If so, Cassel was the main town that lay in their path. It was the place that *must* be held, while the BEF scrambled up the corridor to Dunkirk.

Bridgeman got back to Prémesques late that evening to learn he had a new job. He was now Operations Officer for Lieutenant-General Sir Ronald Adam, who had just been appointed to command the Dunkirk perimeter. So far both the perimeter and the troops holding it existed only on paper, but Bridgeman himself had drawn up the defense plans. Now he would have a chance to see how they worked. If practical, both Dunkirk and the area around it might be held long enough to get the BEF to the coast. After that, it would be the Navy's job to get them home.

But did the Navy, or anyone in London, understand the size of the job? So far, Gort had little reason to feel that they did. The trumpet blasts from Churchill, the fruitless telephone talks with the War Office, Ironside's visit on the 20th, even Dill's visit on the 25th—none were very reassuring. Normally the most tactful of men, Dill actually left the impression that London felt the BEF wasn't trying hard enough. Now Gort had a message that indicated to him that the Navy was assigning only four destroyers to the evacuation.

That afternoon—the 26th—he summoned RAF Group Captain Victor Goddard to the Command Post at Prémesques. Normally Goddard was Gort's Air Adviser, but there were no longer any air operations to advise him on. In fact, there was only one RAF plane left in northern France. It was an Ensign transport that had brought in a special consignment of antitank shells. As it approached, it had been shot down by trigger-happy British gunners but fortunately crash-landed in a potato field just where the ammunition was needed.

Learning that the plane could be repaired, Gort asked Goddard to catch a ride in it to London that night and attend the meeting of the Chiefs of Staff the following morning as Gort's personal representative. The Navy must be told that somehow a much bigger effort was needed. It would be improper for Goddard to speak directly to anybody at the Admiralty, and useless to speak to Ironside alone, but to speak to Ironside in the presence of the Chief of Naval Staff, Admiral of the Fleet Sir Dudley Pound, might accomplish something.

"It must be done," stressed Gort, "in the presence of Dudley Pound. He *must* be there. He certainly will be in the Chiefs-of-Staff daily meeting, and he *must* be confronted with the task. You can't tell the Admiral what to do, but you *can* tell Ironside what I want him to get the Admiral to do!"

Goddard quickly packed his kit and at 11:30 p.m. arrived in a staff car at the potato field where the crippled plane had landed. With him were five other airmen—the last of the RAF staff attached to Gort's headquarters. They too were no longer needed. A brief search in the dark, and the plane was found. The crew were still working on it, but the pilot said he should be ready in an hour. The field was long enough—400 yards—all he needed were lights to guide him down the "runway." The RAF car's headlights would do nicely.

At 1:00 a.m. they were off, roaring down the field, barely clearing the hedges, leaving behind the car, abandoned with motor running and lights still burning. It was a brand new Chevrolet, and Goddard mused about the wastefulness of war.

By 3:00 they were over the Channel ... 4:30, and they touched down briefly at Manston ... 7:00, and they were at Hendon, outside London. A staff car whisked Goddard into town, and it was about 8:10 when he arrived at Whitehall.

Thanks to a combination of lucky meetings with old friends, some persuasive talk, and the aura that went with an officer "just back from the front," shortly after 9:00 Goddard was escorted down to the basement, ushered through a heavily guarded door marked CHIEFS OF STAFF ONLY, and into a large, rectangular, windowless room.

There they all were, the war leaders of the British Empire, seated at a number of tables arranged to form a hollow square. Here and there papers lay scattered over the dark blue tablecloth. The only unexpected twist: Ironside wasn't there. He had just been replaced as Chief of the Imperial General Staff by General Dill.

Admiral Pound was presiding, and he was discussing the limited number of destroyers that could be used at Dunkirk—the very point that had so upset Gort. Unfortunately Dill had already contributed whatever he had to say, and there was no chance to give him the message from Gort that Pound was meant to hear. For a relatively junior RAF officer to appeal directly to the Chief of Naval Staff was, as Goddard well knew, an unpardonable breach of protocol.

Pound finished, asking, "Any more on that?" Only silence as Goddard watched his opportunity slip away, his mission turn into dismal failure. "Well, then," said Pound, "we'll go on to the next item."

Suddenly Goddard heard his own voice speaking, directly to the Admiral of the Fleet: "I have been sent by Lord Gort to say that the provision made is not nearly enough. . . ." Pound gave him a startled look; the room rustled; and all eyes swung to him. Across the table Sir Richard Peirse, the Vice-Chief of Air Staff, sat bolt upright, aghast.

It was too late to stop now. Goddard went on and on, detailing the requirements of the hour, going far beyond anything Gort had told him to say. "You must send not only Channel packets, but pleasure steamers, coasters, fishing boats, lifeboats, yachts, motorboats, everything that can cross the Channel!"

He was repeating himself now: "Everything that can cross the Channel must be sent . . . *everything* . . . even rowing boats!"

At this point Peirse got up from his seat, slipped over, and whispered, "You are a bit overwrought. You must get up and leave here, now."

Goddard knew that all too well. He rose, made a slight bow in Pound's direction, and managed to leave the room with a reasonable degree of composure. But he felt utterly ashamed of his outburst, coupled with dejection at his failure to win any kind of sympathy or response.

Perhaps he would not have felt so badly had he known that at this very moment other men were acting along the lines he had proposed. They were men of the sea—Britain's element—but they were not Chiefs of Staff, or famous admirals, or even sailors on ships. They were working at desks all over southern England, and it was their unannounced, unpublicized intention to confound the gloomy predictions of the warriors and statesmen.

3

"Operation Dynamo"

When W. Stanley Berry reported to the London offices of Admiral Sir Lionel Preston on the morning of May 17, he didn't know quite what to expect. A 43-year-old government clerk, he had just been engaged as the Admiral's assistant secretary, and this was his first day on the job.

Admiral Preston was Director of the Navy's Small Vessels Pool, a tiny blob on the organization chart that supplied and maintained harbor craft at various naval bases. Useful, but hardly glamorous. It was not, in fact, prestigious enough to be located in the Admiralty building itself, but rather in space leased in the adjoining Glen Miles bank block. Berry had no reason to suppose that he faced anything more than mundane office work.

He was in for a surprise. Six sacks of mail were waiting to be opened and sorted. These were the first answers to a BBC broadcast May 14 calling on "all owners of self-propelled pleasure craft between 30 and 100 feet in length to send all particulars to the Admiralty within 14 days. . . ." The call had been prompted not by events in Flanders but by the magnetic mine threat. To counter this, the country's boatyards were absorbed in turning out wooden minesweepers. Finding its normal sources dried up, the Small Vessels Pool was requisitioning private yachts and power boats to meet its own expanding needs.

Stanley Berry dived into the job of processing the mountain of replies to the BBC announcement. He and the Admiral's Secretary, Paymaster Lieutenant-Commander Harry Garrett, sorted them out by both type of vessel and home port. Garrett, a Newfoundlander, found himself getting a crash education in British geography.

This same day Winston Churchill for the first time began thinking of the possibility of evacuation. No one was more offensive-minded than Churchill—nobody prodded Gort harder—but every contingency had to be faced, and his visit to Paris on the 16th was a sobering experience. Now he asked Neville Chamberlain, former Prime Minister and currently Lord President of the Privy Council, to study "the problems which would arise if it were necessary to withdraw the BEF from France. . . ."

At a lower level, other men were taking more concrete measures. On May 19 General Riddell-Webster presided over a meeting at the War Office, taking up for the first time the possibility of evacuation. There was no feeling of urgency, and a representative from the Ministry of Shipping felt that there was plenty of time to round up any vessels that might be needed.

Calais, Boulogne, and Dunkirk would all be used, the meeting decided. The basic plan had three phases: starting on the 20th, "useless mouths" would be shipped home at a rate of 2,000 a day; next, beginning on the 22nd, some 15,000 base personnel would leave; finally, there was just possibly "the hazardous evacuation of very large forces," but this was considered so unlikely that the conferees did not waste their time on it.

The Admiralty put Vice-Admiral Bertram Ramsay in charge of the operation. He was Vice-Admiral, Dover—the man on the spot—the logical man in the logical place. He had 36 vessels, mostly cross-Channel ferries, to work with.

Next day, the 20th, when Ramsay called a new meeting at Dover, events had changed everything. The panzers were pointing for the coast . . . the BEF was almost trapped . . . Gort himself was talking evacuation. "The hazardous evacuation of very large forces" no longer sat at the bottom of the agenda; now "the emergency evacuation across the Channel of very large forces" stood at the top.

The situation was still worse when the same group met on the

21st, this time in London again. Another plan was hammered out; more neat, precise figures. Ten thousand men would be lifted every 24 hours from each of the three ports—still Boulogne, Calais, and Dunkirk. The ships would work the ports in pairs, no more than two ships at a time in any of the three harbors. To do the job, Ramsay was now allotted 30 cross-Channel ferries, twelve steam drifters, and six coastal cargo ships—a bit better than yesterday.

By the following day, the 22nd, everything had changed again. Now the panzers were attacking Boulogne and Calais; only Dunkirk was left. There would be no more of these meticulous plans; no more general meetings of all concerned. Ramsay, an immensely practical man, realized that the battlefront was changing faster than meetings could be held. By now everybody knew what had to be done anyhow; the important thing was to be quick and flexible. Normal channels, standard operating procedures, and other forms of red tape were jettisoned. Improvisation became the order of the day; the telephone came into its own.

Ramsay himself was at his best in this kind of environment. He was a superb organizer and liked to run his own show. This quality had nearly cost him his career in 1935 when, as Chief of Staff to Admiral Sir Roger Backhouse, commanding the Home Fleet, he felt the Admiral had not given him enough responsibility. Always outspoken, he asked to be relieved and ended up on the Retired List. He stayed on the shelf for three years, enjoying horses and a tweedy country life with his wife Mag and their three children.

Then, with the sudden expansion of the Navy on the eve of World War II, he had been called back into service and put in charge at Dover. He knew the area well, had been skipper of a destroyer in the old Dover Patrol during the First War. At first the new job had not been too taxing—mainly antisubmarine sweeps, mine-laying, and trying to work out ways to counter the enemy's new magnetic mines. The German breakthrough changed all that—Dover was only twenty miles from the French coast, practically in the front lines.

His staff was small but good. Ramsay did not suffer fools gladly—never was the cliché more applicable—and his officers were expected to show initiative. He was good at delegating responsibility, and they were good at accepting it. His Flag Lieutenant James Stopford, for instance, waged a monumental single-handed battle to get a direct telephone connection with Boulogne, Calais, and Dunkirk. It would cost £500 a year, the Admiralty complained, but Stopford persisted and finally got his way. Now, with the BEF pinned against the French coast, this phone line was a priceless asset.

As Vice-Admiral, Dover, Ramsay lived and worked at Dover Castle, but his office these days was not part of the magnificent ramparts and keep that towered over the port. Rather it was *under* the Castle, buried in the famous chalk cliffs just east of the town. During the Napoleonic wars French prisoners had cut a labyrinth of connecting casemates in the soft chalk as part of England's coastal defense. Now they were being used to meet the threat of a new, twentieth-century invasion.

An inconspicuous entrance within the castle walls led down a long, steep ramp, which in turn joined a honeycomb of passages. Down one corridor leading toward the sea, a visitor came to a large gallery, then several offices separated by plywood, and finally to the Admiral's own office, with a balcony cut right into the face of the cliff.

It was not the sort of office normally associated with a vice-admiral. The floor was concrete, partly covered by a thin strip of threadbare carpet. A couple of framed charts were all that decorated the whitewashed walls. A desk, a few chairs, a conference table, and a cot in one corner completed the furnishings. But the room did have one amenity. The balcony made it the only place in the whole complex that had any daylight, except for a small window in the women's "head." Here the WRENS, as the distaff members of the Royal Navy were nicknamed, could stand on the "thunder-box" and enjoy a view of the Channel every bit as good as the Admiral's.

By far the biggest room was the large gallery that had to be passed going to and from Ramsay's office. Its main piece of furniture was a huge table covered with a green cloth. Here Ramsay's staff gathered to organize the evacuation. A hard-driving naval captain named Michael Denny was in charge, presiding over a compact collection of sixteen men and seven telephones.

During World War I this cavelike room had housed an auxiliary lighting system for the castle, and it became generally known as the "Dynamo Room." By the same process of association, on May 22 the Admiralty designated the evacuation now being planned as "Operation Dynamo."

The basic need was ships and men. It was clear that the 30 to 40 vessels originally allocated by the Admiralty wouldn't be nearly enough. A closer estimate would be everything that could float. By now Ramsay had practically a blank check to draw whatever he needed; so the staff in the Dynamo Room went to work on their phones—calls to the Ministry of Shipping to collect available vessels along the east and south coasts . . . calls to The Nore Command for more destroyers . . . calls to the Southern Railway for special trains . . . calls to the Admiralty for tugs . . . medical supplies . . . ammunition . . . rations . . . engine spare parts . . . grassline rope . . . diesel fuel . . . blank IT124 forms . . . and, above all, calls for men.

It was a knock on the door at 4:00 a.m., May 23, that awakened Lieutenant T. G. Crick in his quarters at Chatham Naval Depot. A messenger brought instructions that Crick was to be ready for "an appointment at short notice"—nothing more. At 6:30, word came to report at once to the Barracks. On arrival Crick found that he was one of 30 officers required to go to Southampton and man some Dutch barges lying there. Why? They were to "run ammunition and stores to the BEF."

These barges, it turned out, were broad, self-propelled craft of 200 to 500 tons, normally used to carry cargo on the network of canals and waterways that laced Holland. After the German invasion some 50 of them had escaped with their crews across the Channel and were now lying at Poole and in the Thames estuary.

Captain John Fisher, the salty Director of Coastal and Short Sea Shipping at the Ministry of Shipping, knew about these *schuitjes*, as the Dutch called them, in the normal course of his work. It occurred to him that with their shallow draught they would be ideal for working the beaches off Dunkirk. Forty of them were immediately requisitioned for "Dynamo." The striped flag of the Netherlands came down; the Royal Navy's white ensign went up. The Dutch crews marched off; British tars took their place. And with the change in flag and crew came a change in name. The British couldn't possibly master a tongue-twister like *schuitje*; from now on these barges were invariably called "skoots."

At the Ministry of Shipping the search for the right kind of tonnage went on. The burden of the work fell on Captain Fisher's shop and on W. G. Hynard's Sea Transport Department, which controlled all overseas shipping used by the military. In lining up additional ferries and personnel vessels, the problem wasn't so difficult. The Department knew all the passenger carriers, had used them in getting the BEF to France.

But there weren't enough ferries in all the British Isles to do the job. What other vessels might be used? What ships had the right draught, the right capacity, the right speed? The Department alerted sea transport officers in every port from Harwich on the North Sea to Weymouth on the Channel: survey local shipping . . . list all suitable vessels up to 1,000 tons.

Back at the Department's offices on Berkeley Square, staff members Basil Bellamy and H. C. Riggs worked around the clock, napping on a cot in the office, grabbing an occasional bite at "The Two Chairmen" pub around the corner. Life became an endless chain of telephone calls as they checked out the possibilities. Would the drifter *Fair Breeze* do? How about the trawler *Dhoon*? The coaster *Hythe*? The eel boat *Johanna*? The hopper dredge *Lady Southborough*?

At this moment acting Second Mate John Tarry of the *Lady Southborough* had no idea that his ship was under such careful scrutiny. She looked like a vessel that was good for absolutely nothing except what she was doing—dredging the Channel in Portsmouth harbor. There was no reason to suppose she would ever go to sea. She wasn't even painted wartime gray. Her rust-streaked funnel still sported the red and yellow stripes of the Tilbury Dredging Company.

It was quite a jolt to Tarry when the company agent Anthony Summers came aboard one evening and called the nine-man crew together. There was trouble across the Channel, he explained, and the *Lady Southborough* was needed. Who would volunteer to go? Nobody knew what to expect, but to a man they volunteered.

All Portsmouth harbor was coming alive. Besides the *Lady Southborough*, four other Tilbury dredges were alerted. The Hayling Island ferries, Pickford's fleet of small coasters, Navy patrol boats, the battleship *Nelson*'s launch—all bustled with activity, loading fuel and supplies.

Little ships would be especially important if it came to evacuation from the shore itself. The larger vessels couldn't get close enough to the gently shelving Flemish beaches. During the past week Ramsay's requirements for small boats had been widely (though quietly) circulated, yet at dawn on May 26 he still had only four Belgian passenger launches, several Contraband Control boats from Ramsgate, and a few Dover harbor craft. Early that morning Rear-Admiral Sir Tom Phillips, the Vice-Chief of Naval Staff, held a meeting at the Admiralty, trying to speed things up. Among those present was Admiral Preston of the Small Vessels Pool.

The meeting had broken up and Preston was already back at the shop when the Admiral's assistant secretary, Stan Berry, reported for work that morning. It was Sunday; most of the staff were off. Berry was looking forward to a quiet day, but the duty officer, Lieutenant Berrie, offered an ominous greeting: "Thank God you've come. I wouldn't be in your shoes for a pension!"

"Why?" asked Berry.

"I don't know what's up, but the Old Man is here." Whatever it was, it must be serious. Peacetime customs die slowly, and admirals normally didn't come to the office on Sunday.

Preston himself said nothing to clear up the mystery. He simply greeted Berry, asking where was the regular secretary, Commander Garrett? Berry explained that Garrett was off, but the arrangement was for him to call in every two hours.

"Tell him to report immediately." And the Admiral ordered Berry to call in all the rest of the staff, too.

This was no easy matter. For instance, Lieutenant-Commander Pickering, in charge of drifters and trawlers, was in Brighton. When Berry tried to phone him, word came back that he had gone to the cinema. Which cinema? Nobody knew. So Berry had him paged at every cinema in town until he was finally located.

Messages were now flying all over England, breaking into the normal routine of ships and men. Surgeon-Lieutenant James Dow was having a very pleasant war on the minesweeper *Gossamer*, based on the Tyne. The hours were easy, shore leave generous, the local girls all attractive. Suddenly on May 25 an Admiralty signal intruded: "Raise steam with all despatch. Proceed to Harwich. Do not wait for liberty men, who will rejoin at Harwich." The ship buzzed with rumors, but nobody really knew what was up.

At Liverpool the destroyer *Somali* had just docked after a battering in Norwegian waters. Sub-Lieutenant Peter Dickens was counting on a little break, but the *Somali* had barely tied up when he was handed an Admiralty message: report to Chatham Barracks immediately. That meant going to the other end of England—why?

Chatham itself was in turmoil—or as near to turmoil as a Royal Navy training base ever gets. Seaman G. F. Nixon was attending gunnery school when his battalion was ordered to fall in at 4:00 a.m. on the 26th. At 7:00 they left for Dover in busses, singing, "We'll Hang Out the Washing on the Siegfried Line." No one had a clue as to what was going on.

Deep within the white cliffs of Dover the staff of the Dynamo Room worked on. "No bed for any of us last night and probably not for many nights. I'm so sleepy I can hardly keep my eyes open," Admiral Ramsay wrote his wife Mag on the 23rd. As he worked in his office, he would scribble a line or so between visitors, then stuff the letter into his desk drawer as some new crisis arose. Mag, in return, kept up a flow of gingerbread, asparagus from the garden, and tender words of support.

"Days and nights are all one," he wrote her on the 25th, and indeed the men in the Dynamo Room had lost all track of time. The usual measuring rods were gone. Buried deep in their chalk cliff, they had no chance to know whether it was day or night. They had no regular meals—just an occasional sandwich or mug of tea taken on the run. There was no pace to their work; they were going flat out all the time. There was no variety; only a feeling of unending crisis that finally numbed the senses.

The strange fleet of ferries, hoppers, dredges, barges, coasters, and skoots now converging on Dover raised a whole set of new problems. First, they would have to be moored somewhere. Sheerness, on the Thames estuary, gradually became the main collecting point where the smaller ships were sorted out and prepared for the sea. Ramsgate became the final assembly point, where fuel tanks would be topped off, supplies loaded, and convoys organized.

Problems were solved, only to spawn new problems equally pressing. Mechanics had to be found who understood balky engines that defied the Navy's experience . . . coal had to be obtained for some of the ancient coasters . . . 1,000 charts were needed for skippers who rarely went to sea. Routes could be marked on them, but data on the beaches was vague at best. Responding to a call for help from the Dynamo Room, Colonel Sam Bassett—head of the Interservice Topographical Department—toured London's travel agencies, collecting brochures that might describe the French beaches in some detail. There had been nine months of war since the last holiday tripper made that sort of request; the clerks must have thought he was crazy.

Arms were another problem. This peacetime fleet had to have some sort of protection, and the Lewis machine gun seemed the best bet. But there was no single depot that could supply all Ramsay's needs. They had to be scrounged from here and there—11 from London . . . 10 from Glasgow . . . 1 from Cardiff . . . 7 from Newcastle . . . 105 altogether.

If the Dynamo Room was a scene of "organized chaos," as one staff officer later recalled, the majestic cliffs successfully hid the fact from the rest of the world. Dover never looked lovelier than it did this 26th of May. The guns could be heard rumbling across the Channel—Boulogne was gone; Calais was falling—but it all seemed very far away to the crews of the vessels riding peacefully at anchor in the Downs.

On the minesweeper *Medway Queen*, a converted paddle steamer lying just off the cliffs, Chief Cook Thomas R. Russell leaned against the rail, shooting the breeze with his assistant, a young man he knew only as "Sec." It was strange, they decided, that the whole flotilla was in port this morning—no one at all was out sweeping. Right after breakfast a launch had made the rounds, picked up the captain, first officer, and wireless man from every ship, and taken them to the flagship for some sort of palaver. Now a naval barge eased alongside the *Medway Queen* and delivered case after case of food—far more than her 48 men could possibly eat. "Enough grub has been put aboard us," observed Sec, "to feed a ruddy army."

The men trapped in Flanders knew little more than the crew of the *Medway Queen*. Later this day, the 26th, Major-General E. A. Osborne, commanding the 44th Division near Hazebrouck, would get a quiet briefing from Brigadier G. D. Watkins of III Corps headquarters, but those of less exalted rank had to depend on rumor. Reginald Newcomb, a chaplain with the 50th Division, had a crony in Intelligence who hinted darkly that the BEF would make for the coast and embark for home—"that is, if Jerry doesn't get there first." Rumor spread through the 1st Fife and Forfar Yeomanry that they were going back to the sea, where they would embark, land farther down the coast, and attack the Germans from the rear.

Orders, when they finally came, were usually by word of mouth. In the varied units of the Royal Army Service Corps, especially, there was not much to go on, and many of the RASC officers simply vanished. The men of the 4th Division Ammunition Supply Company were merely told, "Every man for himself; make for Dunkirk, and good luck!" The No. 1 Troop Carrying Company was instructed to "get as near Dunkirk as you can, destroy vehicles, and every man for himself." And again, for the 573rd Field Squadron, Royal Engineers, the familiar words: "Every man for himself. Make for Dunkirk."

Often the orders came almost without warning. It was shortly after dawn in a small Belgian village when Sergeant George Snelgar, attached to a transport company, was awakened by voices shouting, "Get on Parade!" He heard the sound of marching feet, and looking out the window of the café where he was billeted, he saw his unit marching off to the vehicle park. Catching up, he learned that the orders were to smash their cars and motorcycles and go to Dunkirk. They couldn't miss it: just head for that column of smoke.

At midnight it was harder. Corporal Reginald Lockerby of the 2nd Ordnance Field Park was groping north in a truck when an officer stepped out in the road and waved him down. He was heading right for the German lines 500 yards away. When Lockerby asked for directions to Dunkirk, the officer pointed to a star hovering above the horizon and said, "Just follow that star." Others were guided by the gun flashes that lit up the night sky. By now they were on almost all sides. There was only one little gap to the north that remained black. That was Dunkirk.

Major Peter Hill, a transport officer, was one of the few who had a map. Not army issue—for some reason all rear area maps had been called in at the start of the campaign. What he did have was a map put out by the *Daily Telegraph* to help its readers follow the war.

Private W. S. Walker of the 5th Medium Regiment, Royal Artillery, could have better used an English-French dictionary. Coming to a signpost that pointed to "Dunkerque," he wondered whether that was the same place as Dunkirk.

He need not have worried. Any road north would do, as long as it kept within the corridor held on the east by the Belgians and British; on the west by the French and the British; and at the foot—all the way south—by the French clinging grimly to Lille.

All the roads were still packed with troops in every sort of order and disorder—ranging from Welsh Guardsmen marching smartly with rifles at the slope to stragglers like Private Leslie R. Page, an artillery officer's batman with the 44th Division. He had lost his unit when it scattered to dodge some strafing. Now he was plodding north alone, mixed with a crowd of soldiers and refugees. A big, open Belgian farm cart rumbled by. It was loaded with fleeing civilians, and there up front beside the driver, Page saw—of all people—his own father.

"What's this, our Sunday school outing?" Page cracked as he climbed aboard for a brief family reunion. It turned out that the father, a warrant officer with the infantry, was just as lost as the son. Then the Luftwaffe struck again . . . the two were separated . . . and once more young Page wandered on alone. "Where are we going?" he asked someone and got the usual answer: "See that smoke in the sky? That's Dunkirk. Make for it!"

There were women, too, in this great trek—not all of them ordinary refugees. A French liaison officer with the 2nd Ordnance Field Park brought along his mistress. Driver Gordon A.

Taylor of the RASC tried to look after a young French girl he had found whimpering alone in the dark in a suburb of Lille. He managed to find a lorry, put her in it, and got her out of town. He felt quite the white knight and protector—until he lost her when the lorry got stuck in a traffic jam and they had to take to their feet. He never saw her again and would always wonder whether his "protection" did her more harm than good.

Private Bill Hersey of the 1st East Surreys had better luck. He had married the daughter of a French café owner in Tourcoing, and Augusta Hersey proved a determined bride indeed. As the East Surreys retreated through Roncq, she suddenly appeared and begged Bill to take her along. With the connivance of his company commander, Captain Harry Smith, Augusta was packed off in the headquarters truck.

Another war bride wasn't as lucky. When Jeanne Michez married Staff Sergeant Gordon Stanley in February 1940, she became the first French girl to wed a member of the BEF. Stanley was attached to GHQ Signals at Arras; Jeanne moved into his quarters; and until May they lived an almost peacetime domestic life. When "the balloon went up," he moved with Advanced GHQ into Belgium, and she went home to sit out the war at her mother's café in the nearby village of Servins.

Jeanne Stanley knew very little of what was happening during the next two weeks, and she was astonished when suddenly one afternoon Gordon rolled up in a staff car with a machine gun mounted on the roof. The Germans were coming, he told her; they must leave right away. Jeanne flung a few things into a suitcase, plus two bottles of rum stuffed in by her mother. In an hour she was ready to go, dressed almost as if she was taking the afternoon train to Paris—blue dress, blue coat, matching blue broad-brimmed hat.

Off they went, the two of them up front and a corporal named Trippe in back. The roads were one huge traffic jam, and it didn't help when Jeanne's broad-brimmed hat blew out the window. Gordon stopped, and as he walked back to pick it up, the first Stukas struck.

They missed . . . the hat was rescued . . . the Stanleys drove on. They spent the first night in the car; other nights mostly in some ditch. Once they slept in the big barn of a Belgian farmer.

He wouldn't give them permission, but Gordon shot off the barn-door lock, and they settled in anyway.

Sleeping in the hay, diving into ditches to escape the Stukas, they got dirtier and dirtier. Once Jeanne managed to buy a bucket of water for ten francs, but most of the time there was no chance to wash. The broad-brimmed hat crumbled and vanished.

Eventually they reached the little French town of Bailleul. Here they stopped at the comfortable house of an elderly woman, Mlle. Jonkerick. Unlike many of the people they met, she was all hospitality and took them in for the night. Next day they moved on, still hounded by the inevitable Stukas.

Jeanne was now completely exhausted, her clothes in shreds. Gordon tried to put her in his battledress, complete with tin hat, but nothing fit. She finally told him that it was no use; she couldn't go on. He took her back to Mlle. Jonkerick, who proved as hospitable as ever: Jeanne was welcome to stay till the roads cleared and she could return safely to Servins.

Now it was time to say good-bye. Gordon was a soldier; he had his duty; she understood that. Still, it was a hard moment, made just a little easier when he promised to come back and get her in two months. He would keep that promise, except for the part about two months. Actually it took him five years.

Jeanne Stanley was not the only one near the breaking point. A young lieutenant trying to lead a unit of the 2nd Ordnance Field Park got lost so many times he finally burst into tears. Corporal Jack Kitchener of the RASC found himself in a horrendous traffic jam, which turned into a pushing and shoving match between British and Belgian drivers. When a BEF officer tried to break it up, someone pushed him, too. He pulled his revolver and fired, hitting Kitchener in the left leg. "You've shot *me*, not the bloke who pushed you!" Kitchener exploded.

Private Bill Bacchus was driver-batman for a chaplain attached to the 13th Field Ambulance, and their trip north turned into an odyssey of bitterness and recrimination. Bacchus considered the padre a drunken coward; the padre charged Bacchus with neglect of duty and "dumb insolence." Several times the padre drove off alone, leaving Bacchus to shift for himself. On two occasions Bacchus reached for his rifle, as if to use it on the padre. It seemed that even a man of God and his helper were not immune to the strain of defeat, the constant danger, the hunger and fatigue, the bombs, the chaos, the agony of this unending retreat.

Private Bill Stone had felt it all. He was a Bren gunner with the 5th Royal Sussex and had been in continuous action for two days holding off Jerry on the eastern side of the escape corridor. Now his section was ordered to make one more stand, giving time for the rest of the battalion to withdraw and reorganize farther to the rear.

They hung on for an hour, then pulled out in a truck kept for their getaway. It was dark now, and they decided to find some place where they could rest—they hadn't had any sleep for three nights. They pulled up at a building which turned out to be a monastery. A robed monk appeared from out of the night, beckoned them to follow him, and led them inside.

It was another world. Monks padded quietly about in their robes and sandals. Flickering candles lit the stone passageways. All was tranquillity, and the war seemed a thousand years away. The abbé indicated that it would be a pleasure to give food and rest to these new visitors, along with a party of Royal Engineers who had also discovered this heavenly oasis.

They were all led into the cloisters and seated at a long refectory table. Each British soldier had a monk to wait on him and attend to his needs. They had food and wine that the monks had produced themselves, and after days of army biscuits and bully beef, the meal was like a royal banquet.

There was only one hitch. The Engineers explained that they were going to blow every bridge in the area next morning. Stone and his mates would have to be on their way by 5:00 a.m. They didn't mind; the stone floor of the cloisters seemed like a feather bed after what they had been through.

At dawn they were on their way. Driving over the bridges, they slowed to a crawl, lest they prematurely set off the demolition charges already laid. The men of the Royal Sussex were well clear of the area when the distant boom of explosives told them that their brief idyll was over and they were back in the war.

Along with blowing up bridges, canal locks, power stations,

and other facilities of possible use to the Germans, the BEF was now demolishing its own equipment. To a good artilleryman, it seemed almost sacrilegious to destroy the guns he had so lovingly fussed over for years. As they smashed the breechblocks and destroyed the dial sights, many were openly crying.

Bombardier Arthur May of the 3rd Medium Regiment felt the agony even more deeply than the others. He had been posted to the same battery of howitzers his father had fought with in World War I, and this was a matter of infinite pride. Even the guns were the same, except that they now had rubber tires instead of the old steel rims. The battlefields were the same too. Armentières and Poperinge were familiar names long before this spring. In more ways than one, May felt he was following in Father's footsteps.

But even in the darkest days of the First War things had never been so bad that the battery had to blow up its own guns. A gnawing conscience told him that somehow he had "let the old man down."

There was little time for such sad reflections in the rush of self-destruction that now swept the BEF. In towns like Hondschoote and Oost Cappel on the road to Dunkirk, the paraphernalia of a whole army was going up in flames. Thousands of lorries, half-tracks, vans, heavy-duty trucks, motorcycles, Bren gun carriers, mobile kitchens, pick-ups, and staff cars were lined up in fields, drained of oil and water, with motors left running till they seized. Mountains of blankets, gas capes, shoes, wellingtons, and new uniforms of every kind lay burning in the fields. Passing one clothing dump about to be blown up, Lance Corporal W. J. Ingham of the Field Security Police raced in, ripped open a few bales, found his size in battledress, changed, and within a few minutes rejoined his unit—"the only well-dressed soldier in our mob."

NAAFI stores—the source of the BEF's creature comforts—lay deserted, open for the taking. Bombardier May walked off with his valise crammed with 10,000 cigarettes.

The chaplains, too, joined the orgy of destruction. Reginald Newcomb of the 50th Division kept busy smashing typewriters and mimeograph machines, while his clerk went to work on the company movie projector. Later, Newcomb burned two cases of army prayerbooks. It was Sunday, May 26, but there would be no Divine Service today.

The smoke that towered over Dunkirk twenty miles to the north was no part of any BEF demolition scheme. Hermann Göring was trying to keep his promise that the Luftwaffe could win the battle alone. For nearly a week the Heinkels, Dorniers, and Stukas of General Kesselring's Luftflotte 2 had been pounding the town. At first the damage was spotty, but on May 25 a giant raid damaged the main harbor lock, knocked out all electric power, and left the port a wreck, with its forest of cranes leaning at crazy angles.

Corporal P. G. Ackrell, a 42-year-old Ordnance Corps man, had been waiting to evacuate with other "useless mouths"; now his unit was hastily drafted to help unload an ammunition ship by hand. The derricks weren't working, and the regular stevedores had vanished.

Toward noon Ackrell's mind began drifting to other matters. The enemy planes were gone for the moment, and he noticed some inviting warehouses nearby. He drifted over for a look-around and spied some large cardboard boxes that seemed especially enticing. He opened one up, but it didn't contain wristwatches or cameras or anything like that. It was full of marshmallows.

Making the best of things, Ackrell took a carton of marshmallows back to the dock, where they proved an instant hit. Returning to the warehouses for more, he discovered a barrel of red wine. He filled his water bottle, then began to sample it. Once again he remembered his friends and took some wine back to them, too. They liked it enough to go back for more, and by the end of the day barely half the ammunition had been unloaded.

Next day, the 26th, the men went back to work, and once again Ackrell's eye began to wander. This time he found a freight car full of underwear. Still exploring, in another car he located some shoes that were a perfect fit. Once again he shared his good fortune with his friends; once again the dock work stopped. That evening the ship put to sea with part of her cargo still unloaded.

Discipline was gone. Dunkirk was a shambles, and clearly the port could not be used much longer. As the Luftwaffe roamed the skies unchecked, bombing at will, a small British naval party launched an experiment that somehow symbolized the futility of the whole air defense effort. Commander J. S. Dove had arrived on the 25th, ordered by the Admiralty to erect what was called "a lethal kite barrage" around the port area. The kites would be flown somewhat in the manner of barrage balloons and, it was hoped, would ensnare unwary German planes. To accomplish this purpose, Dove had on hand 200 "lethal kites" and a small staff of assistants.

There was not enough wind to fly a kite on the morning of May 26, but early in the afternoon the breeze freshened, and Dove's crew managed to rig two kites from the top of the two biggest cranes in the harbor. One bobbed uselessly up and down, but the other rose majestically to 2,000 feet.

No one ever knew what would happen if a Stuka flew into it, because jittery Tommies, ignorant of the experiment and leery of anything flying in the sky, brought it down with a fusillade of small arms fire. Commander Dove stayed on to help with the evacuation; his little team joined the ever-growing horde waiting for transportation home.

The Luftwaffe continued its methodical destruction. On the morning of the 26th alone it dropped 4,000 bombs on the city, plastering the docks, the ships, the roads leading to the port, the disorganized thousands streaming toward it.

"Where is the RAF?" The familiar cry went up again and again. In their exasperation one column turned on a hapless stray wearing air-force blue, who had fallen in with Corporal Lockerby's unit. He was no pilot—just a clerk from some disbanded headquarters—but that didn't help him. The enraged troops pushed and threatened him—the symbol of all their pent-up bitterness.

The man seemed in such danger that Lockerby tried to find a spare army uniform for him to change to, but ironically the search was interrupted by yet another Stuka attack. By the time it was over, the man had vanished, perhaps looking for more congenial companions.

Yet the RAF was there, although often out of sight and not yet very effective. For several days Fighter Command had been shifting its carefully hoarded squadrons of Hurricanes and Spitfires to airfields closer to the Channel, planning for a major effort to cover the evacuation.

When 19 Squadron was moved from Horsham to Hornchurch on May 25, Flying Officer Michael D. Lyne was immediately struck by the totally different atmosphere. Horsham had been all practice—little trace of the war—but at Hornchurch the field was full of battle-damaged planes, and the mess buzzed with talk of combat and tactics. For a young pilot with only 100 hours in Spitfires, it was a sobering change.

Early morning, May 26, Lyne was off on his first patrol over the beachhead. There was no special pep talk or briefing; the squadron just took off for France, as though they did it every day. They met some Stukas and Messerschmitt 109's near Calais, gave better than they took, but lost two of their own, including the squadron commander.

That afternoon Lyne was back over Dunkirk on his second patrol of the day. Off Calais they again met a squadron of Me 109's, and Lyne himself came under fighter fire for the first time, without at first even realizing it. Mysterious little spirals of smoke whisked past his wings; then came the steady *thump-thump* of an Me 109 cannon. It finally dawned on him that he, personally, was somebody's target.

Lyne managed to dodge, but shortly afterward found himself in a duel with two Me 109's circling above him. Trying to maneuver, he stalled, then went into a spin as a bullet or shell fragment hit his knee. The radio conked out . . . the cockpit filled with glycol fumes and steam . . . his engine quit.

His first thought was to crash-land in France and spend the rest of the war in some POW camp. On second thought he decided he didn't want that; instead he'd splash down in the Channel, hoping someone would pick him up. Then he decided against that too—"I didn't want to get wet"—and finally, his spirits returning, he decided he just might be able to nurse the plane back to the British coast.

He made it—barely. Gliding in a few feet above the sea, he crash-landed on the shale beach at Deal in a cloud of flying rocks and pebbles. Bloody and oil-soaked, he staggered from the cockpit into a totally different world.

It was Sunday, and Deal beach was filled with strolling couples—military men in their dress uniforms, girls in their frilliest spring creations—all enjoying a leisurely promenade under the warm May sun. Barging into this dainty scene, Lyne felt he was more than an interruption: he was an unwelcome intruder, thoughtlessly reminding the crowd that only twenty miles away there was a very different world indeed.

He was right. The people of Deal and Dover—all England, for that matter—were still living a life of peace and tranquillity. The government had not yet announced any emergency, and the distant rumble of the guns across the Channel was not enough to break the spell. It was a typical, peacetime weekend: a Dover town team defeated the officers of the Dover Detachment at bowls, 88 to 35 . . . the local football club lost a match to Sittingbourne . . . roller skaters whirled about the rink at the Granville Gardens Pavillion . . . the weekly Variety show announced a new bill featuring those "comedy knockabouts" The Three Gomms.

The mood was different at Whitehall. A chilling awareness gripped the government that Britain was now on the brink of an appalling disaster. Reynaud, in town for a conference with Churchill, was gloomy, too. He felt that Pétain would come out for a cease-fire if a large part of France were overrun.

The time had come to act. At 6:57 p.m. this Sunday, May 26, the Admiralty signaled Dover: "Operation Dynamo is to commence."

At this point Admiral Ramsay had 129 ferries, coasters, skoots, and small craft to do the job, but more were on the way and the staff in the Dynamo Room was clicking smoothly. Still, it was a monumental task. The Admiralty itself did not expect to lift more than 45,000 men in two days. After that, the evacuation would probably be terminated by enemy action.

"I have on at the moment one of the most difficult and hazardous operations ever conceived," Ramsay wrote Mag late that night (actually 1:00 a.m. on the 27th), "and unless the *bon Dieu* is very kind there are certain to be many tragedies attached to it. I hardly dare think about it, or what the day is going to bring. . . ."

Yet the biggest crisis at the moment lay beyond Ramsay's control. The crucial question was whether more than a smattering of men could get to Dunkirk at all. Hitler's "halt order" had been lifted; the German armor was rolling again; thousands of Allied soldiers were still deep in France and Belgium. Could the escape corridor be kept open long enough for these troops to scramble to the coast? What could be done to help the units holding the corridor? How to buy the time that was needed?

4

Buying Time

To Winston Churchill, Calais was the key. The ancient French port, 24 miles west of Dunkirk, was besieged but still in British hands. The Prime Minister decided that it must be held to the last man. Taking it would chew up Rundstedt's troops, slow down his advance, and buy the time needed to get the BEF back to the coast.

Still, it was not an easy decision. It meant deliberately sacrificing 3,000 highly trained troops at a time when Britain could ill afford to lose them. Rescuing any large part of the BEF was a long shot at best. Might not these men be better used on the home front in case of invasion?

For Anthony Eden the decision was especially bitter. He had long served in the King's Royal Rifle Corps, one of the regiments at Calais. Ordering them to fight to the end meant condemning to death or captivity some of his best friends.

It was a gloomy dinner at Admiralty House on the evening of May 25 when the step was finally taken. Churchill silently picked at his food, and on leaving the table, remarked to no one in particular, "I feel physically sick." At 11:30 a last telegram went off to Brigadier Claude Nicholson, commanding the Calais garrison:

Every hour you continue to exist is of greatest help to the BEF. Government has therefore decided you must continue to fight. Have greatest possible admiration for your splendid stand.

For Brigadier Nicholson this was the latest in a bewildering series of messages that had tugged him this way and that. Until late April, his 30th Infantry Brigade had been slated for Norway. With the collapse of that campaign, Churchill decided it should be used to raid the German flanks along the French coast, the way his old Marine Brigade did in World War I.

The 30th was a brigade that should give the Germans a lot of trouble. Two of its three battalions—the 2nd King's Royal Rifle Corps and the 1st Rifle Brigade—were crack regulars. The remaining battalion—the 1st Queen Victoria's Rifles—was a Territorial unit of weekend soldiers; but one of the best in England. All were mechanized. To beef them up still more, Churchill added the 3rd Royal Tank Regiment, already heading for Calais under separate orders.

The tank companies and the Queen Victoria's Rifles left first, sailing from Dover for Calais at 11:00 a.m. on May 22. In the rush to get going, the QVR left all their vehicles behind. The 3rd Tank Regiment brought their tanks, but they were stowed in the bottom of the ship, and unloading them at Calais seemed to take forever.

This work had scarcely begun when a disconcerting figure arrived on the scene. Lieutenant-General Brownrigg, Gort's Adjutant General, had been in Boulogne setting up a rear GHQ. Now he suddenly appeared in Calais, en route to England. Acting on his own authority as senior officer present, he ordered the tanks to head west for Boulogne and join the troops defending that port. It was just as well that the battalion was still unloading, since Boulogne was already cut off.

Later that night Major Ken Bailey arrived from Gort's headquarters with entirely different orders for the tanks: they were to head south, not west, and join the BEF at Saint-Omer. Then from Brownrigg, now at Dover: they were to go to Boulogne, as previously ordered. Pulled this way and that, a squadron of the tanks finally set out for Saint-Omer at 1:30 p.m. on the 23rd, but were hurled back by a panzer column blocking the way.

That afternoon Brigadier Nicholson reached Calais with the rest of the 30th Infantry Brigade. He too had orders from General Brownrigg to head west for Boulogne, but while his troops were still unloading, the War Office ordered him to head east for Dunkirk (the opposite direction) with 350,000 rations for Gort's army. During the night of May 23–24 the convoy set off, but soon ran into the inevitable panzers. In a slam-bang night action three of the escorting tanks broke through to Gort's lines, but the rest of the convoy was destroyed or thrown back to Calais.

Clearly the town was cut off. Whatever Brownrigg or the others ordered, there would be no forays in any direction. Nicholson would have his hands full holding Calais itself. This he proposed to do, deploying his own three battalions, plus the 21 remaining tanks, plus some scattered units to form an "outer" and "inner" perimeter defending the port.

Some 800 French troops also rallied around, manning the town's ancient Citadel and four old forts. Built in the seventeenth century by the great French military engineer Vauban, they were still amazingly strong. A few antique coastal defense guns, worked by French marines, completed the garrison.

Nicholson's plan was to stand fast as long as possible. When enemy pressure became too great, he would gradually pull back toward the harbor. He would then be in position for a fast getaway, since a new message sent by the War Office at 2:48 a.m. on the 24th said that evacuation had been agreed on "in principle."

By afternoon his orders had changed again. During the day Churchill had agreed to the appointment of French General Fagalde as overall commander of the defense of the Channel ports. Adhering to Weygand's idea that these ports should be held indefinitely as fortified bridgeheads on the Continent, Fagalde forbade any evacuation of Calais. Normally British commanders were given some loophole in such a situation, but not this time. At 11:23 p.m. on the 24th, the War Office sent Nicholson new instructions:

> In spite of policy of evacuation given you this morning, fact that British forces in your area now under

Fagalde who has ordered no repeat no evacuation, means that you must comply for sake of Allied solidarity. Your role is therefore to hold on, harbour being for present of no importance to BEF. . . .

When Winston Churchill saw this message on the morning of May 25, he exploded in indignation. To him, the role of Calais was to tie up as many Germans as possible. The French said no evacuation, and that could well mean no escape. If so, "Allied solidarity" and calling Calais harbor "of no importance" were not the arguments to use to make troops fight to the end.

Churchill now drafted the kind of message he felt was needed. It was full of ringing phrases, which Anthony Eden deftly edited into a strong personal appeal from himself to Nicholson. As a former member of the King's Royal Rifle Corps, Eden carried special weight:

Defence of Calais to the utmost is of highest importance to our country as symbolizing our continued cooperation with France. The eyes of the Empire are upon the defence of Calais, and H. M. Government are confident you and your gallant regiments will perform an exploit worthy of the British name.

Nicholson understood without being told. At the very moment when Eden was sending his message—2:00 p.m. on the 25th—a Lieutenant Hoffmann of the 10th Panzer Division was being escorted under a flag of truce into the British lines by a French officer and a Belgian soldier. They guided Hoffmann to Nicholson's headquarters, now at the Citadel. The Lieutenant came to the point immediately: unconditional surrender, or Calais would be destroyed.

Nicholson was equally quick in writing his reply:

1. The answer is no, as it is the British Army's duty to fight as well as it is the German's.
2. The French captain and the Belgian soldier, having not been blindfolded, cannot be sent back. The Allied commander gives his word that they

will be put under guard and will not be allowed to fight against the Germans.

The weary garrison fought on. For three days they had battled the Wehrmacht's tanks and Stukas, gradually yielding inch by inch. Now they were holed up in Calais-Nord, the old part of town by the harbor. The noise of battle gradually faded—Germans have to sleep too—and the only sound was the incongruous trill of nightingales in the Jardin Richelieu.

London's last message had wider distribution than anyone in Whitehall thought. It was picked up and read with the greatest interest by German radio intelligence—especially the ringing exhortation, "Every hour you continue to exist is of the greatest help to the BEF." It was the first convincing evidence that the British planned to evacuate. Until now there had been much speculation that the increased shipping activity in the Channel might be due to some Allied plan to make a surprise landing behind the German advance. Others felt that it meant preparations for a permanent Allied beachhead based at Dunkirk. But this new message seemed to rule all that out. The phrasing pointed to evacuation and nothing else.

The message was interesting for another reason, too. The British obviously regarded holding Calais as more important than the Germans did. Army Group A had warned Guderian not to get involved in costly house-to-house fighting there. Guderian himself regarded the port as a distinctly secondary objective—of "less military than prestige importance." He had taken it from the 1st Panzer Division, leading his advance, and reassigned it to the 10th Panzers trailing behind because it had "only local importance and no influence upon general operations."

And now this curious intercept. For some reason London was calling on Calais to fight to the end. Around noon on May 26 Colonel Blumentritt, Operations Officer at Army Group A, phoned 10th Panzer Division headquarters, where Guderian was conferring with the Division commander, General Lieutenant Ferdinand Schaal. Blumentritt reminded them that the Division must not be wasted on Calais. If the going got tough, Calais should be left to the Luftwaffe.

Schaal felt that wouldn't be necessary. He said his attack was "promising" and asked to be kept in the fight. He expected to have Calais by nightfall.

He had good reason for optimism. The day had begun with a devastating Stuka raid. Most of the British had never been through this ordeal before, and the screech of the planes was predictably terrifying. Private T. W. Sandford of the King's Royal Rifle Corps ran for a cellar, scooping up an equally frightened small dog. Sandford and his mates crouched in the dark, while the dog lay cowering in a corner. They patted it and fussed over it, until it finally wagged its tail, which somehow made them feel better.

After the raid, they emerged into a street littered with bricks and broken glass. The bombing broke up many of the defending units, and Sandford never did find his own company again. At 10:50 a.m. the Germans broke into Calais-Nord and began systematically splitting up the defenders into pockets of resistance.

Communications collapsed, and Brigadier Nicholson was soon isolated in the Citadel with his staff and a handful of French defenders. By 3:00 p.m. it was completely surrounded, and around 3:30 a detachment of Schaal's infantry broke through the south gate. That did it. With the enemy inside the walls, resistance vanished. Hands up, Brigadier Nicholson emerged from his command post to meet his captors.

Down by the harbor a few isolated units fought on. Colour Sergeant Fred Walter of the Queen Victoria's Rifles found himself in a tunnel that ran through Bastion 1, a strong-point near the docks. Troops from other units were packed in here too, milling around, totally disorganized. An ever-growing number of wounded were also crowding into the place, part of which had been set aside as a first aid post.

A cool-headed officer finally appeared and sorted the men out. Some he sent to a nearby fort; others, including Walter, he stationed on top of the tunnel with a French machine gun. They kept it firing as the Germans drew steadily closer, mopping up resistance. The Gare Maritime went; then the nearby fort. At last a British staff officer appeared and told Walter's group to cease fire: arrangements were being made to surrender.

They refused to obey. Lieutenant-Colonel L. A. Ellison-McCartney, commanding the QVR, now appeared, and the men appealed to him. Did he know of any cease-fire order? Ellison-McCartney said no; in fact he understood that if they could hold out another half-hour, the Navy would come in and get them. He asked if the group wanted to give in, and received a rousing "NO!"

Ellison-McCartney then left to find out who had given the cease-fire order ... and why. He soon returned, and his news was all bad: they were the last group holding out; the Germans had them completely surrounded. Enemy guns enfiladed both ends of the tunnel, which was now choked with wounded, and these guns would immediately open fire if there was any further resistance. In addition, the Germans had all their artillery and tanks in position, and the Stukas stood ready to pay a return visit.

The surrender terms had already been concluded by another officer, the Colonel added, and the only thing he could do was follow along. The men must lay down their arms.

The group began breaking up their weapons, until a German officer suddenly appeared brandishing a pistol. He angrily told them to stop, and to march out of the bastion, hands up. In this way the surviving troops filed out, stumbling between two lines of German infantry, every other enemy soldier holding a machine pistol.

To Fred Walter, it was the most humiliating experience he could imagine. He didn't even dare glance at his comrades, for fear he would see in their faces the same utter hopelessness he felt in all his heart and body.

Yet there were British soldiers still free in Calais. Signalman Leslie W. Wright had arrived from Dover on May 21 for communications duty. By the 26th his wireless set was destroyed and he was fighting as an infantryman with the QVR. Midafternoon, he found himself on the eastern breakwater of the harbor. A Red Cross launch had tied up there, and Wright was helping load it with wounded.

He and his mates saw the launch safely off, then started back along the breakwater toward the docks. But before they reached the jetty that led to the shore, the Germans captured that part of the harbor, marooning Wright's group on the breakwater. They settled down among the piles and supporting beams, where they hoped they would be less conspicuous.

They forgot about the tide. It was rising, and soon the men would be forced into the open. Discouraged, the rest of the group headed for shore to surrender—but not Wright. He had heard the Germans didn't take prisoners; so he decided to hang on a little longer. If discovered, at least he would die a free man.

Half an hour, and he changed his mind. He grew so lonely he decided he'd rather die with his friends. He too might as well give up. He worked his way among the piles toward the shore, where a large swastika flag now flew from the jetty. He had almost reached the first German outpost when a couple of British destroyers standing offshore began shelling the jetty.

This put new hope into him. In a flash he again changed his mind. Turning around, he now clambered seaward, scrambling from pile to pile at irregular intervals in order to confuse the enemy. At one point, where mortar fire had cut a gap in the breakwater, he tumbled into the sea. Swimming across the gap, he climbed back among the piles and continued on.

At the seaward end of the breakwater he was overjoyed to find a cluster of 46 British servicemen, hiding like himself among the piles and beams. Over their heads stood a small structure, normally used by port authorities, which served as an observation post. This had been taken over by a Royal Marines captain who was the senior rank present.

The sun was going down now, and it turned bitterly cold. Wright, still wet from his tumble into the harbor, suffered dreadfully. His new companions pulled off his clothing and crowded around him, trying to keep him warm. One young subaltern literally hugged him, and their helmets came together with a fearsome clang that seemed certain to attract the attention of every German in Calais.

But they were still undetected at nightfall, when Wright and most of the others climbed an iron ladder and joined the Royal Marines captain in the port authorities' room. Clearly an enterprising man, he somehow made hot coffee for them all. Outside, a signalman with a lamp kept flashing an SOS, hoping some British ship would see it. Wright, warm at last but now hobbled by a badly bruised foot, dozed under a table.

"They are coming!" was the cry that woke him up. It was around 2:00 a.m., and a small British vessel was entering the harbor. It failed to spot the men on the breakwater and tied up down by the jetty. A landing party went ashore but wasn't gone long. German machine guns opened up, and the shore party raced back to the boat. It slipped its lines and headed back to sea.

As the vessel again drew near, the men on the breakwater whooped and yelled and frantically waved their light. Never mind if the Germans saw them; this was their last chance. The boat again passed them by . . . then at the last possible moment turned and eased alongside the breakwater. Wright and the others scrambled aboard. Next instant they were off, pounding into the open sea, as every gun in the harbor erupted behind them.

Their craft was the naval yacht *Gulzar*, commanded by Lieutenant C. V. Brammall. Not knowing that Calais had fallen, he had taken his boat into the port, hoping to pick up some wounded. He was too late for that, but not for the little group on the breakwater. As the *Gulzar* chugged toward Dover, someone handed Wright a snack and some coffee. Safe at last, he decided it was the best meal he had ever had in his life.

Lieutenant Brammall wasn't the only man that night who failed to realize Calais was gone. The top command in London were as much in the dark as ever. At 4:30 a.m. Winston Churchill telegraphed Gort suggesting—as he had so often done before—that "a column directed upon Calais while it is still holding out might have a good chance."

Finally, at first light on the 27th, a force of 38 Lysanders flew over Calais on a drop mission. They lost three planes but managed to drop 224 gallons of water, 22,000 rounds of ammunition, and 864 grenades. Waiting below, the Germans were appropriately grateful.

The British people were deeply moved by the stand at Calais. For 400 years they had felt a special tie to the place. Every schoolchild knew how Queen Mary—"Bloody Mary"—had lost the port in 1558 through monumental carelessness, and how she died "with the word Calais written on my heart." Now the city had been lost again, but this time in the noblest way for the noblest cause—to buy time for Gort's army.

Yet that certainly wasn't the original goal. At various times Nicholson's force was to be used for raids on the enemy flanks . . . for relieving Boulogne . . . for defending Saint-Omer . . . for escorting rations to Dunkirk . . . for demonstrating "Allied solidarity." It was only in the last 36 hours that buying time became the guiding purpose.

And how much time did it really buy? The best evidence suggests very little. The Germans used only one division at Calais, the 10th Panzer, and it could not have reached the Aa Canal Line before the "halt order" was issued. The advance did not resume until after Calais had been taken. The other panzer troops were idle throughout the siege.

One panzer division, the 1st, did take a passing swipe at Calais, as it led the dash eastward on the 23rd. It hoped to take the port by surprise without a fight. Finding this was impossible it was told not to waste any more time, but to continue the advance east. Calais, never considered very important, could be cleaned up by the 10th Panzers, still trailing behind everyone else.

Even after Calais had been taken, the 10th was not rushed forward to join the troops attacking Dunkirk. It was, in fact, sent the other way for the almost nominal task of guarding the coast from Calais to Audresselles. Another 24 hours would pass before Guderian decided that maybe he could use the Division's tanks at Dunkirk after all.

Actually, OKH felt they already had enough troops to take the port. And this was certainly true at the time the "halt order" was issued. Six crack panzer divisions were poised on the Aa Canal Line, with the 1st and the 6th Divisions less than twelve miles from Dunkirk. This was easily enough to overwhelm the sprinkling of Allied defenders.

All these panzer divisions were still in place when the halt order was lifted on May 26. In the interim the French 68th Division had moved into the Gravelines area, and Gort had set up his system of "stops" and strong-points. But most of the BEF were still deep in France and Belgium, reeling back toward the coast.

To save them it was still necessary to buy time, but it would not be bought by the heroic defenders of Calais. That was all over. The job would have to be done by the troops holding the strong-points along the escape corridor. None of these towns and villages had the emotional pull of Calais; some were little more than dots on the map. . . .

At Hazebrouck on the morning of May 27 a discomforting report reached the 229th Field Battery: the panzers had turned the British flank, and there was nothing between the battery and the German Army. High time to get out, but one gun was detached and wheeled into position at a road junction just south of town. A forlorn hope, it might briefly cover the exposed flank. Captain John Dodd, second in command of the battery, climbed to the top of a nearby farmhouse to scan the horizon for any sign of the enemy.

A German tank stood half-hidden behind a hedge 200 yards away. Dodd rushed down the stairs to lay the gun, but Sergeant Jack Baker already had his crew of four giving a drill-hall performance. They got off two rounds before the German tank even replied. Then came an answering hale of machine-gun bullets. Two more tanks rumbled up, and all three blazed away at Baker's gun.

Another British field piece joined in. It was under repair some yards off, but the battery sergeant major found several volunteers, including a cook and a motor mechanic. They swung the gun around and hammered away until they ran out of ammunition.

Baker's gun carried on alone, giving as good as it got. Two of the crew fell; now there were only Baker and his layer left. Then the layer was hit, and there was only Baker. He continued firing, getting off six more shots on his own. Then he too ran out of ammunition.

But the issue was already decided. The three tanks turned and lumbered away. Baker had won. Captain Dodd rushed up, to be greeted by the wounded layer. Excitedly shaking the Captain's hand, he cried, "We got the bugger, sir!"

At Epinette, another Gort strong-point eight miles farther south, the determination was the same, but the weapon was different. Captain Jack Churchill had gone to war with three

May 24-30, The Allied Escape Corridor

ENGLISH CHANNEL

• Ostend

Nieuport

BELGIUM

La Panne
Bray-Dunes•
Furnes
• Dunkirk
Dixmude

• Gravelines
Bergues
Oost Cappel
Noordschote

• Calais
• Bourbourg
Westvleteren

Aa Canal
Houtkerque

Wormhout
Poperinge
Ypres

Ledringhem

Cassel
Kemmel

St.-Omer•
Hazebrouck
Roubaix

Steenbecque
Steenwerck
Prémesque

Merville
Estaires
Lille

Epinette
Le Paradis

FRANCE
Festubert
La Bassée

La Bassée Canal

0   10 miles

☾   defensive "stops" or strong-points

     perimeter

"toys"—his bagpipes, a sword, and a bow and arrow. On the 27th the bagpipes and sword were packed with his gear somewhere, but he had the bow and a few arrows with him as he and about 80 others, mostly 2nd Manchesters, prepared to defend the village.

When the German advance came in sight, Churchill climbed into the loft of a granary and peered through a vertical opening normally used for hauling up sacks of grain. There, only 30 yards away, he saw five enemy soldiers sheltering behind the corner of a house. He quickly fetched up two British infantrymen and ordered them to open rapid fire, but not until he had loosed an arrow at the center man. He lifted his bow, took aim, and let fly. Hearing the twang, the riflemen blasted away.

Churchill had a brief, satisfying glimpse of his arrow hitting home—right in the left side of the center man's chest. The rifles brought down three of the other Germans, but the fifth escaped by dodging around the corner of the house. For perhaps the last time in history, the English bow—the weapon that turned the tide at Crécy and Poitiers six hundred years earlier—had again been used in battle.

Tradition was also in evidence at La Bassée, the southern anchor of Gort's Canal Line defense system. The 1st Queen's Own Cameron Highlanders, holding the town, were the last Scottish regiment to wear kilts in action. It was against regulations, but the Camerons wore them anyway, and in one case, at least, they served a practical purpose. The battalion adjutant, Major Peter Hunt, was hit in the leg, but the bullet's effect was diminished by a fold in his kilt.

For two days the Camerons had been holding out, hurling back every German attempt to cross the canal. But it was a costly business. After one counterattack A Company had only six men left—nowhere near enough to hold the ground so dearly bought.

Now, on the morning of May 27, the enemy again stormed across the canal, and La Bassée was soon engulfed in flames and smoke. "Next door" at Festubert the 2nd Dorsets heard a last faint radio signal: the Camerons were completely surrounded and wanted permission to destroy their wireless.

The Dorsets sensed their turn was next. As the panzers approached, a strange cheerfulness—almost bravado—swept C Company headquarters. Someone wound up an ancient gramophone, and it ground out "Ramona" over and over again. For most people the tune might conjure up visions of moonlight and waterfalls, but 2nd Lieutenant Ivor Ramsay would always connect it with Festubert and those beetlelike tanks.

Making clever use of the village buildings, the Dorsets managed to hold out till dark, when orders were to fight their way back to Estaires. They were now deep in enemy-held territory; using the roads was impossible. They would have to go cross-country—at night, without maps. All that the battalion commander Lieutenant-Colonel E. L. Stephenson had was a compass.

At 10:30 p.m. they started out. Stephenson took the lead, followed by about 250 Dorsets and miscellaneous "odds and sods" who had lost their own units. It was a black, cloudy night, and the men soon had their first contact with the enemy when Stephenson ran head-on into a German infantry sergeant inspecting his own outposts. The Colonel pulled his revolver and killed the man with a single shot. Hearing the commotion, a nearby enemy sentry called, "Heinrich?"—but did nothing else. Relieved, the Dorsets stumbled on through the dark.

Next, they came to a road running directly across their line of retreat, packed with enemy tanks and motor transport. A whole armored division was driving past. Stephenson's little troop lay down in the stubble and watched the show for over an hour—the German vehicles didn't even bother to turn off their lights. Finally, there was a break in the flow, and the Dorsets scooted across the road, plunging back into the underbrush just as the next echelon rolled into view.

Guided by Colonel Stephenson's compass, the men struggled on across ploughed fields, over barbed-wire fences, through ditches waist-deep and stinking of sewage. At dawn they came to a canal too deep to wade. The swimmers formed a human chain to help the nonswimmers across. Somehow they managed it, then had to do it all over again when the canal looped back a quarter-mile further on.

But Stephenson's compass never failed them. Just as he had calculated, at 5:00 a.m. on the 28th the Dorsets stumbled into

Estaires, completing an eight-mile odyssey. French troops were defending the town and cheerfully shared their flasks of *vin rouge* with the exhausted newcomers.

There was not always such a happy ending. German troops surging across the La Bassée Canal caught the 2nd Royal Norfolks at Locon, wiping out most of the battalion. About 100 survivors fell back on a farm in the nearby village of Le Paradis. Trying to keep his men together, the acting CO Major Ryder sent Private Fred Tidey to make contact with some troops holding out on another farm across the road.

Private Tidey accomplished his mission, then couldn't get back. The machine-gun fire was now too heavy for him to cross the road. Ryder and 98 of his men were soon surrounded in a cowshed by troops of the SS Totenkopf Division. The Germans set fire to the farm, ultimately forcing the Norfolks to surrender. They were immediately marched to a nearby barnyard, where a couple of machine guns mowed them down. The SS finished off those still alive with pistol and bayonet—except for Privates Bill O'Callaghan and Bert Pooley. Though fearfully wounded, they managed to survive by hiding beneath the bodies.

Across the road Tidey had the good fortune to be taken prisoner by different troops, who were not SS but in the regular German Army. His war was over too, but at least he was alive. The road, it turned out, was the dividing line between the two different German units, and he still marvels at how this narrow strip of dirt and gravel almost certainly made all the difference between life and death.

Le Paradis . . . Festubert . . . Hazebrouck—it was the fight put up at villages like these that bought the time so desperately needed to get the trapped troops up the 60-mile corridor to Dunkirk. The British 2nd Division, supported by some French tanks, took a merciless beating, but their sacrifice enabled two French divisions and untold numbers of the BEF to reach the coast.

As the battered battalions swarmed up the corridor, the Luftwaffe continued to roam the skies unopposed. Besides bombs, thousands of leaflets fluttered down, urging the Tommies to give up. The addressees reacted in various ways. In the

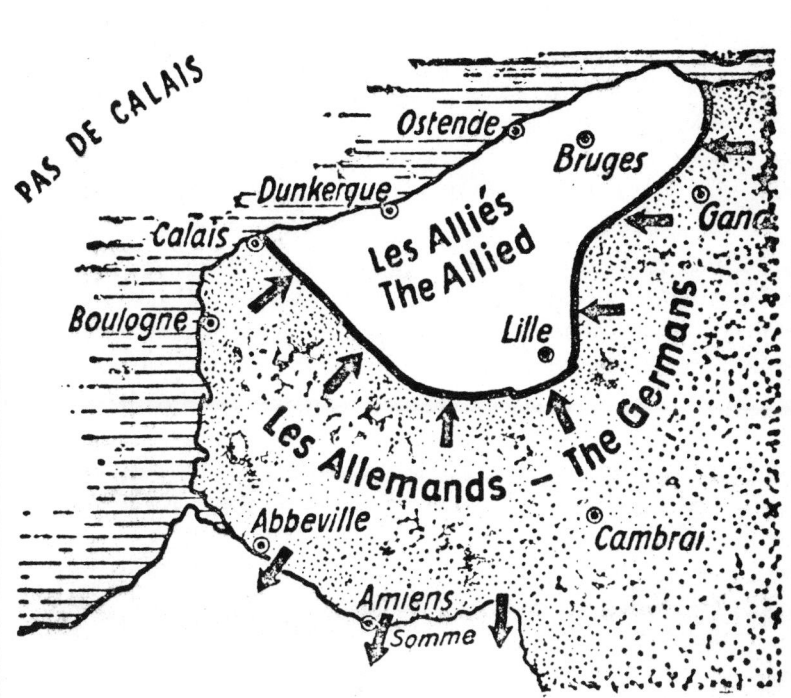

Camarades!

Telle est la situation!
En tout cas, la guerre est finie pour vous!
  Vos chefs vont s'enfuir par avion.
A bas les armes!

British Soldiers!

Look at this map: it gives your true situation!
Your troops are entirely surrounded —
    stop fighting!
Put down your arms!

58th Field Regiment, Royal Artillery, most men treated the leaflets as a joke and a useful supply of toilet paper. Some men in
the 250th Field Company, Royal Engineers, actually felt en-
couraged by a map that featured the Dunkirk beachhead. Until
now, they hadn't realized there was still a route open to the sea
so near at hand. A sergeant in the 6th Durham Light Infantry
carefully read the strident wording several times, then observed
to Captain John Austin: "They must be in a bad way, sir, to de-
scend to that sort of thing."

The jumbled masses were approaching Dunkirk now, coming
in every way imaginable—members of the 1st East Surreys on
borrowed bicycles . . . a farmboy in the 5th Royal Sussex riding
a giant Belgian carthorse . . . a hatless brigadier tramping alone
up the road from Bergues. Just outside Dunkirk, artilleryman
Robert Lee saw one fellow sweep by on roller skates carrying an
umbrella. Another chap was hustling along with a parrot in a
cage. But far more typical was Gunner P. D. Allan. When his
feet developed enormous blisters and he could no longer walk,
two of his comrades acted as crutches, supporting him for the
last five miles.

At Dunkirk nobody was ready for this impending avalanche.
Admiral Jean Abrial, the French naval officer in overall command of the coast, was tucked away in Bastion 32, planning the
defense of the port. Like Weygand and Blanchard, he saw Dunkirk as the base for a permanent foothold on the Continent.
General Adam, appointed by Gort to organize the evacuation,
hadn't arrived yet.

Adam was supposed to act under the orders of General Fagalde, the military commander under Abrial, provided Fagalde's orders "did not imperil the safety or welfare of the
British troops"—an escape clause the size of Big Ben. Already
there had been sharp disagreement over preparing various
bridges for demolition.

In a try for better coordination, the British and French commanders met in Cassel at 7:30 on the morning of May 27. The
town, situated on its isolated hill nineteen miles south of Dunkirk, was one of Gort's most important strong-points, but as yet
had not been attacked.

Adam and Fagalde arrived early, and before the main meet-

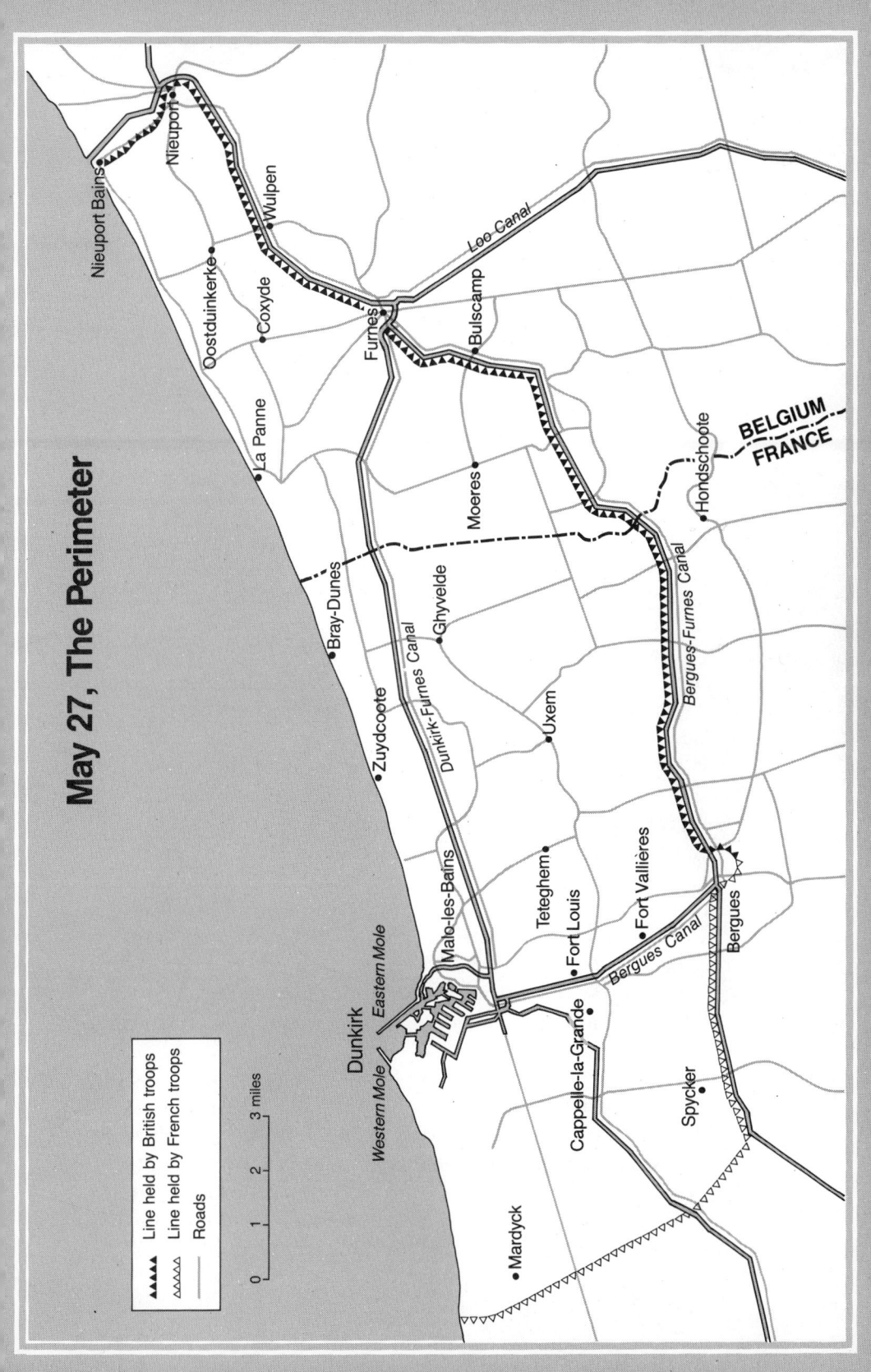

May 27, The Perimeter

Line held by British troops
Line held by French troops
Roads

0   1   2   3 miles

Nieuport Bains
Nieuport
Wulpen
Oostduinkerke
Coxyde
Furnes
Bulscamp
Loo Canal
La Panne
Moeres
BELGIUM
FRANCE
Hondschoote
Bray-Dunes
Ghyvelde
Bergues-Furnes Canal
Zuydcoote
Dunkirk-Furnes Canal
Uxem
Malo-les-Bains
Teteghem
Fort Louis
Fort Vallières
Bergues
Eastern Mole
Dunkirk
Western Mole
Cappelle-la-Grande
Bergues Canal
Spycker
Mardyck

ing began, they worked out between themselves how they would defend the beachhead. They would try to hold the coast from Gravelines on the west to Nieuport on the east—a distance of about 30 miles. Inland, the perimeter would make maximum use of the canals that laced the area, running from Gravelines southeast to Bergues ... then east to Furnes ... and finally northeast to Nieuport. The French would be responsible for the area west of Dunkirk, the British for everything east. As the troops fell back into the perimeter, the French should keep to the west, the British to the east. Nowhere was there any provision for the Belgians, who were desperately fighting still farther east; it was decided their situation was too "obscure."

The main meeting now began in the Hôtel du Sauvage dining room, where several tables had been stripped of their cloths and bunched together. It was a bare, stark setting relieved only by a bottle of Armagnac sitting in the center. Besides Fagalde, the French commanders included Admiral Abrial, General Blanchard, and General Koeltz from Weygand's headquarters. General Adam, representing Gort, had brought along Colonel Bridgeman and Lieutenant-General W. G. Lindsell, the BEF Quartermaster-General.

It turned out that the principal business of the meeting was not defense arrangements but a ringing order of the day from General Weygand, relayed by General Koeltz. It called on the embattled forces to swing over to the offensive and retake Calais. The French generals agreed to try, but the British considered the appeal preposterous. Survival was a matter of hanging on, not advancing. To Bridgeman, Koeltz spoke such nonsense that he stopped taking notes.

"Why aren't you writing?" Lindsell whispered.

"There's nothing being said worth writing down," Bridgeman whispered back.

And so it proved. Far from retaking Calais, General Fagalde's hard-pressed 68th Division had to pull back from the Gravelines end of the perimeter. Late on the 27th the French retired to a new line running from Mardyck to Spycker to Bergues.

But at least the beachhead was now blocked out and the responsibilities for its defense clearly defined. As the poilus hunkered down in the western half of the perimeter, General Adam began organizing the eastern half. Under Bridgeman's plan it was divided into three sectors—one for each corps of the BEF. Specifically, III Corps would hold the Dunkirk end, next to the French; I Corps would be in the middle; and II Corps would defend the eastern end, which stretched across the frontier into Belgium. Two major canals—one running from Bergues to Furnes, the other from Furnes to Nieuport—would be the main defense line. For the most part, the line lay five or six miles back from the coast, which would protect the beaches at least from small arms fire. To command this defense line, Adam had the services of Brigadier the Honorable E. F. Lawson, a competent artilleryman.

There was only one ingredient missing—soldiers. As of 8:00 a.m. on the 27th, when the Cassel meeting broke up, the British defense line existed only on paper. Lawson would have to man it with troops plucked from the horde tumbling into Dunkirk, taking pot luck from what turned up. Later he could replace these pick-up units, when the regular divisions holding open the corridor fell back on the coast; but for the moment improvisation was once again the order of the day.

For immediate help he depended largely on artillerymen who had destroyed their guns during the retreat and could now serve as infantry. Several units manned the line between Bergues and Furnes, bolstered by a party of nineteen Grenadier Guards, who had somehow been separated from their battalion. Farther east, the 12th Searchlight Battery dug in at Furnes, and a survey company of Royal Engineers moved into Nieuport.

While Lawson patched together his defense line, Colonel Bridgeman concentrated on getting the troops back to the coast. Basically his plan called for three main routes—III Corps would head for the beach at Malo-les-Bains, an eastern suburb of Dunkirk . . . I Corps for Bray-Dunes, six miles farther east . . . and II Corps for La Panne, four miles still farther east and across the Belgian frontier. All three towns were seaside resorts and provided an unlikely setting of bandstands, carousels, beach chairs, push-pedal cycles, and brightly painted cafés.

Of the three, La Panne was the logical place to establish headquarters. It was where the telephone cable linking Belgium and England entered the Channel, and this meant direct contact with Dover and London not available anywhere else. Adam set up shop in the *Mairie*, or town hall, and it was from here that Bridgeman did his best to direct the withdrawal.

Naturally his plans meant issuing orders, and this in turn meant paper, and this in turn raised a brand new problem: there was no paper. GHQ's entire supply had gone up in flames, as the BEF destroyed its stores and equipment to keep them from falling into enemy hands.

Major Arthur Dove, a staff officer under Bridgeman, finally managed to buy a pad of pink notepaper at a local stationery store. It was more suitable for *billets-doux*, but it was the only thing available. In payment Dove needed all his diplomacy to persuade Madame the proprietress to accept French instead of Belgian francs.

It's doubtful whether many of the addressees ever saw the Major's pink stationery. Dispatch riders did their best to deliver the orders, but communications were in a bigger shambles than ever. While the three corps did stick basically to their allotted sectors of the beachhead, many units remained unaware of any such arrangement, and thousands of stragglers went wherever whim—or an instinct for self-preservation—took them.

They swarmed into Dunkirk and onto the beaches—lost, confused, and all too often leaderless. In many of the service and rear area units the officers had simply vanished, leaving the men to shift for themselves. Some took shelter in cellars in the town, huddling together as the bombs crashed down. Others threw away their arms and aimlessly wandered about the beach. Others played games and swam. Others got drunk. Others prayed and sang hymns. Others settled in deserted cafés on the esplanade and sipped drinks, almost like tourists. One man, with studied indifference, stripped to his shorts and sunbathed among the rocks, reading a paperback.

And all the time the bombs rained down. The 2nd Anti-Aircraft Brigade was charged with protecting Dunkirk, and soon after arriving at La Panne, Colonel Bridgeman instructed the Brigade's liaison officer, Captain Sir Anthony Palmer, to keep his guns going to the last. Any spare gunners to join the infantry; any incapacitated men to go to the beach. Palmer relayed the order to Major-General Henry Martin, commanding all

Gort's antiaircraft, but somewhere along the line the meaning got twisted. Martin understood that all antiaircraft gunners were to go to the beach.

He never questioned the order, although it's hard to see why any force, as hard-pressed from the air as the BEF, would begin an evacuation by sending off its antiaircraft gunners. Instead, he merely reasoned that if the gunners were to leave, there would be no further use for their guns. Rather than have them fall into enemy hands, he ordered his heavy 3.7-inch pieces to be destroyed.

Sometime after midnight, May 27–28, Martin appeared at Adam's headquarters to report that the job was done. With rather a sense of achievement, one observer felt, he saluted smartly and announced, "All the antiaircraft guns have been spiked."

There was a long pause while a near-incredulous Adam absorbed this thunderbolt. Finally he looked up and merely said, "You . . . fool, go away."

So the bombing continued, now opposed only by some light Bofors guns, and by the troops' Brens and rifles. In exasperation some men even cut the fuses of grenades and hurled them into the air hoping to catch some low-flying plane. More were like Lance Corporal Fred Batson of the RASC, who crawled into a discarded Tate & Lyle sugar box. Its thin wooden sides offered no real protection, but somehow he felt safer.

Their big hope was the sea. The Royal Navy would come and get them. Gallipoli, Corunna, the Armada—for centuries, in a tight spot the British had always counted on their navy to save the day, and it had never disappointed them. But tonight, May 27, was different. . . .

Private W.B.A. Gaze, driver with an ordnance repair unit, looked out to sea from Malo-les-Bains and saw nothing. No ships at all, except a shattered French destroyer beached a few yards out, her bow practically severed from the rest of the hull.

After a bit, a single British destroyer hove into view . . . then three Thames barges, which moored 400 yards out . . . and finally fourteen drifters, each towing a couple of small boats. Not much for this mushrooming crowd on the beach.

The prospect was even worse to the east. At La Panne Captain J. L. Moulton, a Royal Marines officer attached to GHQ, went down to the beach to see what was going on. Three sloops lay offshore, but there were no small boats to ferry anybody out.

After quite a while a motor launch appeared, towing a whaler. As a Marine, Moulton knew something about boats and rushed to grab the gunwhale to keep the launch from broaching to the surf. The skipper, sure that Moulton was trying to hijack his boat, fired a shot over his head.

Somehow Moulton convinced the man of his good intentions, but the incident underscored the ragged inadequacy of the whole rescue effort at this point. More ships were needed, and many more small boats.

Acting on his own, Moulton decided to go to Dover. He persuaded the skipper of the launch to ferry him out to one of the sloops, and then persuaded its captain to take him across the Channel. As a Royal Marine he would have easy access to naval headquarters at the Castle. Perhaps he could explain the true dimensions of the job. Without enough ships, all the time so dearly bought in Flanders would be wasted.

5

"Plenty Troops, Few Boats"

In his office just off the Dynamo Room Admiral Ramsay listened politely as Captain Moulton described the desperate situation at Dunkirk, and the need for a greater naval effort if many men were to be saved. Moulton had the sinking feeling that he wasn't getting his point across ... that this was one of those cases where a mere Marine captain didn't carry much weight with a Vice-Admiral of the Royal Navy.

Actually, Moulton was mistaken. If Ramsay didn't seem responsive, it was only because he didn't need to be told. He already knew his ships weren't accomplishing enough at Dunkirk. Relying mainly on personnel vessels—ferries, pleasure steamers, and the like—he had hoped to dispatch two every three and a half hours, but the schedule soon broke down.

The first ship sent was *Mona's Isle*, an Isle of Man packet. She left Dover at 9:00 p.m., May 26, and after an uneventful passage tied up at Dunkirk's Gare Maritime around midnight. Packed with 1,420 troops, she began her return journey at sunrise on the 27th. Second Lieutenant D. C. Snowdon of the 1st/7th Queen's Royal Regiment lay in exhausted sleep below decks, when he was suddenly awakened by what sounded like someone hammering on the hull. This turned out to be German artillery firing on the vessel. Because of shoals and minefields, the short-est route between Dunkirk and Dover (called Route Z) ran close to the shore for some miles west of Dunkirk. Passing ships of-fered a perfect target.

Several shells crashed into *Mona's Isle*, miraculously without exploding. Then a hit aft blew away the rudder. Luckily, she was twin-screw, and managed to keep course by using her propel-lers. Gradually she drew out of range, and the troops settled down again. Lieutenant Snowdon went back to sleep below decks; others remained topside, soaking in the bright morning sun.

Then another rude awakening—this time by a sound like hail on the decks. Six Me 109's were machine-gunning the ship. All the way aft Petty Officer Leonard B. Kearley-Pope crouched alone at the stern gun, gamely firing back. Four bullets tore into his right arm, but he kept shooting, until the planes broke off. *Mona's Isle* finally limped into Dover around noon on the 27th with 23 killed and 60 wounded. Almost as bad from Ramsay's point of view, the 40-mile trip had taken eleven and a half hours instead of the usual three.

By this time other ships too were getting a taste of those Ger-man guns. Two small coasters, *Sequacity* and *Yewdale*, had start-ed for Dunkirk about 4:00 a.m. on the 27th. As they approached the French coast, a shell crashed into *Sequacity*'s starboard side at the waterline, continued through the ship and out the port side. Another smashed into the engine room, knocking out the pumps. Then two more hits, and *Sequacity* began to sink. *Yew-dale* picked up the crew, and with shells splashing around her, headed back for England.

By 10:00 a.m. four more ships had been forced to turn back. None got through, and Admiral Ramsay's schedule was in hopeless disarray. But he was a resourceful, resilient man; in the Dynamo Room the staff caught his spirit and set about revamp-ing their plan.

Clearly Route Z could no longer be used, at least in daylight. There were two alternatives, neither very attractive. Route X, further to the northeast, would avoid the German batteries, but it was full of dangerous shoals and heavily mined. For the mo-ment, at least, it too was out. Finally there was Route Y. It lay still further to the northeast, running almost as far as Ostend,

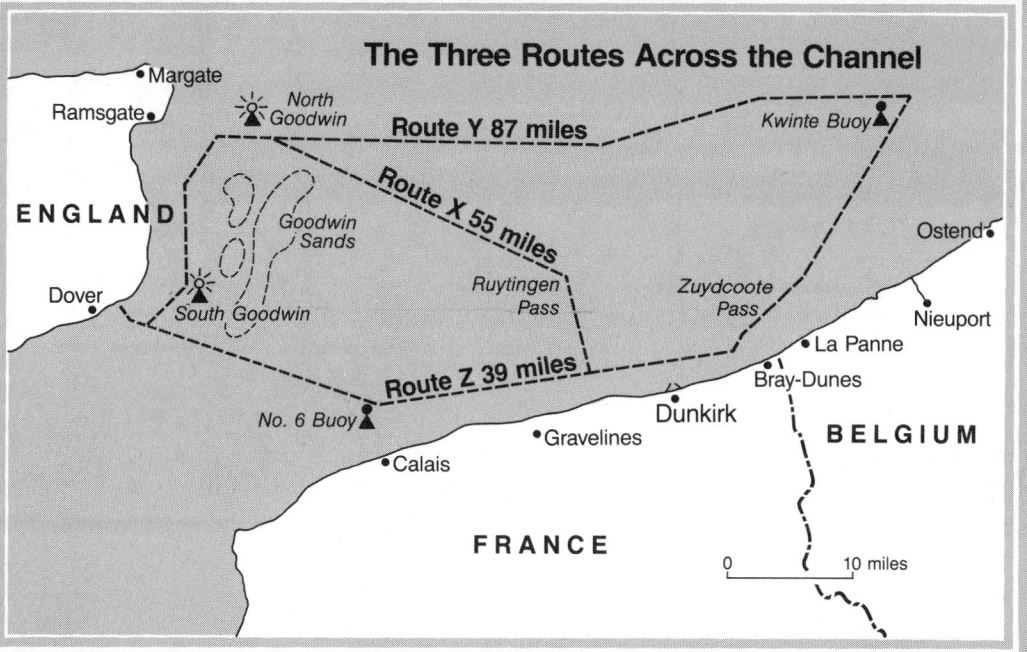

The Three Routes Across the Channel

Margate
Ramsgate
North Goodwin
Route Y 87 miles
Kwinte Buoy
Ostend
ENGLAND
Goodwin Sands
Route X 55 miles
Dover
South Goodwin
Ruytingen Pass
Zuydcoote Pass
Nieuport
La Panne
Bray-Dunes
Route Z 39 miles
No. 6 Buoy
Dunkirk
BELGIUM
Gravelines
Calais
FRANCE
0   10 miles

where it doubled back west toward England. It was easier to navigate, relatively free of mines, and safe from German guns; but it was much, much longer—87 miles, compared to 55 for Route X and 39 for Route Z.

This meant the cross-Channel trip would be twice as long as planned; or, put another way, it would take twice as many ships to keep Ramsay's schedule.

Still, it was the only hope, at least until Route X could be swept clear of mines. At 11:00 a.m. on the 27th the first convoy—two transports, two hospital ships, and two destroyers—left Dover and arrived off Dunkirk nearly six hours later.

The extra effort was largely wasted, for at the moment Dunkirk was taking such a pounding from the Luftwaffe that the port was practically paralyzed. The *Royal Daffodil* managed to pick up 900 men, but the rest of the convoy was warned to stay clear: too much danger of sinking and blocking the harbor. With that, the convoy turned and steamed back to Dover.

During the evening four more transports and two hospital ships arrived by Route Y. The transport *Canterbury* picked up 457 troops at the Gare Maritime, but then the Luftwaffe returned for a nighttime visit, and it again looked as though the harbor might be blocked.

As *Canterbury* pulled out, she received a signal from the shore to turn back any other vessels trying to enter. She relayed the message to several ships waiting outside, and they in turn relayed it to other ships. There was more than one inexperienced signalman at sea that night, and garbles were inevitable. By the time the warning was flashed by a passing ship to the skoot *Tilly*, coming over by Route Y, it said, "Dunkirk has fallen and is in enemy hands. Keep clear."

Tilly was one of six skoots that had sailed together from the Dover Downs that afternoon. Her skipper, Lieutenant-Commander W.R.T. Clemments, had no idea why he was going to Dunkirk. His only clue was a pile of 450 lifejackets that had been dumped aboard just before sailing—rather many for a crew of eleven. Now here was a ship telling him to turn back from a trip he didn't understand anyhow. After consulting with the nearest skoot, he put about and returned to Dover for further orders.

The other skoots hovered off Nieuport for a while. They too received signals from passing ships that Dunkirk had fallen. They too turned back. To cap off the day, two strings of lifeboats being towed over by a tug were run down and scattered.

This chain of mishaps and misunderstandings explained why the men waiting on the beaches saw so few ships on May 27. Only 7,669 men were evacuated that day, most of them "useless mouths" evacuated by ships sent from Dover before Dynamo officially began. At this rate it would take 40 days to lift the BEF.

As the bad news flowed in, Admiral Ramsay and his staff in the Dynamo Room struggled to get the show going again. Clearly more destroyers were needed—to escort the convoys, to fight off the Luftwaffe, to help lift the troops, to provide a protective screen for the longer Route Y. Ramsay fired off an urgent appeal to the Admiralty: take destroyers off other jobs; get them to Dunkirk. . . .

HMS *Jaguar* was on escort duty in the cold, foggy waters off Norway when orders came to return to England at once. . . . *Havant* was lying at Greenock, tucked among the green hills of western Scotland. . . . *Harvester* was a brand new destroyer training far to the south off the Dorset coast. One after another, all available destroyers were ordered to proceed to Dover "forthwith."

Saladin was a 1914 antique on escort duty off the Western Approaches when she got the word. The other escort vessels had similar orders, and all complied at once. The twelve to fourteen ships in the convoy were left to fend for themselves. These were dangerous waters, and Chief Signal Clerk J. W. Martin of the *Saladin* wondered what the commodore of the convoy thought as he watched his protection steam away.

On the destroyers few of the men knew what was up. On the *Saladin* Martin, who saw much of the message traffic, caught a reference to "Dynamo," but that told him nothing. He just knew it must be important if they were leaving a convoy in this part of the Atlantic.

Speculation increased as the destroyers reached Dover and were ordered to proceed immediately to "beaches east of Dunkirk." On the *Malcolm* the navigation officer, Lieutenant David Mellis, supposed they were going to bring off some army unit that had been cut off. With luck they should finish the job in a few hours. The *Anthony* passed a motor boat heading back to England with about twenty soldiers aboard. The officer of the watch shouted across the water, asking if there were many more to come. "Bloody thousands," somebody yelled back.

It was still dark when the *Jaguar* crept near the French coast in the early hours of May 28. As dawn broke, Stoker A. D. Saunders saw that the ship was edging toward a beautiful stretch of white sand, which appeared to have shrubs planted all over it. Then the shrubs began to move, forming lines pointed toward the sea, and Saunders realized they were men, thousands of soldiers waiting for help.

The whole stretch of beach from Dunkirk to La Panne shelved so gradually that the destroyers couldn't get closer than a mile, even at high tide. Since no small craft were yet on the scene, the destroyers had to use their own boats to pick up the men. The boat crews weren't used to this sort of work, the soldiers even less so.

Sometimes they piled into one side all at once, upsetting the craft. Other times too many crowded into a boat, grounding or swamping it. All too often they simply abandoned the boat once they reached the rescue ship. Motors were clogged with sand, propellers fouled by debris, oars lost. Operating off Malo-les-Bains in the early hours of May 28, *Sabre*'s three boats picked up only 100 men in two hours. At La Panne, *Malcolm*'s record was even worse—450 men in fifteen hours.

"Plenty troops, few boats," the destroyer *Wakeful* radioed Ramsay at 5:07 a.m. on the 28th, putting the problem as succinctly as possible. All through the day *Wakeful* and the other destroyers sent a stream of messages to Dover urging more small boats. The Dynamo Room in turn needled London.

The Small Vessels Pool was doing its best, but it took time to wade through the registration data sent in by owners. Then H. C. Riggs of the Ministry of Shipping thought of a short-cut. Why not go direct to the various boatyards along the Thames? With a war on, many of the owners had laid up their craft.

At Tough Brothers boatyard in Teddington the proprietor, Douglas Tough, got an early-morning phone call from Admiral Sir Lionel Preston himself. The evacuation was still secret, but Preston took Tough into his confidence, explaining the nature of the problem and the kind of boats needed.

The Admiral couldn't have come to a better man. The Tough family had been in business on the Thames for three generations. Douglas Tough had founded the present yard in 1922 and knew just about every boat on the river. He was willing to act for the Admiralty, commandeering any suitable craft.

The first fourteen were already in the yard. Supervised by Chief Foreman Harry Day, workmen swiftly off-loaded cushions and china, ripped out the peacetime fittings, put the engines in working order, filled the fuel tanks.

Tough himself went up and down the river, picking out additional boats that he thought could stand the wear and tear of the job ahead. Most owners were willing; some came along with their boats. A few objected, but he commandeered their vessels anyhow. Some never realized what was happening, until they later found their boats missing and reported the "theft" to the police.

Meanwhile volunteer crews were also being assembled at Tough's, mostly amateurs from organizations like the Little Ships Club or a wartime creation called the River Emergency Service. These gentleman sailors would get the boats down the river to Southend, where the Navy would presumably take over.

The Small Vessels Pool, of course, did not confine its efforts to Tough's. It tried practically every boatyard and yacht club from Cowes to Margate. Usually no explanation was given—just the distance the boats had to go. At William Osborne's yard in Littlehampton the cabin cruisers *Gwen Eagle* and *Bengeo* seemed to fill the bill; local hands were quickly rounded up by the harbor master, and off they went.

Often the Small Vessels Pool dealt directly with the owners in its files. Technically every vessel was chartered, but the paperwork was usually done long afterwards.

Despite a later legend of heroic sacrifice, some cases were difficult. Preston's assistant secretary Stanley Berry found himself dealing interminably with the executor of a deceased owner's estate, who wanted to know who was going to pay a charge of £3 for putting the boat in the water. But most were like the owner who asked whether he could retrieve some whisky left on board. When Berry replied it was too late for that, the man simply said he hoped the finder would have a good drink on him.

By now the Dynamo Room was reaching far beyond the Small Vessels Pool. The Nore Command of the Royal Navy, based at Chatham, scoured the Thames estuary for shallow-draft barges. The Port of London authorities stripped the lifeboats off the *Volendam*, *Durbar Castle*, and other ocean liners that happened to be in dock. The Royal National Lifeboat Institution sent everything it had along the east and south coasts.

The Army offered eight landing craft (called ALC's), but some way had to be found to bring them from Southampton. Jimmy Keith, the Ministry of Shipping liaison man in the Dynamo Room, phoned Basil Bellamy at the Sea Transport Division in London. For once, the solution was easy. Bellamy flipped through his cards and found that the cargo liner *Clan MacAlister*, already in Southampton, had exceptionally strong derrick posts. She began loading the ALC's on the morning of the 27th, and was on her way down the Solent by 6:30 p.m.

On board was a special party of 45 seamen and two reserve officers. They would man the ALC's. Like the crews for the skoots, they were drawn from the Chatham Naval Barracks. Sometimes a ship was lucky and drew an experienced crew. More often it was like the skoot *Patria*, which had a coxswain who couldn't steer and an engineer making his first acquaintance with marine diesels.

In the Dynamo Room, Admiral Ramsay's staff worked on.

There seemed a million things to do, and all had to be done at once: Clear Route X of mines. . . . Get more fighter cover from the RAF. . . . Find more Lewis guns. . . . Dispatch the antiaircraft cruiser *Calcutta* to the scene. . . . Repair damaged vessels. . . . Replace worn-out crews. . . . Send over water for the beleaguered troops. . . . Prepare for the wounded. . . . Get the latest weather forecast. . . . Line up some 125 maintenance craft to service the little ships now gathering at Sheerness. . . . Put some men to work making ladders—fast.

"Poor Morgan," Ramsay wrote Mag, describing the effect on his staff, "is terribly strained and badly needs a rest. 'Flags' looks like a ghost, and the Secretary has suddenly become old. All my staff are in fact completely worn out, yet I see no prospect of any let up. . . ."

For Ramsay himself there was one ray of light. Vice-Admiral Sir James Somerville had come down from London, volunteering to take over from time to time so that Ramsay could get a bit of rest. Somerville had an electric personality, and was worshiped by junior officers. He was not only a perfect stand-in but a good trouble-shooter as well. Shortly after his arrival on May 27 morale collapsed on the destroyer *Verity*. She had been badly shelled on a couple of trips across the Channel, her captain was seriously wounded, and the crew had reached the breaking point. One sailor even tried to commit suicide. When the acting skipper reported the situation to Dover Castle, Somerville went back with him and addressed the ship's company. Knowing that words can only accomplish so much, he also rested *Verity* overnight. Next morning she was back on the job.

To Somerville, to Ramsay—to the whole Dynamo Room contingent—the evacuation had become an obsession. So it seemed like a visit from another world when three high-ranking French naval officers turned up in Dover on the 27th to discuss, among other things, how to keep Dunkirk supplied.

From General Weygand on down, the French still regarded the port as a permanent foothold on the Continent. Admiral Darlan, the suave naval Chief of Staff, was no exception, and his deputy, Captain Paul Auphan, had the task of organizing a supply fleet for the beachhead. Auphan decided that trawlers and fishing smacks were the best bet, and his men fanned out over

Normandy and Brittany commandeering more than 200 vessels.

Meanwhile, disturbing news reached Darlan. A liaison officer attached to Gort's headquarters reported that the British were considering evacuation—with or without the French. It was decided to send Auphan to Dover, where he would be joined by Rear-Admiral Marcel Leclerc from Dunkirk and by Vice-Admiral Jean Odend'hal, head of the French Naval Mission in London. A firsthand assessment might clarify the situation.

Auphan and Odend'hal arrived first, and as they waited for Leclerc in the officers' mess, Odend'hal noticed a number of familiar British faces. They were strictly "desk types"—men he saw daily at the Admiralty—yet here they were in Dover wearing tin hats. Odend'hal asked what was up. "We're here for the evacuation," they replied.

The two visitors were astonished. This was the first word to reach the French Navy that the British were not merely "considering" evacuation—they were already pulling out. Leclerc now arrived, and all three went to see Ramsay. He brought them up to date on Dynamo. Auphan began rearranging the plans for his fleet of fishing smacks and trawlers. Instead of supplying the beachhead, they would now be used to evacuate French troops. The two navies would work together, but it was understood that each country would look primarily after its own.

Back in France next day, the 28th, Auphan rushed to French naval headquarters at Maintenon and broke the news to Darlan. The Admiral was so amazed he took the Captain to see General Weygand. He professed to be equally surprised, and Auphan found himself in the odd position of briefing the Supreme Allied Commander on what the British were doing.

It's hard to understand why they all were so astounded. On the afternoon of May 26 Churchill told Reynaud that the British planned to evacuate, urging the French Premier to issue "corresponding orders." At 5:00 a.m. on the 27th Eden radioed the British liaison at Weygand's headquarters, asking where the French wanted the evacuated troops to be landed when they returned to that part of France still held by the Allies. At 7:30 a.m. the same day the French and British commanders meeting at Cassel discussed the "lay-out of the beaches" at Dunkirk—they could only have been talking about the evacuation.

Informally, the French had been aware of Gort's thinking a good deal sooner. As early as May 23 a British liaison officer, Major O. A. Archdale, came unofficially to say good-bye to his opposite number, Major Joseph Fauvelle, at French First Army Group headquarters. Fauvelle gathered that evacuation was in the wind and told his boss, General Blanchard. He in turn sent Fauvelle to Paris to tell Weygand. The information was in the Supreme Commander's hands by 9:00 a.m., May 25.

And yet, surprise and confusion on the 28th, when Captain Auphan reported that the British had begun to evacuate. Perhaps the best explanation lies in the almost complete breakdown of French communications. The troops trapped in Flanders were no longer in touch with Weygand's headquarters, except by wireless via the French Navy, and their headquarters at Maintenon was 70 miles from Paris.

As a result, vital messages were delayed or missed altogether. The various commands operated in a vacuum; there was no agreement on policy or tactics even among themselves. Reynaud accepted evacuation. Weygand thought in terms of a big bridgehead including a recaptured Calais. Blanchard and Fagalde wrote off Calais, but still planned on a smaller bridgehead built around Dunkirk. General Prioux, commanding First Army, was bent on a gallant last stand down around Lille.

In contrast, the British were now united in one goal—evacuation. As Odend'hal noted, even senior staff officers from the Admiralty were manning small boats and working the beaches—often on the shortest notice.

One of these was Captain William G. Tennant, a lean, reserved navigation expert who normally was Chief Staff Officer to the First Sea Lord in London. He got his orders on May 26 at 6:00 p.m.; by 8:25 he was on the train heading for Dover. Tennant was to be Senior Naval Officer at Dunkirk, in charge of the shore end of the evacuation. As SNO he would supervise the distribution and loading of the rescue fleet. To back him up he had a naval shore party of eight officers and 160 men.

After a brief stopover at Chatham Naval Barracks, he arrived in Dover at 9:00 a.m. on the 27th. Meanwhile buses were coming from Chatham, bringing the men assigned to the shore party. Most still had no idea what was up. One rumor spread that

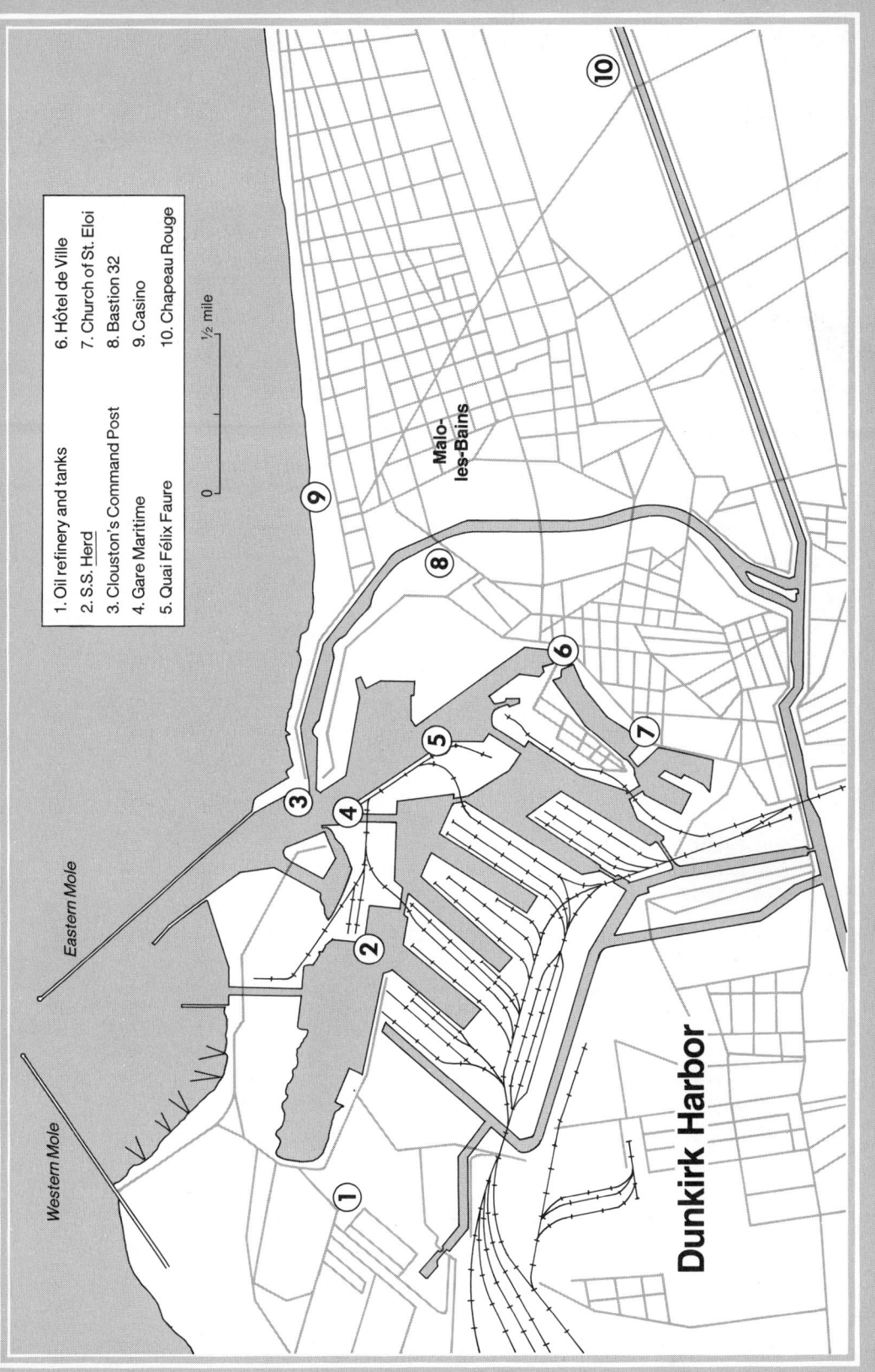

Western Mole

Eastern Mole

1. Oil refinery and tanks
2. S.S. Herd
3. Clouston's Command Post
4. Gare Maritime
5. Quai Félix Faure
6. Hôtel de Ville
7. Church of St. Eloi
8. Bastion 32
9. Casino
10. Chapeau Rouge

0   ½ mile

Malo-
les-Bains

Dunkirk Harbor

they were going to man some six-inch guns on the Dover cliffs. Seaman Carl Fletcher was delighted at the prospect: he then would be stationed near home.

He soon learned better. On arrival at Dover the men were divided into parties of twenty, each commanded by one of Tennant's eight officers. Fletcher's group was under Commander Hector Richardson, who explained that they would shortly be going to Dunkirk. It was a bit "hot" there, he added, and they might like to fortify themselves at a pub across the way. To a man they complied, and Seaman Fletcher belted down an extra one for the trip over.

The destroyer *Wolfhound* would be taking them across, and shortly before departure her skipper, Lieutenant-Commander John McCoy, dropped by the wardroom to learn what his officers knew about conditions at Dunkirk. Sub-Lieutenant H. W. Stowell piped up that he had a friend on another destroyer who was there recently and had a whale of a time—champagne, dancing girls, a most hospitable port.

At 1:45 p.m. *Wolfhound* sailed, going by the long Route Y. At 2:45 the first Stukas struck, and it was hell the rest of the way. Miraculously, the ship dodged everything, and at 5:35 slipped into Dunkirk harbor. The whole coastline seemed ablaze, and a formation of 21 German planes rained bombs on the quay as *Wolfhound* tied up. Commander McCoy dryly asked Sub-Lieutenant Stowell where the champagne and dancing girls were.

The *Wolfhound* was too inviting a target. Captain Tennant landed his shore party and dispersed them as soon as possible. Then he set off with several of his officers for Bastion 32, where Admiral Abrial had allotted space to the local British command.

Normally it was a ten-minute walk, but not today. Tennant's party had to pick their way through streets littered with rubble and broken glass. Burned-out trucks and tangled trolley wires were everywhere. Black, oily smoke swirled about the men as they trudged along. Dead and wounded British soldiers sprawled among the debris; others, perfectly fit, prowled aimlessly about, or scrounged among the ruins.

It was well after 6:00 p.m. by the time they reached Bastion 32, which turned out to be a concrete bunker protected by earth and heavy steel doors. Inside, a damp, dark corridor led through a candle-lit operations room to the cubbyhole that was assigned to the British Naval Liaison Officer, Commander Harold Henderson.

Here Tennant met with Henderson, Brigadier R.H.R. Parminter from Gort's staff, and Colonel G.H.P. Whitfield, the Area Commandant. All three agreed that Dunkirk harbor couldn't be used for evacuation. The air attacks were too devastating. The beaches to the east were the only hope.

Tennant asked how long he would have for the job. The answer was not encouraging: "24 to 36 hours." After that, the Germans would probably be in Dunkirk. With this gloomy assessment, at 7:58 p.m. he sent his first signal to Dover as Senior Naval Officer:

> Please send every available craft East of Dunkirk immediately. Evacuation tomorrow night is problematical.

At 8:05 he sent another message, elaborating slightly:

> Port continually bombed all day and on fire. Embarkation possible only from beaches east of harbour.... Send all ships and passenger ships there. Am ordering *Wolfhound* to anchor there, load and sail.

In Dover, the Dynamo Room burst into action as the staff rushed to divert the rescue fleet from Dunkirk to the ten-mile stretch of sand east of the port....

> 9:01, *Maid of Orleans* not to enter Dunkirk but anchor close inshore between Malo-les-Bains and Zuydcoote to embark troops from beach....

> 9:27, *Grafton* and Polish destroyer *Blyskawicz* to close beach at LaPanne at 0100/28 and embark all possible British troops in own boats. This is our last chance of saving them....

> 9:42, *Gallant* [plus five other destroyers and cruiser *Calcutta*] to close beach one to three miles east of Dunkirk with utmost despatch and embark all possi-

ble British troops. This is our last chance of saving
them.

Within an hour the Dynamo Room managed to shift to the
beaches all the vessels in service at the moment: a cruiser, 9 destroyers, 2 transports, 4 minesweepers, 4 skoots, and 17 drifters—37 ships altogether.

In Dunkirk, Captain Tennant's naval party went to work
rounding up the scattered troops and sending them to the nearest beach at Malo-les-Bains. Here they were divided by Commander Richardson into packets of 30 to 50 men. In most cases
the soldiers were pathetically eager to obey anybody who
seemed to know what he was doing. "Thank God we've got a
Navy," remarked one soldier to Seaman Fletcher.

Most of the troops were found crowded in the port's cellars,
taking cover from the bombs. Second Lieutenant Arthur
Rhodes managed to get his men into a basement liberally
stocked with champagne and foie gras, which became their sta-
ple diet for some time. But this did not mean they were enjoying the good life. Some 60 men, two civilian women, and
assorted stray dogs were packed in together. The atmosphere
was heavy . . . made even heavier when one of the soldiers fed
some foie gras to one of the dogs, and it promptly threw up.

Some of the men took to the champagne, and drunken shouts
soon mingled with the crash of bombs and falling masonry that
came from above. From time to time Rhodes ventured outside
trying to find a better cellar, but they all were crowded and he
finally gave up. Toward evening he heard a cry for "officers."
Going up, he learned that the Royal Navy had arrived. He was
to take his men to the beaches; ships would try to lift them that
night.

Cellars couldn't hold all the men now pouring into Dunkirk.
Some, looking desperately for cover, headed for the sturdy old
French fortifications that lay between the harbor and the beach-
es east of town. Bastion 32 was here, with its small quota of
British staff officers, but the French units holed up in the area
were not inclined to admit any more visitors.

Terrified and leaderless, one group of British stragglers
wasn't about to turn back. They had no officers, but they did

have rifles. During the evening of the 27th they approached Bastion 32, brandishing their guns and demanding to be let in. Two Royal Navy officers came out unarmed and parlayed with them. It was still touch and go when one of Tennant's shore parties arrived. The sailors quickly restored order, and this particular crisis was over.

Seaman G. F. Nixon, attached to one of these naval parties, later recalled how quickly the troops responded to almost any show of firm authority. "It was amazing what a two-badge sailor with a fixed bayonet and a loud voice did to those lads."

Captain Tennant, making his first inspection of the beaches as SNO, personally addressed several jittery groups. He urged them to keep calm and stay under cover as much as possible. He assured them that plenty of ships were coming, and that they would all get safely back to England.

He was invariably successful, partly because the ordinary Tommy had such blind faith in the Royal Navy, but also because Tennant *looked* like an officer. Owing to the modern fashion of dressing all soldiers alike, the army officers didn't stand out even when present, but there was no doubt about Tennant. In his well-cut navy blues, with its brass buttons and four gold stripes, he had authority written all over him.

And in Tennant's case, there was an extra touch. During a snack at Bastion 32 his signal officer, Commander Michael Ellwood, cut the letters "S-N-O" from the silver foil of a cigarette pack, then glued them to the Captain's helmet with thick pea soup.

Unfortunately no amount of discipline could change the basic arithmetic of Dunkirk. Far too few men were being lifted from the beaches. Tennant estimated he could do the job five or six times faster if he could use the docks. Yet one glance at Dunkirk's blazing waterfront proved that was out of the question.

But he did notice a peculiar thing. Although the Luftwaffe was pounding the piers and quays, it completely ignored the two long breakwaters or moles that formed the entrance to Dunkirk's harbor. Like a pair of protective arms, these moles ran toward each other—one from the west and one from the east—with just enough room for a ship to pass in between. It was the eastern mole that attracted Tennant's special attention.

Made of concrete piling topped by a wooden walkway, it ran some 1,400 yards out to sea. If ships could be brought alongside, it would speed up the evacuation enormously.

The big drawback: the mole was never built to be used as a pier. Could it take the pounding it would get, as the swift tidal current—running as high as three knots—slammed ships against the flimsy wooden planking? There were posts here and there, but they were meant only for occasional harbor craft. Could large vessels tie up without yanking the posts loose? The walkway was just ten feet wide, barely room for four men walking abreast. Would this lead to impossible traffic jams?

All these difficulties were aggravated by a fifteen-foot tidal drop. Transferring the troops at low or high water was bound to be a tricky and dangerous business.

Still, it was the only hope. At 10:30 p.m. Tennant signaled *Wolfhound*, now handling communications offshore, to send a personnel ship to the mole "to embark 1,000 men." The assignment went to *Queen of the Channel*, formerly a crack steamer on the cross-Channel run. At the moment she was lifting troops from the beach at Malo-les-Bains, and like everyone else, her crew found it slow going. She quickly shifted to the mole and began loading up. She had no trouble, and the anxious naval party heaved a collective sigh of relief.

By 4:15 a.m. some 950 men crammed the *Queen*'s decks. Dawn was breaking, when a voice called out from the mole asking how many more she could take. "It's not a case of how many more," her skipper shouted back, "but whether we can get away with what we already have."

He was right. Less than halfway across the Channel a single German plane dropped a stick of bombs just astern of the *Queen*, breaking her back. Except for a few soldiers who jumped overboard, everyone behaved with amazing calm. Seaman George Bartlett even considered briefly whether he should go below for a new pair of shoes he had left in his locker. He wisely thought better of it, for the ship was now sinking fast. He and the rest stood quietly on the sloping decks, until a rescue ship, the *Dorrien Rose*, nudged alongside and transferred them all.

The *Queen of the Channel* was lost, but the day was saved. The mole worked! The timbers did not collapse; the tide did not interfere; the troops did not panic. There was plenty of room for a steady procession of ships. The story might be different once the Germans caught on, but clouds of smoke hung low over the harbor. Visibility was at a minimum.

"SNO requires all vessels alongside east pier," the destroyer *Wakeful* radioed Ramsay from Dunkirk at 4:36 a.m. on the 28th. Once again the staff in the Dynamo Room swung into action. They had spent the early part of the night diverting the rescue fleet from the harbor to the beaches; now they went to work shifting it back again. On the beach at Malo-les-Bains Commander Richardson got the word too and began sending the troops back to Dunkirk in batches of 500.

But even as the loading problem was being solved, a whole new crisis arose. Critical moments at Dunkirk had a way of alternating between the sea and the land, and this time, appropriately enough, the setting once again reverted to the battle-scarred fields of Flanders.

At 4 a.m.—just as the *Queen of the Channel* was proving that the mole would work—Leopold III, King of the Belgians, formally laid down his arms. The result left a twenty-mile gap in the eastern wall of the escape corridor. Unless it could be closed at once, the Germans would pour in, cut the French and British off from the sea, and put an abrupt end to the evacuation.

6

The Gap

General Gort heard the news by chance. Hoping to confer with General Blanchard about the evacuation, he had driven to Bastion 32 around 11 o'clock on the night of May 27. No sign of Blanchard, but General Koeltz from Weygand's headquarters was there, and casually asked whether Gort had heard that King Leopold was seeking an armistice.

Gort was amazed. He felt sure that the Belgians weren't capable of prolonged resistance, but he didn't expect them to crumble so soon. "I now found myself suddenly faced with an open gap of 20 miles between Ypres and the sea through which enemy armoured forces might reach the beaches."

General Weygand was even more astonished. He got the word during a conference at Vincennes, when somebody handed him a telegram from his liaison officer with the Belgians. "The news came like a thunderclap, as nothing had enabled me to foresee such a decision, no warning, not a hint of it."

Even Winston Churchill, who had his own special man, Admiral Sir Roger Keyes, at Leopold's headquarters, seems to have been caught off-guard. "Suddenly," the Prime Minister told a hushed House of Commons a few days later, "without prior consultation, with the least possible notice, without the advice

of his ministers, and upon his own personal act, he sent a pleni-
potentiary to the German command, surrendered his Army, and
exposed our whole flank and means of retreat."

The mystery is why they were so surprised. As early as May 25
Leopold had telegraphed King George VI that Belgian resistance was on the point of being crushed, "and so the assistance
which we can give to the Allies will come to an end if our Army
is surrounded." He added that he considered it his duty to remain with his people and not set up a government in exile.

On the 26th and 27th both Gort and the War Office received
from their Belgian liaison contacts seven separate messages
warning that the end was near, unless the British could counterattack—which was clearly impossible. In addition, Admiral
Keyes telephoned Churchill on the morning of May 27 that "he
did not think that the Belgian army's resistance could be maintained much longer." Keyes then wired Gort that Leopold

> fears a moment is rapidly approaching when he can
> no longer rely upon his troops to fight or be of any
> further use to the BEF. He wishes you to realize that
> he will be obliged to surrender before a debacle.

Leopold, on the other hand, had been told nothing about Allied
intentions. Although Gort felt that an active, fighting Belgian
Army was "essential for our extraction," its leaders were never
consulted, and not one ship was allocated for the use of Belgian
troops.

Finally, after a nudge from Eden, Churchill telegraphed Gort
on the morning of May 27, "It is now necessary to tell the Belgians. . . ." He then included a personal message for Admiral
Keyes, spelling out the approach to take with Leopold: "Impart
following to your friend. Presume he knows that British and
French are fighting their way to coast. . . ." Thus London explained away its failure to inform the King by simply "presum-
ing" that he already knew.

Churchill's message also urged Keyes to make sure that Leopold left the country and ended with a vague offer to include
Belgian troops whenever the BEF returned to France.

The message never reached Keyes, but it didn't matter. By

now Leopold had other ideas. Never an attractive personality—
a haughty, aloof man who made his ministers stand in his presence—the King nevertheless had a strong sense of duty. On the
mistaken assumption that he would continue to have influence
under German occupation, he decided to surrender and remain
with his people.

At 5:00 p.m. on the 27th a trusted staff officer, Major-General
Derousseau, set out with a white flag for the German lines. Any
hopes he had for favorable terms were quickly dashed. The
Fuehrer insisted on unconditional surrender. Leopold agreed,
and at 4:00 a.m. on May 28 Belgium formally laid down her
arms.

Here and there a few fought on. After an exhausting day of
retreat, Captain Georges Truffant of the 16th Infantry Division
was sleeping in the great hall of the chateau at Ruddervoorde
when he woke up with a start at 4:30 a.m. The lights were on,
and people were moving about. "The army has capitulated,"
somebody explained.

"What?"

"The liaison officer attached to Corps headquarters has just
brought the order."

"Then I'm deserting." Truffant, a member of Parliament and
one of the young leaders of the Walloon Socialist Party, was no
man for blind obedience to military orders.

He "borrowed" a staff car and was soon on his way to Dunkirk. Coming to a French outpost, he learned that staying in the
war would be no easy matter. Enraged by the Belgian surrender, the officer in charge called him a traitor, a coward, and
warned that the guard would start shooting if he came any
closer.

Turned back, Truffant now tried another road farther south
. . . and ran head-on into a German column. Racing north again,
he reached the sea at Coxyde. Here he cautiously approached a
British officer and carefully explained he was no traitor. Could
he enter the lines?

"I'm afraid it's impossible, sir. Sorry."

On to Nieuport, which he found full of Belgian soldiers, some
as frustrated as himself. Here Truffant and a few others appro-
priated a fishing smack lying in the fairway. They had trouble

with the engine, with the sail, and with a lone German plane that swooped down and buzzed them. It apparently decided they weren't worth the ammunition, for it flew off and they safely reached the open sea.

It was now dark, and to attract attention they lit rags soaked in petrol. There were plenty of ships, but no one wanted to stop in these dangerous waters. Finally a British destroyer did pick them up, and once again Truffant faced a hostile reception.

This time he managed to sell his case. In fact, the destroyer was on its way to Dunkirk and could use these sturdy Belgians with their boat. It had been a long, hard day, but Georges Truffant was at last back in the war.

There were not many like him. Private W.C.P. Nye of the 4th Royal Sussex was on sentry duty at the Courtrai airfield when he saw a mass of men coming down the road away from the front. Hundreds of Belgian soldiers on bicycles swept by, shouting that the war was over. Tramping toward the coast from the River Lys, the men of the 2nd North Staffordshire passed swarms of disarmed Belgians standing by the roadside watching the retreat. Some looked ashamed, but many shouted insults and shook their fists at the weary Tommies. At Bulscamp a plump gendarme appeared at British headquarters, announced that Belgium had surrendered and he had been ordered to confiscate all British weapons. There is no record of the language used in reply.

All over the countryside white bedsheets blossomed from windows and doorways. At Watou Lieutenant Ramsay of the 2nd Dorsets started to enter an empty house to get a bit of rest. A woman who lived nearby rushed up crying, "*Non, non, non!*"

"*C'est la guerre,*" explained Ramsay, using the time-honored expression that had served so well in two world wars to explain any necessary inconvenience.

"*C'est la guerre, oui, mais pas pour nous!*" she retorted.

To most Belgians it was now indeed somebody else's war, and they were relieved to be out of it. Many felt their country had become just a doormat, to be stamped on by larger, stronger neighbors in an apparently endless struggle for power. "*Les anglais, les allemands, toute la même chose,*" as one weary peasant woman put it.

Technically, the Belgian surrender suddenly created a huge gap at the northeastern end of the Allied escape corridor. Actually, the gap had been steadily growing as Belgian resistance crumbled, and for the past 48 hours Lieutenant-General Brooke, the II Corps commander defending the line, had been juggling his forces, trying to fill it. He worked miracles, but on the afternoon of May 27 (just when Leopold was tossing in his hand) there were still no Allied troops between the British 50th Division near Ypres and some French on the coast at Nieuport—a gap of over twenty miles.

All Brooke had left was Major-General Montgomery's 3rd Division down by Roubaix near the bottom of the pocket. To do any good, it would have to pull out from its position near the right end of the line . . . move north for 25 miles across the rear of three other divisions . . . then slide back into place on the far left. The shift would be that most difficult of military maneuvers: a giant side-step by 13,000 men, made at night along back lanes and unfamiliar roads, often within 4,000 yards of the enemy. And it all had to be completed by daylight, when the moving column would make a prime target for the Luftwaffe.

Montgomery wasn't in the least fazed by the assignment. Although virtually unknown to the public, he was probably the most discussed division commander in the BEF. Cocky, conceited, abrasive, theatrical, he had few friends but many admirers in the army. Whatever they thought of him, all agreed that he was technically a superb soldier and a master at training and inspiring troops. All winter his men had practiced this sort of night march. They had drilled and drilled, until every detail was down pat, every contingency foreseen. Now "Monty" was sure he could pull it off.

Late afternoon, his machine gunners and armored cars went ahead as a light advance force. Then at last light the red-capped Military Police moved out to mark the way and keep the traffic properly spaced. Finally, after dark, the main body—2,000 vans, lorries, pick-ups, staff cars, and troop carriers. There were, of course, no regular lights. Every driver had to watch the rear axle of the vehicle in front of him. It was painted white, faintly illuminated by a small shielded lamp. Monty himself was riding in his regular Humber staff car, with his bodyguard Sergeant Elkin close by on his motorcycle. On their right the front, running parallel, was marked by the constant flicker of guns. On their left some British artillery kept up a lively fire from Mont Kemmel. Shells and tracers were passing overhead in both directions, forming a weird archway for the moving troops. Once a British battery, positioned by the roadside, let loose just as Monty was passing. It practically blew the Humber off the road, but the General didn't bat an eye.

By daylight on the 28th the 3rd Division was moving into position. Thanks to Montgomery's giant side-step, British troops now held the eastern wall of the escape corridor as far north as Noordschote. For the rest of the way to the sea—some thirteen miles—he counted on the remaining Belgians, for they were still in the war, as far as he knew. Then, shortly after 7:30 a.m., he learned for the first time of Leopold's capitulation.

"Here was a pretty pickle!" Montgomery later recalled in his memoirs. "Instead of having a Belgian Army on my left, I now had nothing. . . ." He quickly slapped together a scratch force of machine gunners plus some British and French armored cars. These fanned out and held the line until more substantial help could be mustered. It was often touch and go. Lieutenant Mann of the 12th Lancers barely managed to blow the bridge at Dixmude before Bock's advance entered the town.

Then, in the afternoon, more bad news. The Germans were at Nieuport, the eastern anchor of the perimeter. The Belgians were gone; Montgomery was stretched to the limit; there was no organized unit to defend the line from Wulpen to Nieuport and the sea.

Once more, improvisation. Brigadier A. J. Clifton happened to be available. Brooke packed him off to Wulpen to organize the defense. On arriving, he took over a scratch force of 200 artillerymen, bolstered from time to time by "unemployed" fitters, surveyors, transport drivers, and headquarters clerks. The unit never had a name; the officers came from five different regiments. Most of the men had never seen their officers before, and the officers had never worked with Clifton.

Somehow he welded them together and they marched off to the front in amazingly good spirits. Along the way, they met the disbanded Belgians trooping back. The Belgians were throwing away their weapons and shouting that the war was over. Taking advantage of the windfall, Clifton's men scooped up the discarded rifles and ammunition, and added them to their own meager arsenal. Positioned along the Furnes-Nieuport canal and the River Yser, they kept the enemy at bay for the next 30 hours. The hottest fighting swirled around the bridge at Nieuport. The Belgians had failed to blow it before the cease-fire, and the British sappers couldn't reach the demolition wires at the eastern end. Again and again the Germans tried to cross, but Clifton concentrated all his "heavy stuff" (four 18-pounders and some Bren guns) at this point and managed to fend them off. Once again the eastern wall held.

The west held too. At Wormhout, a strong-point twelve miles south of Dunkirk, the British 144th Brigade held off Guderian's troops all May 27 and most of the 28th. Every man was used. At the local chateau that served as Brigade headquarters, Private Lou Carrier found himself teaching some cooks and clerks how to prime a Mills bomb—even though he had never seen one before in his life.

Successfully completing this hazardous assignment, he was ordered to help man the chateau wall. As he made his way through the garden, he heard a terrible scream. Thinking some poor blighter had been hit, he spun around . . . and discovered that it came from a peacock perched in a tree.

"That is one bird who will frighten no one else," Carrier said to himself as he raised his rifle to bring it down. Before he could fire, a young lieutenant knocked the rifle aside, saying that he should know better. Didn't he realize it was unlucky to shoot peacocks? The officer added that Carrier would be courtmartialed if he disobeyed and shot the bird.

The next step was predictable. Carrier waited until the lieutenant moved out of sight, then took careful aim and fired. If shooting a peacock brought bad luck, he never noticed it.

But a large dose of bad luck did come to some men defending Wormhout who had probably never harmed a peacock in their lives. After a hard fight most of the 2nd Royal Warwicks were broken up and forced to surrender around 6:00 p.m. on the 28th. Prodded by their captors, the SS Leibstandarte Adolf Hitler Regiment, about 80 men and one officer were herded into a small open-ended barn just outside the village.

As they crowded in, the officer Captain J. F. Lynn-Allen protested that there wasn't enough room for the wounded. Speaking fluent English with a strong American accent, one of the SS guards snapped back, "Yellow Englishman, there will be plenty of room where you're all going to!"

With that, he hurled a stick grenade into the barn, and the carnage was on. For fifteen minutes the guards blasted away with grenades, rifles, tommy guns, and pistols. As an extra touch two batches of prisoners were brought outside and executed by an impromptu firing squad. Amazingly, some fifteen men somehow survived amid the jumble of bodies.

Eight miles farther south Cassel continued to hold. Perched on its hill, it had become—as Colonel Bridgeman foresaw—the "Gibraltar" of the western wall. For two days Kleist's tanks, artillery, and mortars battered the town ... waves of Stukas pounded it ... and still it stood. It was a minor miracle, for the principal defenders—the 5th Gloucesters—had little to fight with. Told to build a barricade, Lieutenant Fane could find only one farm wagon, one plough, a pony trap, and a water cart. When a tank broke into a nearby garden, he tried to stop it with a Boyes rifle—and watched his shots bounce off the armored plate.

The town was surrounded, yet on the evening of May 28 the Gloucesters' quartermaster Captain R.E.D. Brasington managed to get some rations through. The defenders settled down to an odd meal of bully beef washed down by vintage wine.

All the way south, at the bottom of the pocket, units of General Prioux's First Army still held Lille. In contrast to most of the French, they fought with passionate commitment, holding off six German divisions ... meaning six fewer divisions to harass the BEF farther up the corridor.

Most of the escaping troops were now well on their way. The time had come to abandon the strong-points farthest south, and pull the defending units back toward the coast as a sort of rear guard.

On the morning of the 28th Corporal Bob Hadnett, in charge of dispatch riders at 48th Division headquarters, was ordered to get a message to the troops holding Hazebrouck, one of these southern strong-points. The defenders were to disengage and make for Dunkirk that night. Hadnett had already lost two messengers on missions to Hazebrouck; so this time he decided to go himself.

The main roads were jammed with refugees and retiring troops, but he had been a motorcycle trials driver in peacetime and had no trouble riding cross-country. Bouncing over fields and along dirt lanes, he reached Hazebrouck and delivered his message at 143rd Brigade headquarters. After helping the staff work out an escape route north, he mounted his motorcycle and started back.

This time he ran smack into a German column that was just moving into the area. No way to turn, he decided to ride right through. Bending low over the handlebars, accelerator pressed to the floorboards, he shot forward. The startled Germans scattered, but began firing at him as he roared by.

He almost made it. Then suddenly everything went blank, and when he came to, he was lying in the grass with a shattered leg and hand. An enemy officer was standing over him, and a trooper was holding a bottle of brandy to his lips. "Tommy," the officer observed in English, "for you the war is over."

As the British troops streamed up the corridor toward the coast, General Gort's headquarters moved north too. On May 27 the Command Post shifted from Prémesques to Houtkerque, just inside the French border and only fourteen miles from the sea. For the first time since the campaign began, headquarters was not on the London-Brussels telephone cable. It made little difference: Gort wasn't there much anyhow.

He spent most of the 27th looking for General Blanchard, hoping to coordinate their joint withdrawal into the perimeter. He never did find him, and finally returned to Houtkerque weary and frustrated at dawn on the 28th. Then, around 11:00 a.m., Blanchard unexpectedly turned up on his own.

There was much to discuss, and Gort began by reading a telegram received from Anthony Eden the previous day. It confirmed the decision to evacuate: "Want to make it quite clear that sole task now is to evacuate to England maximum of your force possible."

Blanchard was horrified. To the amazement of Gort and Pownall, the French commander hadn't yet heard about the British decision to evacuate. He still understood that the strategy was to set up a beachhead based on Dunkirk which would give the Allies a permanent foothold on the Continent. Somehow Churchill's statement to Reynaud on May 26, Eden's message to the French high command on the 27th, the decisions reached at Cassel and Dover the same day, the information given Abrial and Weygand early on the 28th—all had passed him by. Once again, the explanation probably lay in the complete collapse of French communications.

Now that Blanchard knew, Gort did his best to bring him into line. He must, Gort argued, order Prioux's French First Army to head for Dunkirk too. Like the BEF, they must be rescued to come back and fight again another day. With the Belgians out of the war, there was no longer any possibility of hanging on. It was a case of evacuation or surrender.

Blanchard wavered briefly, but at the crucial moment a liaison officer arrived from Prioux, reporting that the First Army was too tired to move anywhere. That settled it. Blanchard decided to leave the army in the Lille area.

Gort grew more exasperated than ever. Prioux's troops, he exclaimed, couldn't be so tired they were unable to lift a finger to save themselves. Once again, evacuation was their only chance.

Blanchard remained adamant. It was all very well, he observed ruefully, for the British to talk evacuation. "No doubt the British Admiralty had arranged it for the BEF, but the French Marine would never be able to do it for French soldiers. It was, therefore, idle to try—the chance wasn't worth the effort involved."

There was no shaking him. He ended by asking whether the British would continue to pull back to Dunkirk, even though they knew that the French would not be coming along. Pownall exploded with an emphatic *"OUI!"*

Down at French First Army headquarters at Steenwerck a somewhat similar conversation took place that afternoon between General Prioux himself and Major-General E. A. Osborne, commanding the British 44th Division. Osborne was planning the 44th's withdrawal from the River Lys and came over to coordinate his movements with the French, who were on his immediate left. To his surprise, he learned that Prioux didn't plan to withdraw at all. Osborne tried every argument he knew—including the principle of Allied solidarity—but he too got nowhere.

Yet Prioux must have had second thoughts, for sometime later that afternoon he released General de la Laurencie's III Corps, telling them to make for the coast if they could. He himself decided to stay with the rest of his army and go down fighting.

The idea of a gallant last stand—saving the honor of the flag, if nothing else—seemed to captivate them all. "He could only tell us the story of the honor of the *drapeaux*," Pownall noted in his diary after hearing it from Blanchard one more time.

"I am counting on you to save everything that can be saved—and, above all, our honor!" Weygand telegraphed Abrial. "Blanchard's troops, if doomed, must disappear with honor," the General told Major Fauvelle. Weygand pictured an especially honorable role for the high command when the end finally came. Rather than retreat from Paris, the government should behave like the Senators of ancient Rome, who had awaited the barbarians sitting in their curule chairs.

This sort of talk, though possibly consoling at the top level, did not inspire the poilus in the field. They had had enough of antiquated guns, horse-drawn transport, wretched communications, inadequate armor, invisible air support, and fumbling leaders. Vast numbers of French soldiers were sitting around in ditches, resting and smoking, when the 58th Field Regiment, Royal Artillery, passed by on May 28. As one of them explained to a French-speaking Tommy, the enemy was everywhere and there was no hope of getting through; so they were just going to sit down and wait for the Boches to come.

Yet there were always exceptions. A French tank company, separated from its regiment, joined the 1st Royal Irish Fusiliers at Gorre and proved to be a magnificent addition. The crews bristled with discarded British, French, and German weapons and were literally festooned with clanking bottles of wine. They fought with tremendous *élan,* roaring with laughter and pausing to shake hands with one another after every good shot. When the Fusiliers were finally ordered to pull back, the tank company decided to stay and fight on. *"Bon chance!"* they called after the departing Fusiliers, and then went back to work.

General de la Laurencie was another exuberant Frenchman not about to fold his tent. Exasperated by the indecision and defeatism of his superiors, on two separate occasions he had already tried to get his III Corps transferred to Gort's command. Now, released by Prioux, he hurried toward Dunkirk with two divisions.

The first of the fighting contingents were already entering the perimeter. The 2nd Grenadier Guards moved into Furnes, still marching with parade-ground precision. The steady, measured tread of their boots echoed through the medieval market square. Here and there a uniform was torn, a cap missing, a bandage added; but there was no mistaking that erect stance, that clean-shaven, expressionless look so familiar to anyone who had ever watched the changing of the guard at Buckingham Palace.

Not far behind came the 1st/7th Middlesex. They were a Territorial unit far removed from the professionalism of the Guards, but raffishly engaging in their own way. They too had seen their share of rear-guard action. Now they continued through Furnes, finally halting at Oostduinkerke three miles to the east. Here they were a mile or so from Nieuport, the eastern anchor of the perimeter and the point most exposed by the Belgian surrender. Colonel Clifton's "odds and sods" were already in position, but spread very thin. The Middlesex battalion would beef up the line.

Spreading their camouflage nets and digging slit trenches, the new arrivals settled down in the dunes and scrub. As yet there was no sign of the enemy, and it was wonderful to flake out at last and sleep undisturbed. The war of movement had ended, and until the Regimental Sergeant-Major, "Big Ike" Colton, caught up with them and devised some new torment, it was a chance to soak up oceans of missed sleep. Private Francis Ralph Farley only hoped that "Big Ike" didn't find them too soon.

General Gort was also moving into the perimeter. At 6:00 p.m., May 28, GHQ opened up at La Panne, housed in a beachside villa at the western end of town. The place was well chosen. It had been the residence of King Albert during the dark days of the First War, and later served as a summer home for the old King during the twenties. As a result it had a large, reinforced cellar, ample wiring, and the London-Brussels telephone cable, which ran practically by the front door. Once again Gort was only a phone call away from Churchill, the War Office, and Ramsay at Dover.

The Corps commanders also moved into the perimeter on the 28th: III Corps at Dunkirk, II Corps at La Panne, and I Corps in between at Bray-Dunes. Lieutenant-General Michael Barker, commanding I Corps, was by now utterly exhausted. An elderly veteran of the Boer War, he was no man to cope with a *blitzkrieg*. Reaching corps headquarters at the western end of the beach promenade, he retired to the cellar. From here he constantly called up to his assistant quartermaster, Major Bob Ransome, to come and tell him what was going on.

Ransome found the scene on the beach appalling. A mob of officers and men from various service units milled around, firing haphazardly at German planes. Ransome tried to get the crowd into some sort of order but had no luck, even though he jammed his pistol into some very senior ribs. Finally he sent for Captain Tom Gimson, an assistant operations officer at III Corps headquarters. Gimson was an old Irish Guardsman, and his solution was to order the mob to fall in, as on parade. He then solemnly drilled them, running through all the usual commands. Surprisingly, the men complied, and order was soon restored. To Ransome the incident revealed not only what drill could accomplish but also the workings of that most austere of human mechanisms, a Guardsman's mind.

Reports of the confusion at Bray-Dunes soon reached Captain Tennant, busy organizing the embarkations at Dunkirk. So far he had no naval shore parties operating that far up the beach. But the eastern mole and Malo-les-Bains were now under control, and clearly Bray was the next problem to tackle. There were said to be 5,000 troops there, most without officers or any leadership.

Around 5:00 p.m. on the 28th Tennant met with Commander Hector Richardson and two of his other officers, Commanders Tom Kerr and John Clouston. He explained that he wanted an officer to lead a party to Bray and embark the 5,000 men waiting there. At the moment all three commanders were available; so they decided to cut a deck of cards for the assignment—loser to get Bray-Dunes. Richardson lost, but said it was such a big job he really needed another officer to go with him. Kerr and Clouston then cut again. This time Kerr lost. Clouston, the "winner," took what all three considered the easiest assignment—pier master of the mole.

Richardson and Kerr then set off for Bray with fifteen men in a lorry. It was only seven miles, but the roads were so clogged with traffic and pitted with craters that it took an hour to get there. Arriving around 9:00 p.m., the party headed down to the beach to start organizing the embarkation.

It was dusk now, and in the fading light Seaman G. F. Nixon saw what he first thought were several breakwaters, extending from the sand out into the water. Then he realized that the "breakwaters" were actually columns of men, eight thick, leading from the shore right into the sea. The men in front were standing up to their waists, and even to their shoulders, in water.

Five thousand troops? It was more like 25,000. Richardson immediately signaled the situation to Dover and the Admiralty via a destroyer hovering offshore. Once again, an urgent appeal for small boats and motor launches.

Meanwhile they must "make do." Richardson set up headquarters in the back of the lorry. Some of his seamen began breaking up the troops into batches of 50; others rigged lifelines running down into the sea. The beach shelved so gradually that even small boats had a hard time getting in close.

"What a terrible night that was," Kerr wrote his wife a few days later, "for we had got hold of the odds and ends of an army, not the fighting soldiers. There weren't many officers, and those that were, were useless, but by speech and promise of safety and the sight of our naval uniforms we got order out of the rabble."

Those manning the boats were having an equally difficult time. The skoot *Hilda* had arrived early in the afternoon, and because of her shallow draft, her skipper Lieutenant A. Gray managed to nurse her within wading distance of the shore. Troops swarmed out, surrounding the boat completely, trying to scramble up ladders tossed over the bow. But the ladders weren't firmly secured; the men were exhausted; and the tide was rising. They began falling back into the sea. It took super-human efforts by the *Hilda*'s crew to haul them up and over the rail—a collection of inert, sopping bundles.

By 7:00 p.m. Gray had 500 men aboard—not many, considering that 25,000 were waiting—but all he could carry. These he ferried to a destroyer lying farther out, then returned for another load. The tide was now ebbing, and the *Hilda* soon sat on the sand in only two feet of water. Some 400 soldiers surged aboard, and he had another full load by the time the next tide refloated him around 1:30 a.m.

Not far away the skoot *Doggersbank* was doing similar work. Earlier her skipper Lieutenant Donald McBarnet had let go a kedge anchor, then ran himself aground. But he drew more than the *Hilda*, and he still lay in six feet of water—too deep for wading. He lowered his boat and a raft to ferry men out to the ship. On reaching shore, both were immediately mobbed and swamped. Bailed out, they went to work, and by 8:00 p.m. McBarnet had about 450 aboard. Enough. He then used the kedge to pull himself off the beach. Once afloat, he too carried his load to a destroyer farther out, then returned for more.

This became the pattern all along the beach—Bray, Malo-les-Bains, and La Panne as well. Dinghies, rowboats, and launches would load at water's edge and ferry the troops to small ships waiting offshore. These would then ferry the men to the growing fleet of destroyers, minesweepers, and packets lying still farther out. When filled, these would head for England—and one more bit of the army would be home.

It was a practical, workable scheme, but it was also very slow. Each skoot, for instance, averaged only 100 men an hour. No wonder nerves were frayed.

Most of the troops were not up front where they could see what was going on. They stood far back in line or waited in the dunes behind the beach. They couldn't imagine why it all took so long. In the blackness of the night they could see nothing, except the occasional silhouette of some boat caught in the glittering phosphorescence of the water. They could hear only the steady rhythm of the surf and every now and then the clank of oarlocks.

They were tired, cold, and hungry. May nights are chilly along the coast of Flanders, and the men longed for the greatcoats they had thrown away during the hot, dusty retreat. Regular rations had vanished, and it was no longer possible to live off the land. When Corporal R. Kay, a GHQ signalman, found a seven-pound tin of peas near the beach, it was a major discovery. He and a few lucky mates ate them with their fingers, like expensive chocolates.

At Malo-les-Bains Lieutenant-Colonel John D'Arcy was another who fretted over the seemingly endless delay. He had gathered his artillery regiment in a brickyard behind the dunes—splendid cover but no place to see what was going on. He finally ordered one of his officers, Lieutenant C. G. Payne, to take a signal lamp and "go down to the beach and call up the Navy."

Payne had no idea how to go about this, but he did find a signal manual with a section headed, "Call to an Unknown Ship." Pointing his lamp to sea, he carefully followed the instructions, little expecting any results. To his amazement, an answer came flashing out of the night. Instructed to bring the unit to the beach, he hurried back to the Colonel in triumph.

Around 1:30 a.m. on the 29th a stiff breeze sprang up, meaning much greater surf and even slower going. At Bray-Dunes Commander Richardson was making so little progress that he decided to suspend any further embarkations and began sending the troops back to Dunkirk. Maybe the mole would be faster.

Indeed so. Over 24 hours had now passed since Captain Tennant began using the eastern mole or breakwater of Dunkirk harbor as an improvised pier, and the gamble was paying off. A steady stream of destroyers, minesweepers, ferries, and other steamers eased alongside, loaded troops, then backed off and headed for England. The flow of men was regulated by Commander Clouston, who had won the "easy" assignment—pier master of the mole—when he, Richardson, and Kerr cut cards to decide who would be stuck with Bray-Dunes.

Clouston was a Canadian—big, tough, athletic, amusing. He was a fine ice hockey player, and when stationed at Portsmouth, typically he had organized the staff into a hockey team. He was a man bursting with energy, and in his new job he needed all of it.

Word of the mole had gotten around, and now thousands of

disorganized troops were flocking there, queuing up for a chance to embark. To Private Bill Warner, a headquarters clerk with the Royal Artillery, it was like the endless queue at the cinema when talkies first came in. To others it was more like London at rush hour or a rugby scrum. Planting himself at the foot of the mole, Clouston squarely faced the crowd. Megaphone in hand, he shouted instructions, matching the flow of men to the flow of ships.

At first they were mostly destroyers. During the morning of May 28 no fewer than eleven loaded up, and Commander Brian Dean of the destroyer *Sabre* showed how fast they could work. Earlier he had lifted 100 men off the beaches in two hours. His turn-around at Dover took only 58 minutes, and now he was back again, tying up at the mole at 11:30 a.m. This time he loaded 800 men, and headed back to Dover at 12:30 p.m.—a rate of 540 men an hour, compared to 50 men an hour at the beaches.

And he wasn't through yet. Reaching Dover at 6:20 p.m., he refueled and was on his way back to the mole at 10:30—his third trip of the day. This time he stayed only 35 minutes, picking up another 500 troops.

Dusk on the 28th, and the destroyers were joined by an assortment of other craft. The fleet minesweeper *Gossamer* arrived at 9:45 p.m., departed half an hour later with 420 aboard. The sweeper *Ross* loaded another 353 about the same time. The skoot *Tilly*, leading a procession of six small motor vessels, tied up at 11:15; they took on hundreds more. The paddle steamer *Medway Queen* arrived around midnight and picked up nearly 1,000. Her skipper Lieutenant A. T. Cook had warned Chief Cook Russell to expect "several hundred men who will no doubt feel somewhat peckish." The warning scarcely prepared Russell for the assault on his galley. These men weren't "peckish"—they were ravenous.

All through the night of May 28–29 the ships kept coming, while the men streamed out the long wooden walkway like an endless line of ants. For a while the ebb tide slowed the pace—it was hard for untrained soldiers to crawl down the makeshift ladders and gangplanks—but the flow never stopped. Tennant estimated that Clouston was getting men off at a rate of 2,000 an hour.

At 10:45 p.m. he sent Dover his first optimistic situation report:

> French general appreciation is that situation in port tomorrow will continue as for today. Provided aircraft fighters adequate, embarkation can proceed full speed. . . .

The Dynamo Room began to hope that more than a handful might be saved. The total evacuated on May 28 reached 17,804—more than twice the figure for the 27th. They would have to do far better than that, but at least they were moving in the right direction.

There was other good news too: the Admiralty had now released to Ramsay *all* destroyers in home waters. . . . Route X had at last been cleared of mines, cutting the passage to Dunkirk from 87 to 55 miles. . . . The beachhead was holding despite the Belgian surrender. . . . The surf was subsiding; a threatening storm veered away. . . . Smoke from the blazing oil refinery hid the port from the Luftwaffe. . . . Casualties were mercifully low.

Besides the *Queen of the Channel*, the only serious loss of the day was the little paddle steamer *Brighton Belle*. A charming antique looking like something out of a toy store, she was thrashing her way home with 800 men plucked from the sea at La Panne. Sapper Eric Reader huddled in the boiler room drying off, when the ship hit a submerged wreck with a frightful jolt. "Never touched us," an old cockney stoker called out cheerfully, but the sea gurgled in and the *Brighton Belle* began to sink. The troops tumbled on deck as the whistle tooted an SOS. Happily other ships were nearby and took everybody off—even the captain's dog.

If casualties could be kept at this level, there were valid grounds for the Dynamo Room's optimism. On the whole the evacuation was proceeding smoothly, and the greatest crisis of the day—the gap created by the Belgian surrender—had been successfully met. For the troops still pouring up the escape corridor, there was additional reason to hope. On either side of the raised roadways, the fields were beginning to fill with water.

The French were flooding the low-lying land south of the coast. Even German tanks would find the going difficult.

But already a new crisis had arisen, shifting the focus back from the land to the sea. It had been brewing for several days without anybody paying much attention. Now, in the early hours of May 29, it suddenly burst, posing a fresh challenge to Admiral Ramsay and his resourceful staff.

7

Torpedoes in
the Night

What could the German Navy do to help prevent an evacuation?
General Keitel asked Vice-Admiral Otto Schniewind, Chief of
the Naval War Staff, in a phone conversation on May 26. Not
much, Schniewind felt, and he formally spelled out the Navy's
views in a letter to OKW on the 28th. Large ships were not suitable in the narrow, confining waters of the English Channel; the
destroyers had been used up in Norway; U-boats were restricted
by shallow water and the enemy's very effective antisubmarine
measures.

There remained the *Schnellboot,* the small fast German motor
torpedo boat. These "S-boats" were especially suited to narrow
seas like the Channel, and new bases were now available in Holland, closer to the scene of action. The only problems were the
possibility of bad weather and the short nights this time of year.

Overall, the prospects seemed so bright that SKL—the naval
war command—had already shifted two flotillas, totaling nine
boats, from the German island of Borkum to the Dutch port of
Den Helder, 90 miles closer to Dunkirk. From here Captain-
Lieutenant Birnbacher's 1st Flotilla and Captain-Lieutenant Pe-
terson's 2nd Flotilla began operating along the coast.

They drew first blood on the night of May 22–23. The French

destroyer *Jaguar*, approaching Dunkirk, rashly radioed that she would be arriving at 12:20 a.m. German intelligence was listening in, and when *Jaguar* turned up on schedule, an unexpected reception committee was waiting. *S 21* and *S 23* sank her with a couple of well-placed torpedoes, then slipped away unseen.

On the Allied side nobody was sure what caused the loss. A submarine seemed most likely. The British were still unaware of the S-boats' nightly patrols as the destroyer *Wakeful* lay off the beach at Bray-Dunes, loading troops on the evening of May 28. Her skipper Commander Ralph Lindsay Fisher was chiefly worried about an air attack. This might require some violent maneuvering; he packed the troops as low in the ship as possible to get maximum stability. They crowded into the engine room, the boiler room, the store rooms, every inch of empty space.

At 11:00 p.m. *Wakeful* weighed anchor with 640 men aboard—all she could carry—and headed for Dover via the long Route Y. It was a black night, but the phosphorescence was brilliant. Under such conditions bombers often spotted ships by their wake; as Commander Fisher headed northeast on the first leg of his trip, he kept his speed down to twelve knots to reduce this danger.

Around 12:30 he spotted the winking light of Kwinte Whistle Buoy, where he would swing west for the final run to Dover. It was an important buoy; so important that it remained lit even in these dangerous times. It was also the most exposed point of the homeward journey—easy to reach for enemy planes, U-boats, or any other menace.

Fisher began to zigzag and increased his speed to twenty knots. You couldn't get by Kwinte too soon.

Not far away other vessels were also watching the winking light of Kwinte Whistle Buoy. The two German *Schnellboote* flotillas were now alternating their nightly patrols, and tonight was the turn of Captain-Lieutenant Heinz Birnbacher's 1st Flotilla. On *S 30* the skipper, Lieutenant Wilhelm Zimmermann, searched the night with his binoculars. There ought to be plenty of targets out by the buoy, but so far he saw nothing.

Then suddenly, about 12:40, he spotted a shadow even

darker than the night. "There, dead ahead!" He nudged the helmsman, standing right behind him. The shadows quickly took shape as a darkened ship rushing toward them. Zimmermann sized it up as a destroyer.

A few brief orders, and *S 30* turned toward the target, leading it slightly. On a *Schnellboot* the torpedo was aimed by aiming the boat itself. The gap quickly narrowed between the two vessels as the S-boat crew tingled with excitement. Would they get close enough before they were seen?

Another order from Zimmermann, and two torpedoes slapped into the sea. The crew began counting the seconds, waiting interminably. . . .

On the bridge of the *Wakeful*, Commander Fisher saw them coming—two parallel streaks, one slightly ahead of the other, racing toward his starboard side. They gleamed like silver ribbons in the phosphorescence. He ordered the helm hard-a-port, and as the ship began to swing, the first torpedo passed harmlessly across his bow.

The second hit. It exploded with a roar and a blinding flash in the forward boiler room, breaking *Wakeful* in half. She sank in fifteen seconds . . . the severed ends resting on the bottom, the bow and stern sticking out of the water in a grotesque V.

The troops far below never had a chance. Trapped by the slanting decks, engulfed by the sea, they were all lost—except one man who happened to be topside sneaking a cigarette.

A few hundred yards away Lieutenant Zimmermann watched with satisfaction as his torpedo finally hit. He had almost given up hope. He toyed with the idea of picking up survivors for questioning, then thought better of it. Occasional shadows and flashes of phosphorescence suggested that other ships were rushing to the scene—certainly alert and maybe even looking for him. Withdrawal seemed his best bet. The *S 30* eased off into the night and resumed its prowl.

Back at the wreck Commander Fisher floated clear of his ship, as did most of the gun crews. About 30 men ended up on the stern, some 60 feet out of the water. Fisher and the rest paddled about, hoping some friendly vessel would find them.

In half an hour they got their wish. Two small drifters, *Nautilus* and *Comfort*, appeared out of the night. Normally engaged in minesweeping, they were now part of Admiral Ramsay's rescue fleet, bound for La Panne via Route Y. As they approached Kwinte Buoy, crew members heard voices crying "Help!" and saw heads bobbing in the sea.

Nautilus managed to pick up six men, *Comfort* another sixteen, including Commander Fisher. Other rescue ships began to appear: the minesweeper *Gossamer*, packed with troops from the eastern mole . . . next the sweeper *Lydd*, also crowded . . . then the destroyer *Grafton*, with a full load from Bray-Dunes. All lowered their boats and stood by. Few yet knew what happened— only that a ship had sunk—and there were a number of flares and flashing signal lights.

Hidden by the night, a thousand yards away Lieutenant Michalowski, commanding the German submarine *U 62*, watched the confusion of lights with interest. Like the *Schnellboot*, he had been lying near Kwinte Buoy, waiting for some fat target to come along. These were indeed shallow waters for a U-boat— but not impossible. The *U 62* glided toward the lights.

Commander Fisher sensed the danger. Picked up by the *Comfort*, he had taken over from her regular skipper. Now he moved here and there warning the other ships. Hailing *Gossamer*, he shouted that he had been torpedoed and the enemy was probably still nearby. *Gossamer* got going so fast she left her skiff behind. *Comfort* picked up its crew, ordered *Nautilus* to get going too, then moved over to warn *Grafton* and *Lydd*. Easing alongside *Grafton*'s starboard quarter, Fisher once again called out his warning.

Too late. At that moment, 2:50 a.m., a torpedo crashed into *Grafton*'s wardroom, killing some 35 army officers picked up at Bray-Dunes. *Comfort*, lying alongside, was hurled into the air by the blast, then dropped back into the sea like a toy boat. Momentarily swamped, she bobbed back to the surface, but all the crew on deck were washed overboard, including Commander Fisher.

With no one at the helm, but her engines set at full speed, *Comfort* now moved into a wide circle that took her off into the night. Fisher grabbed a rope's end and hung on for a brief, wild ride. But she was going too fast, and there was no one to pull him aboard. He finally let go.

Just as well. *Comfort*, still in her circle, came back into view and was sighted by the nearby *Lydd*. Her skipper, Lieutenant-Commander Rodolph Haig, had been warned by a *Wakeful* survivor that an enemy torpedo boat, rather than submarine, was probably to blame. Now this seemed confirmed by what he saw in the dark: a small vessel dashing about at high speed.

Lydd opened up with her starboard guns, raking the stranger's wheelhouse and producing a satisfying cloud of sparks. The torpedoed *Grafton* joined in, and the stranger appeared disabled.

Swimming in the sea again, Commander Fisher realized that *Lydd* had mistaken *Comfort* for the enemy; but there was nothing he could do. On *Comfort* herself three survivors huddled below decks, equally helpless. Her engines had stopped now, probably knocked out by gunfire, and she wallowed clumsily in the Channel swell.

Suddenly something big loomed out of the night, racing toward her. It was *Lydd* again, coming to finish off the "enemy" by ramming. As her steel prow knifed into *Comfort*'s wooden side, two figures burst out of the hatch and leapt for *Lydd*'s bow.

"Repel boarders!" The ancient rallying cry rose above her decks as members of the crew grabbed rifles and pistols and blazed away. They fortunately missed the two survivors of *Comfort* who had climbed aboard, but a stray shot fatally wounded Able Seaman S. P. Sinclair, one of their own men. The mix-up was finally ironed out, and *Lydd* set course for home.

Meanwhile, confusion on the stricken *Grafton*. The torpedo hits (there was apparently a second) knocked out all her lights, and the 800 troops aboard blindly thrashed about. Among them was Captain Basil Bartlett of the Field Security Police, one of the last to board the ship at Bray-Dunes. There was no space left in the ward room, where the officers were assigned; he settled for a corner of the captain's cabin. Stunned by the explosion, he came to, groping for some way out. There seemed practically no chance of escape; still he was not overly worried. He remembered similar scenes in countless American war movies. "Gary Cooper always finds a way out," he consoled himself.

He finally stumbled onto the open deck, and found the night alive with gunfire. *Grafton* had joined *Lydd* in pounding the luckless *Comfort*, and probably other nearby ships were firing, too. Stray shots ripped into the *Grafton*'s bridge, killing the skipper, Commander Charles Robinson.

Gradually the firing died down, and a semblance of order returned. Word reached the sick bay to start sending the wounded up, and Private Sam Sugar, an RASC driver who had injured his hand, bolted for the ladder. He was stopped in his tracks by an orderly, who gave him a flashlight and told him to stay a bit. Someone was needed to hold the light while the orderly fixed a tourniquet on a sailor who had just lost both legs. Sugar had been on the verge of panic, but the sight of the orderly calmly going about his business at this desperate moment showed the power of example. He had to stay calm too; he just couldn't let this good man down.

By the time Sugar reached deck, the ferry *Malines* lay alongside taking off the troops. The *Grafton* was listing now, slowly sinking, but the men kept in ranks, patiently waiting for their turn to transfer. Captain Bartlett was one of the last to cross over. Gary Cooper had found a way out.

The destroyer *Ivanhoe* finished off *Grafton* with two well-placed shells, and at last there was time for postmortems. For Bartlett there was the lucky break of getting on board so late. Any earlier, and he would have died with the other officers in the ward room.

For Sergeant S. S. Hawes, 1st Division Petrol Company, there was a more ironical twist. He had briefly left his unit at Bray-Dunes to help a wounded comrade. Understandable, but orders were to stick together. By the time he got back, the others had put out in a launch, heading for a destroyer lying offshore. It was the *Wakeful*, and every man in the company was lost. For disobeying orders, Hawes was rewarded with his life.

The luckiest man of all was the indestructible Commander Fisher. Washed off *Wakeful*, he was one of the few picked up by *Comfort;* washed off *Comfort*, he was again picked up, this time by the Norwegian freighter *Hird*. A battered old steamer out of Oslo, *Hird* was engaged in the timber trade and was not even part of Admiral Ramsay's rescue fleet. She had made a routine stop at Dunkirk on May 13, and for the past two weeks had been taking her share of punishment as the Luftwaffe pounded the port. Now only one engine worked, and she could barely make six knots.

But these were desperate times. As the panzers approached, *Hird* was requisitioned by the French Navy to transfer some of the trapped poilus to Cherbourg, 180 miles to the southwest and presumably out of danger. They crowded aboard all through the evening of May 28, unofficially joined by some of the British soldiers pouring into Dunkirk. Sapper L. C. Lidster found the gangplank blocked by a queue of Frenchmen, so he grabbed a rope ladder hanging down. He and his mates scrambled aboard while the waiting poilus shouted in anger. In various ways other Tommies made it too—Private Sam Love of the 12th Field Ambulance . . . Corporal Alf Gill of the 44th Division . . . Staff Sergeant Reg Blackburn of the Military Police . . . maybe 1,000 men altogether.

The *Hird* finally crept out of the harbor about midnight, packed with 3,000 Allied troops and a handful of German prisoners. At six knots, her master Captain A. M. Frendjhem wasn't about to challenge the enemy batteries planted along the coast to the west, so he first steered east along Route Y. At Kwinte Whistle Buoy he would then swing west and make his run down the Channel, beyond the range of the German guns.

It was while rounding Kwinte that he picked up Commander Fisher and several other swimmers—all probably survivors of the *Wakeful*. Exhausted, Fisher slumped against the after cargo hatch among a crowd of French colonial troops. He saw no British soldiers, nor did it occur to him that any might be aboard.

Regaining his strength, he went to the bridge to urge that he be landed at Dover. Important charts might have floated clear when the *Wakeful* sank, and Admiral Ramsay must be warned. Captain Frendjhem replied that his orders were to go straight to Cherbourg. Fisher didn't persist: he knew that the *Hird* had to pass close to Dover breakwater anyhow; surely he could catch a ride into the harbor from some passing ship.

And so it proved. As the *Hird* approached the breakwater, Fisher hailed a passing naval trawler. It came alongside, and he jumped aboard.

Meanwhile on the *Hird*'s foredeck the British troops watched Dover draw near with mounting anticipation. It had been an exhausting trip—no food or water—made worse when one Tommy fell down an open hatch and lay groaning all night. Now at last life began perking up. The famous white cliffs never looked better.

Then to everyone's surprise the *Hird* turned out again and headed westward along the coast, past Folkestone ... Eastbourne ... Brighton. The men decided they must be going to Southampton and settled back to make the best of things. Sapper Lidster tried eating a tin of uncooked fish roe. It tasted awful, "but God! I was so hungry!"

Then another surprise. The *Hird* didn't go to Southampton after all. Instead, she veered off past the Isle of Wight and headed across the Channel toward France again. Howls of rage rose from the foredeck. Some men aimed rifles at the bridge, hoping to "persuade" Captain Frendjhem to change his mind. At the crucial moment an elderly British major named Hunt stood up in front of the Captain to protect him and try to calm the troops. He explained that the *Hird* was under French control, that the senior French officer aboard had ordered her to Cherbourg, that the poilus were desperately needed there, and finally that he personally would see that every British soldier got back to England. It was an inspiring performance, coming from an officer who was not a trained combat leader, but rather a mild father figure in the 508th Petrol Company of the supply troops.

The spell of mutiny was broken. The *Hird* continued on to Cherbourg, where the British troops each received two slices of dry bread and jam, then marched off to a transit camp outside of town. Here they settled down in tents, until Major Hunt—true to his word—got them all back to England.

Admiral Ramsay and the Dynamo Room staff were blissfully ignorant of the meandering *Hird*, but they were very much aware of the disastrous events off Kwinte Whistle Buoy. With characteristic energy they dived into the business of countermeasures.

At 8:06 a.m. on the 29th Ramsay radioed his entire armada: "Vessels carrying troops not to stop to pick up survivors from ships sunk but are to inform other near ships."

Next he took two minesweepers off troop-carrying duties and ordered them to search the area around Kwinte for any lurking torpedo boats. This was a drastic but realistic move. He needed every possible ship for lifting the BEF, but what good did it do, unless he could get them safely home?

There was still some suspicion that U-boats might be involved, so the Admiral also established an antisubmarine patrol in the waters west of Kwinte. In addition, antisubmarine trawlers patrolling off the Thames estuary were brought down to the critical area east of Margate and Ramsgate. A speedboat flotilla at Harwich was ordered to stand by as a striking force in case these various probes turned anything up.

Most important of all, the middle Route X was finally cleared of mines and opened to traffic. During the morning three destroyers tried it out, pronounced it safe from the German shore batteries both east and west of Dunkirk. At 4:06 p.m. Ramsay ordered all ships to start using the new route exclusively in daylight hours. This not only shortened the trip from 87 to 55 miles, but shifted the traffic 26 miles farther west of Kwinte Buoy—meaning 26 miles farther away from the S-boats' favorite hunting ground.

By midafternoon all possible countermeasures had been taken, and the Dynamo Room returned to what one staff officer called "its normal state of organized chaos." There were always fresh problems. New German batteries were shelling the mole from the southeast—could the RAF mount a quick strike? The Army's medical service had completely broken down on the beaches—could the Navy send over a team of good doctors? Refueling was becoming a major bottleneck. Peacetime Dover refueled commercial traffic at a leisurely pace of one ship at a time—how to cope with dozens of vessels, all clamoring for oil at once? The Admiralty reported twenty Thames barges, towed by five tugs, would be arriving at Ramsgate at 5:30 p.m.—could they be used on the beaches as an improvised pier?

Tennant was consulted about the barges, and he turned the idea down. The beach shelved so gradually that twenty barges weren't enough to make a decent pier. Better to use them for ferrying troops out to the destroyers and coastal steamers waiting offshore. He still didn't have the small boats he really needed for this work, but the barges were better than nothing.

Meanwhile the problems grew. Men were pouring onto the beach at a far faster rate than they could be lifted off. When Captain S. T. Moore led a mixed bag of 20 officers and 403 men into La Panne around 10:00 a.m. he hadn't the faintest idea what he was meant to do with them. Someone suggested he check II Corps headquarters; he left his charges in a hotel garden and trudged to the headquarters dugout about a mile up the beach.

Inside, it was another world—three lieutenant-colonels, about six staff assistants, a battery of telephones, and papers being shuffled back and forth. He was given a ticket, neatly filled out, authorizing him to embark 20 officers and 403 men from "Beach A." Presumably it was to be handed to some collector at some gate to some particular beach.

Then back to the beach the way it really was: no signposts, no ticket takers, just bewildered waiting. At La Panne, Bray-Dunes, and Malo-les-Bains, ever-growing lines of men curled over the sand and into the sea. The queues seemed almost stationary, and the troops whiled away the hours as best they could. The padre of the 85th Command Ammunition Depot moved among his flock, inviting them to join him in prayers and hymns. Some antiaircraft gunners at Bray-Dunes were calmly playing cards; they had run out of ammunition long ago. On the promenade east of the mole a group pedaled about on brightly-colored mini-bikes borrowed from some beachfront concession. Near Malo a soldier lay face down, clutching handfuls of sand and letting it run through his fingers, repeating over and over, "Please, God, have mercy . . ."

Some discovered a stiff drink could help. Corporal Ackrell of the 85th Command Ammunition Depot asked a comrade for a drink from his water bottle. He discovered, not entirely to his sorrow, that it was filled with rum. A few swigs, and he passed out. Others like Private Jack Toomey didn't trust the drinking water and had depended on wine and champagne for a fortnight. This morning some *vin blanc* finally caught up with him: "I was drunk as a lord."

As the queues inched into the water, panic sometimes took over. With so many thousands waiting, it was hard to remain calm when some skiff, holding perhaps ten people, finally came within reach. Working the beach at La Panne, Lieutenant Ian Cox of the destroyer *Malcolm* had to draw his revolver and threaten to shoot the next man who tried to rush the boats. Even so, one army officer went down on his knees, begging to be allowed off first. In another rush at La Panne a boat overturned, and seven men were drowned in four feet of water.

Wading out could be hell. Artillery Captain R. C. Austin felt his britches balloon out and fill with water till they were "heavy as masonry." His sodden jacket and water-logged boots seemed to nail him down.

The sea was up to his chin when a ship's lifeboat finally appeared, and Austin wondered how he could ever climb into it. He need not have worried. Strong arms reached out, grabbed him by the armpits and belt, and swung him over the gunwale. He heard someone in the boat shouting, "Come on, you bastards, wake up, blast you!"

Occasionally the more resourceful soldiers devised their own transportation. Separated from his artillery unit, Gunner F. Felstead discovered that none of the queues seemed to want stragglers, so he and six mates decided to go it alone. Walking along the beach, they found a canvas collapsible drifting offshore. It had only one oar, but using their rifles as paddles, the little group put to sea. They were ultimately picked up by a naval cutter and transferred to the paddle steamer *Royal Eagle*.

The minesweeper *Killarney* rescued three other adventurers about this time. Heading across the Channel, she encountered a raft made of a door and several wooden planks. Aboard were a French officer, two Belgian soldiers, and six demijohns of wine. All were safely transferred.

But it was Lieutenant E. L. Davies, skipper of the minesweeper *Oriole*, who had the most practical idea for breaking the bottleneck of the beaches this day. *Oriole* was an old River Clyde paddle steamer with a good, shallow draft. Taking advantage of this, Davies aimed her at the shore and drove her hard aground. For the rest of the day she served as a pier. The troops wading out scrambled aboard her bow and were picked up from her stern by a steady stream of boats from the larger vessels lying further out.

Even so, many of the soldiers stumbled and sank while trying to reach the *Oriole*. Sub-Lieutenant Rutherford Crosby, son of a Glasgow bookseller, dived overboard again and again, pulling them out. He got a rest when the tide went out, leaving the *Oriole* high and dry, but toward evening it flowed in again, ultimately refloating the ship. Her work done, she turned for Ramsgate with a final load of Tommies. Altogether on the 29th, some 2,500 men used her as a bridge to safety.

In Dunkirk Captain Tennant had his own solution to the problem of the beaches. The eastern mole was proving such a success, he asked that the whole evacuation be concentrated there. Admiral Ramsay turned him down. The BEF was now pouring into the perimeter in such numbers the Admiral felt that both the mole *and* the beaches were needed. Beyond that, he wanted to spread the risk. So far he had been lucky. Thanks to the smoke and a low cloud cover, the Luftwaffe had virtually ignored the mole. Ramsay wanted to keep it that way. A large concentration of shipping might draw unwelcome attention.

As it was, a steady stream of vessels pulled in and out all morning. The formula was working: a ship would come alongside . . . the pier master Commander Clouston would send out enough troops to fill it . . . the ship would load up and be off again—sometimes in less than half an hour. Working with Clouston was Brigadier Reggie Parminter, formerly of Gort's staff and now army embarkation officer. Totally imperturbable, he disdained a helmet and jauntily sported a monacle in his left eye.

All the time the queue of men waiting at the foot of the mole continued to grow. To keep it manageable, Parminter devised a "hat-check" system. The waiting men were divided into batches of 50; the leader of each batch was assigned a number; and when that number was called, it was time to go.

"Embarkation is being carried out normally now," Captain Tennant radioed Dover at 1:30 p.m. on the 29th. And everything was indeed "normal"—except for the number of ships alongside the mole. There were more than usual. On the harbor side the destroyers *Grenade* and *Jaguar*, the transport *Canterbury*, and a French destroyer were all loading troops. On the seaward side, the Channel packet *Fenella* was also loading.

Now at 1:30, just as Tennant was sending his message, six

more ships arrived. Lieutenant Robin Bill was leading in a flotilla of small trawlers. Normally engaged in minesweeping, today they were bringing some badly needed ladders for the mole. They too tied up on the harbor side, between the two British destroyers and the *Canterbury*.

Then a big paddle steamer, the *Crested Eagle*, also arrived, tying up on the seaward side, just astern of the *Fenella*. Altogether, there were now twelve ships clustered around the end of the mole.

At the same time the weather began to clear and the wind changed, sending the smoke inland instead of across the harbor. It was turning into a sparkling afternoon.

All these details were unknown in the Dynamo Room, but the message traffic was certainly reassuring. Every possible precaution had been taken against those torpedo attacks in the night. There had been no serious ship loss since early morning, when *Mona's Isle* had struck a mine. Fortunately, she was empty at the time. No fresh information was coming in from Dunkirk, but news from there was always late.

By the end of the afternoon spirits were soaring. At 6:22 p.m. Major-General H. C. Lloyd, doing liaison work with Ramsay, telegraphed the War Office in London:

> Naval shipping plan now approaching maximum efficiency. Subject to weather and reasonable immunity enemy action, expect lift about 16,000 Dunkirk, and 15,000 from beaches. . . .

But even as the General wired his optimism, awesome events were unfolding at Dunkirk . . . staggering the rescue fleet, turning the mole into a shambles, and throwing Admiral Ramsay's whole evacuation plan into wild disarray.

8

Assault from
the Sky

To Captain Wolfgang Falck, these would always be "the golden days." As a *Gruppe* commander in Fighter Squadron 26, he flew an Me 110—a new two-engine fighter said to be even better than the fabled Me 109, but nobody really knew because there was so little opposition. So far the campaign had been a picnic: knocking down obsolete British Fairey Battle bombers ... shooting French planes as they sat in neat rows on the ground ... protecting the Stukas, the Heinkel 111's, the Dornier 17's from attacks that never came.

The only problem was keeping up with the panzers. As the army advanced, so did the squadron, and it required superb organization to keep fuel, spare parts, and maintenance flowing. Usually the ground personnel would move forward during the night, leaving a skeleton crew to service the planes before taking off on their morning missions. These skeleton crews would then move on too. When the squadron completed its mission, it would land at the new base, where everything would be set up and waiting.

Food and lodging were always the best. The squadron's administrative officer Major Fritz von Scheve was an old reservist who had a real nose for finding decent billets—and where a good wine cellar might be hidden. He usually selected some local chateau whose owner had fled, leaving everything behind. Falck forbade any looting—the place must be left as they found it—but there was no rule against enjoying life, and the pilots found themselves eating off Limoges china and sleeping in canopied beds.

There was even time for nonsense. Near one captured airfield some member of the squadron found a number of French baby tanks, abandoned but full of petrol. Pilots tend to be good at tinkering, and they soon had the tanks manned and running. The men spent a glorious hour chasing and ramming one another—it was like a giant dodgem concession at some amusement park.

May 27, and the German flyers got their first inkling that the golden days would not last forever. Now the target was Dunkirk itself, and as the Stukas and Heinkels went about their usual business, a new throaty roar filled the air. Modern British fighters—Hurricanes and Spitfires—came storming down upon them, breaking up the neat formations, sending occasional bombers spinning down out of control. These British squadrons had been considered too valuable to base in France, but the fighting was in range of England now, and that was different. Taking off from a dozen Kentish fields, they poured across the Channel.

It's hard to say who was more surprised—the Tommies on the ground or the Germans in the air. The ordinary British soldier had almost given up hope of ever seeing the RAF again; then suddenly here it was, tearing into the enemy. For the Luftwaffe pilots, these new air battles were an educational experience. Captain Falck soon discovered that the Me 110 was not better than the Me 109—in fact, it wasn't as good. On one mission his plane was the only 110 of four to get back to base after tangling with the RAF. He landed, still quivering with fright, to find General Kesselring making an inspection. When they met again years later, the General still remembered Falck's shaky salute.

Like many pilots, Falck was superstitious. On the side of his plane he had painted a large ladybug—the lucky symbol of his squadron in the Norwegian campaign. A big letter "G" also adorned the fuselage. G was the seventh letter of the alphabet and "7" was his lucky number. With the Spitfires around, he needed every talisman he could get.

Even the Me 109's had met their match. The Spitfires could make sharper turns, hold a dive longer, and come out of it faster. They also had a way of appearing without warning—once so suddenly that Captain Adolf Galland, a veteran 109 pilot flying wing on his skipper, lost his usual cool. Momentarily shaken, he made a false turn, leaving the skipper a wide-open target. In anguish, Galland managed to shoot one of the Spitfires down, then returned to his base fearing the worst. But the skipper, a veteran World War I pilot named Max Ibel, turned out to be an indestructible old bird. Run to earth by the Spits, he managed to crash-land and "walked home."

Happily for the Luftwaffe, there were never enough Spitfires and Hurricanes. The RAF's Fighter Command had to think ahead to the coming defense of Britain herself, and Air Chief Marshal Sir Hugh Dowding refused to allocate to Dunkirk more than sixteen squadrons at any one time. Even stretched thin, these planes could not provide full-time cover, and the Luftwaffe took full advantage of those moments when the beaches were without fighter protection. When the score for the 27th was finally added up, there were conflicting claims on British and German losses, but on one point there was complete agreement: the port of Dunkirk was wrecked.

May 28 promised to be an even more productive day for the Luftwaffe. The Belgian surrender, the crumbling French defenses, the capture of Calais—all released additional planes. But the weather turned sour; Fliegerkorps VIII, responsible for Dunkirk, remained on the ground. Its commanding officer General Major Wolfram von Richthofen (distant cousin of the famous Red Baron) had more than the weather to contend with. Hermann Göring was constantly on the phone. The General Field Marshal was now worried about his assurances to Hitler that the Luftwaffe could win the battle alone, and seemed to think that Richthofen could somehow chase away the clouds.

May 29 dawned even worse. A steady drizzle and ceiling only 300 feet. Fliegerkorps VIII steeled itself for another barrage of calls from Göring. But around noon it began to clear up. At 2:00 p.m. Richthofen gave the long-delayed orders to attack.

Gruppe leaders were summoned and briefed. The main point: by agreement with Army Group B only the beaches and shipping would be attacked. No targets inland. There was now too much danger of hitting friendly troops. At 2:45 the planes began taking off from various fields: Major Oskar Dinort's Stukas from Beaulieu . . . Major Werner Kreipe's Dornier 17's from Rocrai . . . Captain Adolf Galland's Me 109's from Saint Pol . . . and so on.

It was no ordinary raid. Fliegerkorps VIII had been specially reinforced: planes from four other *Fliegerkorps* . . . a wing of new Ju 88's from Holland . . . another all the way from Dusseldorf. Altogether some 400 aircraft headed for Dunkirk, led by 180 Stukas.

By 3:00 p.m. they were there. So far no sign of the RAF. Circling so as to come in from the sea, Corporal Hans Mahnert, a gunner-radio operator flying with Stuka Wing No. 3, looked down on a remarkable sight. Ships were crowded together everywhere. It reminded him, oddly enough, of an old print he had once seen of the English fleet gathered at Trafalgar.

Other more practiced eyes were also scanning the sea. They may have missed the eastern mole before, but not today. The smoke was blowing inland now, and there—directly below—was a sight no one could overlook. Clustered alongside the mole were a dozen ships. It was hard to imagine a better target. . . .

Lieutenant Robin Bill could easily see the bombs falling. They looked about the size of 15-inch shells as they tumbled out of the diving Stukas. No more time for comparisons: he threw himself face-down on the mole, as the world exploded around him.

One bomb landed squarely on the mole, twenty feet in front of him, hurling slabs of concrete into the air. A chunk sailed by his ears, killing a soldier further down the walkway. Shaken and covered with dust, Bill felt something oddly moist: it was a stray puppy licking his face.

He glanced to his left, where his six trawlers were moored. They were still all right. But this was just the start. The planes seemed to attack in twos and threes, dropping a couple of

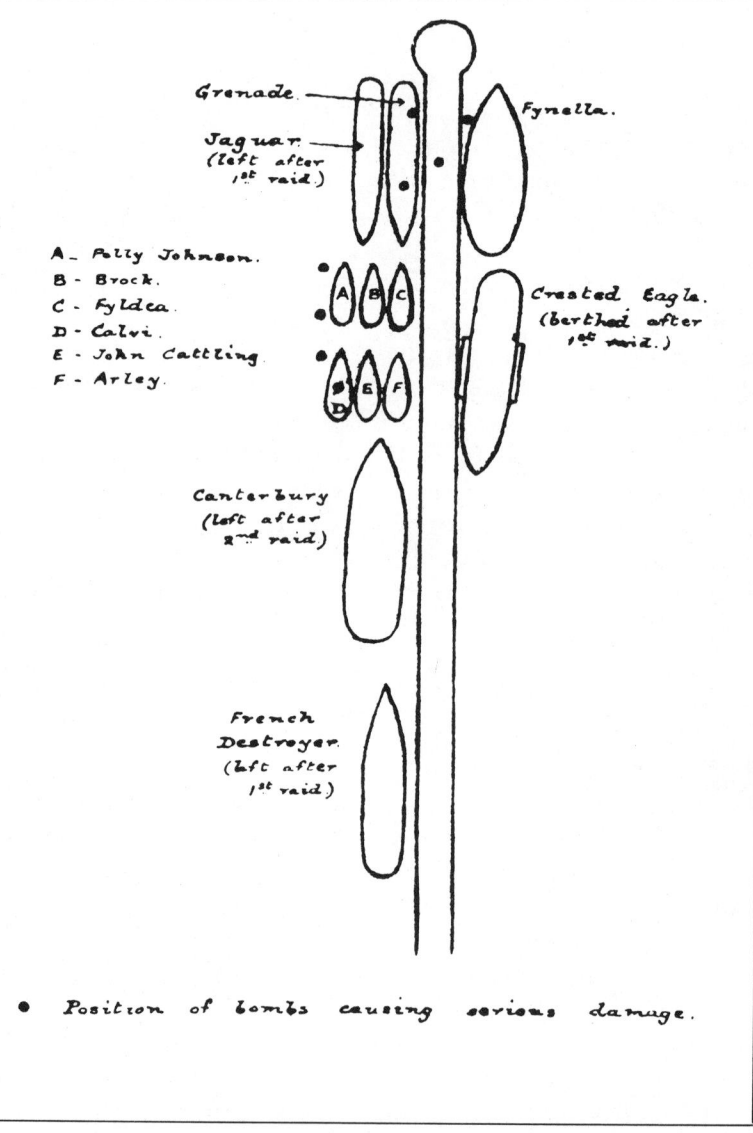

May 29, 2:45 p.m., the eastern mole (drawn at the time by Lieutenant Robin Bill)

bombs every time. There were occasional lulls, but the attack never really stopped.

Lying at the very end of the mole, the destroyer *Jaguar* managed to cast off. Packed with troops, she headed for home as the Stukas dived on her again and again. They scored no direct hits, but several near misses did fearful damage. Shrapnel riddled her port side, slashing open fuel tanks and steam lines. *Jaguar* quickly lost headway and drifted toward the shore. Just in time the destroyer *Express* raced over, towed her clear, and took off the troops. Listing seventeen degrees, *Jaguar* ultimately crawled back to Dover empty—out of the evacuation for good.

At the mole it was the destroyer *Grenade*'s turn next. Standing by the forward capstan, Chief Stoker W. Brown watched a Stuka pass overhead, turn, and race in from the sea. It scored a near miss on the mole, spraying the *Grenade* with shrapnel. Brown fell wounded, and just as the ship's medical officer finished patching him up, along came another Stuka. This time the aim was perfect. One bomb landed aft, another on the bridge, exploding in an oil tank below. A great sheet of flame shot up through the deck as Brown managed to clamber onto the mole.

Seaman Bill Irwin was on the *Grenade* just by chance. One of his mates had been wounded on the mole, and Irwin brought him aboard, looking for medical attention. As they waited in a small compartment on the upper deck, a sudden blast threw them off their feet. Somebody's tin hat—turned literally red-hot—rolled crazily around on its rim as Irwin dodged out of the way.

He managed to get his friend back onto the mole, but had to leave behind a badly wounded petty officer lying in a bunk. Irwin promised to come back for him, but it was a promise he couldn't keep. Already Commander Clouston's men were loosening the ship's lines so that she wouldn't go down at her berth. Still blazing, *Grenade* drifted into the harbor channel. But if she sank here, it could be even worse. She might block the harbor completely. Finally one of Lieutenant Bill's trawlers towed her out of the way. *Grenade* burned on for several hours ... then blew up, vanishing in a mushroom cloud of smoke.

Able Seaman P. Cavanagh managed to scramble from the burning *Grenade* onto the mole just before she cast off. Momentarily he was safe—but only momentarily. A German plane swooped down, machine-gunning the troops that crowded the walkway. A quick-thinking soldier pushed Cavanagh down, then lay on top of him. When the plane had gone, Cavanagh asked the soldier to get off his back, but there was no answer—he was dead. He had given his life to save a man he never even knew.

Cavanagh now went on board the *Fenella*, a large wooden steamer lying on the other side of the mole. "If this gets hit," someone observed, "it will go up like a box of matches." With that, a bomb landed alongside, splintering the ship's hull. Cavanagh hopped off, crossed the mole again, and decided to try one of Lieutenant Bill's trawlers. He picked the *Calvi*, but before he could climb aboard a bomb landed on her, too. She went down at her berth with stately dignity, resting on the bottom completely upright. Her funnel and masts remained above water, her battle ensign still flying from the foremast.

Cavanagh moved on to another of the trawlers—he never knew the name—and this time nobody dropped anything on him. Bombed out of three ships and machine-gunned once (all in 45 minutes), he sat down on the deck for a moment's rest. "Get off your arse and give us a hand," someone called, and he went wearily back to work.

On the *Fenella*, riddled by the near miss alongside the mole, Gunner Mowbray Chandler of the Royal Artillery sat below-decks sipping cocoa. He had been in Commander Clouston's queue since early morning; now that he was at last on board a ship, it was time to relax a little. Not even that near miss could interrupt his cocoa. Then someone looked out a porthole and noticed that the mole seemed to be rising. Since this was impossible, the ship must be settling. So it wasn't time to relax after all. Chandler and his mates hurried back to the mole, as *Fenella* sank at her berth.

Three ships gone—the mole strafed and damaged—it was all very unnerving. This long arm jutting out into the sea, once the goal of everyone, was no longer so popular. Some of the troops waiting at the seaward end wavered, then surged back toward the land. Commander Clouston was at the shore end talking to Lieutenant Bill, but his quick eye caught the movement. Taking Bill with him, he pulled his revolver and hurried out to meet the mob.

"We have come to take you back to the U.K.," he said quietly but firmly. "I have six shots here, and I'm not a bad shot. The Lieutenant behind me is an even better one. So that makes twelve of you." A pause, and then he raised his voice: *"Now get down into those bloody ships!"*

That ended the incident. The men turned back again, most of them boarding the steamer *Crested Eagle*, which lay just astern of the unlucky *Fenella*. A big wooden paddle-wheeler, the *Crested Eagle* was a familiar sight to many of the troops. In happier days she had taken them on excursions up and down the Thames. Going aboard her was almost like going home. By 6:00 p.m. her decks were packed with 600 men, including a number of bedraggled survivors from the *Grenade* and *Fenella*.

Commander Clouston gave the signal to get going, and *Crested Eagle*'s big paddle wheels began churning the sea. Swinging clear of the mole, her skipper Lieutenant B. R. Booth headed east along the coast, planning to go home via Route Y.

It didn't take long for the Luftwaffe to find her. Standing by one of the paddle boxes, Chief Stoker Brown, safely off the *Grenade*, once again heard the familiar screech of a Stuka's bomb. It landed with a crash in the main saloon, sending tables, chairs, and bodies flying.

A deck below, Gunner Chandler, just off the *Fenella*, was watching the engines when the explosion came. It blew him along the deck until he hit the end bulkhead.

On the bridge Commander Booth noted that the paddles were still working, so he tried to hold his course. Maybe they could get out of this yet.

No such luck. The whole after end of the vessel was burning, and the engineer Lieutenant Jones came on the bridge to report that he couldn't keep the paddles going much longer. Booth decided to beach the ship, and turned toward shore opposite the big sanitarium at Zuydcoote, just short of Bray-Dunes. On the beach the troops momentarily forgot their own troubles as they watched this blazing torch of a boat drive hard aground.

"Get off, mate, while you can," a seaman advised Gunner Chandler as he stood uncertainly by the rail. Chandler decided it was good advice; he took off his shoes and jumped. There were other ships around, but none near, so he swam to the beach. It was easy; he had a life jacket and even managed to tow a nonswimmer along.

Once ashore he discovered for the first time how badly burned he was. In the excitement he hadn't noticed that the skin was hanging in shreds from both his hands. He was bundled into an ambulance and taken to the Casino at Malo-les-Bains, currently serving as a collection point for the wounded. It's hard to imagine a fuller day, yet he ended up only a few hundred yards from where he had started in the morning.

Except for the mole, the most inviting target this perilous afternoon was the 6,000-ton cargo liner *Clan MacAlister*. Loaded with eight assault landing craft and their crews, she had come over from Dover the previous night. Her skipper Captain R. W. Mackie felt that the prescribed route was unnecessarily dangerous, but when he complained to Captain Cassidie, in charge of the ALC's, Cassidie simply replied, "If you don't like to go, Captain, give me a course to steer, put the boats in the water, and I'll take them over myself." Mackie took this as a challenge to both his courage and his ability. On they went.

By 9:00 a.m. on the 29th they were lying off Dunkirk Roads discharging the boats. Two were damaged in lowering, but the other six were safely launched and soon hard at work. *Clan MacAlister* herself was told to wait around for further orders.

She was still waiting when the Luftwaffe struck. At 3:45 p.m. the Stukas scored three direct hits and set fire to No. 5 hold. Nearby the destroyer *Malcolm* dodged the same attack, and came alongside to help. Lieutenants Ian Cox and David Mellis leapt aboard the *Clan MacAlister* and began playing the *Malcolm's* fire hose down the blazing hold. Everyone ignored the fact that the hold was full of 4-inch ammunition. If it went off, it would be certain death for both officers—and probably both ships.

Luck was with the brave. The ammunition did not explode—but neither could Cox and Mellis put the fire out.

They finally returned to the *Malcolm*, and the destroyer cast off. With her went the *Clan MacAlister's* wounded and a number of troops who had ferried out to the big steamer on the mistaken assumption that size meant safety. Captain Mackie stuck with his ship, still hoping somehow to get her home. But the Stukas kept attacking, knocked out her steering, and finally Mackie called for help.

The minesweeper *Pangbourne* eased alongside and asked if he wanted to "abandon ship." The sensitive Mackie refused to swallow that phrase. "Well, 'temporarily abandon,' " the *Pangbourne*'s captain tactfully suggested. That was all right, and Mackie crossed over.

There was no need to feel ashamed or embarrassed. The *Clan MacAlister* was just beginning to play her most useful role. She sank upright in the shallow water off the beach, and for the next several days the Luftwaffe would waste tons of bombs on her deserted hulk.

The *Clan MacAlister* was an especially tempting target, but no ship was safe this May 29th. As the minesweeper *Waverley* headed for home with 600 troops around 4:00 p.m., twelve Heinkels plastered her with bombs. For half an hour *Waverley* twisted and turned, dodging everything, but the Heinkels were insatiable. Finally a near miss tore off her rudder; then a direct hit blasted a six-foot hole in the bottom of the ship. The *Waverley* sank by the stern with a loss of over 300 men.

Now it was the *Gracie Fields*'s turn. Formerly a much-beloved Isle of Wight ferry, she left La Panne in the evening with some 750 troops. Forty minutes later a bomb exploded in her boiler room, sending up a huge cloud of steam that enveloped the ship. It was impossible to stop the engines, and with her helm jammed, she began circling at six knots. The skoots *Jutland* and *Twente* rushed over—one on each side—and for a while the three vessels waltzed around and around together, while the troops were transferred.

The minesweeper *Pangbourne*, already loaded with survivors from the *Crested Eagle* and riddled with holes herself, joined the rescue effort. She got a line on *Gracie Fields* and began towing her home. They never got there. With her crew safely removed, "Gracie" finally went down during the night.

The raid tapered off at dusk, and on the mole Commander Clouston surveyed a doleful scene. There was not a sound ship left. The *Fenella* and *Calvi* were sunk at their berths, and the rest of the vessels were gone—some to destruction, others to England with what troops they already had aboard. The bombing and the shelling were over, and the only sound was the barking of stray dogs. Abandoned by their fleeing owners, "half the canine population of France" (as one man put it) had joined the BEF. Some were smuggled on the transports, but many had to be left behind and now forlornly prowled the waterfront—a continuing and melancholy phenomenon of the evacuation.

The mole itself was a sorry sight. Here and there it was pitted with holes and craters, not all of them made by bombs. At least two British ships rammed the walkway in their frantic maneuvers during the raid. Clouston went to work and soon had the gaps bridged with doors, hatch covers, and planking salvaged from the wrecked ships.

In the midst of these labors, the passenger steamer *King Orry* eased alongside. Her steering gear was gone and her hull badly holed by near misses. The last thing Clouston needed was another ship sunk at her berth; during the night her skipper took her out, hoping to beach her clear of the fairway.

He didn't get very far. Outside the harbor, but still in deep water, *King Orry* rolled over and sank. The naval yacht *Bystander* appeared and began picking up survivors. Manning the ship's dinghy, Able Seaman J. H. Elton dived into the sea to help the exhausted swimmers. He alone saved 25 men, and he was not done yet. He was the ship's cook, and once back on board the *Bystander*, he headed straight for his galley. Normally Elton had to feed a crew of seven, but tonight there were 97 aboard. Undaunted, he made meals for them all, then raided the ship's locker for dry clothes and blankets.

Often the evacuated troops were too exhausted to help themselves, but not always. Gunner W. Jennings of the Royal Artillery proved a tower of strength while transferring soldiers from the crippled *Gracie Fields* to the skoots alongside. Again and again he lifted men on his shoulders and carried them across, as if they were children.

When the escort vessel *Bideford* lost her stern off Bray-Dunes, Private George William Crowther, 6th Field Ambulance, gave up his chance to be rescued. He remained instead on the *Bideford*, helping the ship's surgeon. He worked for 48 hours, almost without a break, while the *Bideford* was slowly towed back to Dover.

All through the afternoon of May 29 the Dynamo Room remained blissfully ignorant of these staggering events. As far as the staff knew, the evacuation was proceeding smoothly—"approaching maximum efficiency," as liaison officer General Lloyd telegraphed the War Office at 6:22 p.m.

Three minutes later the roof fell in. The destroyer *Sabre* had been sent over with some portable wireless sets and reinforcements for the naval shore parties. Arriving at the height of the air attack, she wired Dover at 6:25:

> Continuous bombing for 1½ hours. One destroyer sinking, one transport with troops on board damaged. No damage to pier. Impossible at present to embark more troops.

Then, at 7:00 p.m. came a startling phone message. It was from Commander J. S. Dove, calling from La Panne on the direct line that linked Gort's headquarters with London and Dover. Dove had been helping out at Tennant's headquarters since the "lethal kite" fiasco, and was not part of the regular chain of command. He was calling on his own initiative, but it was not his status; it was what he said that seemed important. He reported that he had just come from Dunkirk, that the harbor was completely blocked, and that the whole evacuation must be carried out from the beaches.

Why Dove made this call remains unclear. He had apparently commandeered a car, driven it to La Panne, and talked the military into letting him use the phone—all on his own. He had been in Dunkirk since May 24, and had previously shown great coolness under fire. Perhaps, as Ramsay's Chief of Staff later speculated, he was simply shell-shocked after five extremely hard days.

In any event, the call caused a sensation in the Dynamo Room. Taken together with *Sabre*'s signal ("Impossible at present to embark more troops"), it seemed to indicate that the harbor was indeed blocked and only the beaches could be used.

First, Ramsay tried to make sure. At 8:57 he radioed Tennant, "Can you confirm harbor is blocked?" Tennant replied, "No," but the raid had left communications in a shambles, and the answer never got through. Not hearing from Tennant, he later tried the French commander, Admiral Abrial, but no answer there either.

At 9:28 Ramsay didn't dare wait any longer. He radioed the minesweeper *Hebe*, serving as a sort of command ship offshore:

> Intercept all personnel ships approaching Dunkirk and instruct them not to close harbor but to remain off Eastern beach to collect troops from ships.

Midnight, there was still no word from Dunkirk. Ramsay sent the destroyer *Vanquisher* to investigate. At 5:51 a.m. on the 30th she flashed the good news,

> "Entrance to Dunkirk harbor practicable. Obstructions exist towards outer side of eastern arm."

This welcome information was immediately relayed to the rescue fleet, but a whole night had gone by. Only four trawlers and a yacht used the mole during those priceless hours of darkness, despite calm seas and minimum enemy interference. "A great opportunity was missed," commented Captain Tennant a few days later. "Probably 15,000 troops could have been embarked had the ships been forthcoming."

But for Ramsay, the worst thing that happened on the evening of May 29 was not the false report from Dunkirk; it was a very real decision made in London. The day had seen heavy losses in shipping—particularly destroyers. The *Wakeful*, *Grafton*, and *Grenade* were gone; *Gallant*, *Greyhound*, *Intrepid*, *Jaguar*, *Montrose*, and *Saladin* damaged. The whole "G" class was now knocked out. To the Admiralty there was more than Dunkirk to think about: there were the convoys, the Mediterranean, the protection of Britain herself.

At 8:00 p.m. Admiral Pound reluctantly decided to withdraw the eight modern destroyers Ramsay had left, leaving him with only fifteen older vessels, which in a pinch could be considered expendable.

For Ramsay, it was a dreadful blow. The destroyers had come to be his most effective vessels. Withdrawing a third of them wrecked all his careful projections. Even if there were no further losses, he would now be able to maintain a flow of only one destroyer an hour to the coast—a pace that would lift only 17,000 troops every 24 hours.

The Admiralty's decision couldn't have come at a worse time. Every ship was desperately needed. The fighting divisions—the men who had defended the escape corridor—were now themselves moving into the perimeter. In the little Belgian village of Westvleteren, 3rd Division packed up for the last time. Headquarters was in a local abbey, and before pulling out, General Montgomery sought out the Abbot, Father M. Rafael Hoedt. Could the Father hide a few personal possessions for him? The answer was yes; so the General handed over a box of personal papers and a lunch basket he particularly favored. These were then bricked up in the abbey wall, as Monty drove off promising that the army would be back and he'd pick everything up later.

Only a general as cocky as Montgomery could make such a promise. Brigadier George William Sutton was more typical. He felt nothing but anguish and personal humiliation as he trudged toward Dunkirk, passing mile after mile of abandoned equipment. He was a career officer, and "if this was what it came to when the real thing came to a crisis, all the years of thought and time and trouble that we had given to learning and teaching soldiering had been wasted. I felt that I had been labouring under a delusion and that after all, this was not my trade."

Despite the disaster, some units never lost their snap and cohesion. The Queen's Own Worcestershire Yeomanry marched into the perimeter with the men singing and a mouth organ playing "Tipperary." But others, like the 44th Division, seemed to dissolve. Officers and men tramped along individually and in small parties. Private Oliver Barnard, a signalman with the 44th, had absolutely no idea where he was heading. Eventually Brigadier J. E. Utterson Kelso came swinging by. Barnard fell in behind him with the comforting thought, "He's a brigadier, he must know where he's going."

Parts of the French First Army north of Lille—finally released by General Prioux—were converging on Dunkirk, too. The plan was for the French to man the western end of the perimeter while the British manned the eastern end, but this caused all sorts of trouble where the poilus coming up the escape corridor had to cross over from east to west. It meant going at almost right angles to the generally north-south flow of the British.

There were some unpleasant collisions. As the Worcester-shire Yeomanry approached Bray-Dunes, they met the main body of the French 60th Division moving west on a road parallel to the shore. Part of the Worcesters wriggled by, but the rest had to get down into a rugger scrum and smash their way through.

When a lorry fell into a crater, blocking the road north, Major David Warner of the Kent Yeomanry organized a working party to move it. French troops kept pushing the party aside, refusing to stop while the job was done. Finally, Warner drew his revolver and threatened to shoot the next man who didn't stop when ordered. The poilus paid no attention, until Warner actually did shoot one of them. Then they stopped, and the lorry was moved.

There were clashes even among the brass. General Brooke ordered the French 2nd Light Mechanized Division, operating under him, to cover his eastern flank as II Corps made its final withdrawal on the night of May 29–30. General Bougrain, the French division's commander, announced that he had other orders from General Blanchard, and that he was going to comply with them. Brooke repeated his previous instructions, adding that if the French General disobeyed, he'd be shot, if Brooke ever caught him. Bougrain paid no attention to this either, but Brooke never caught him.

All through this afternoon of tensions and traffic jams, the last of the fighting troops poured into the perimeter. Some went straight to the beaches, while others were assigned to the defenses, taking over from the cooks and clerks who had manned the line the past three days. As the 7th Guards Brigade moved into Furnes, cornerstone of the eastern end of the perimeter, the men spotted General Montgomery standing in the marketplace. In a rare lapse, the General had dropped his normally cocky stance and stood looking weary and forlorn. As the 7th swung by, they snapped to attention and gave Monty a splendid "eyes left." It was just the tonic he needed. He immediately straightened up and returned the honor with a magnificent salute.

Farther west, the 2nd Coldstream Guards were moving into

position along the Bergues-Furnes canal. Running parallel to the coast, about six miles inland, the canal was the main line of defense facing south. The Coldstream dug in along the north bank, making good use of several farm cottages that stood in their sector. The flat land across the canal should have offered an excellent field of fire, but the canal road on that side was littered with abandoned vehicles, and it was hard to see over them.

At the moment this made no difference. There was no sign of the enemy anywhere. The Coldstreamers whiled away the afternoon casting a highly critical eye on the troops still pouring into the perimeter. Only two platoons of Welsh Guards won their approval. These marched crisply across the canal bridge in perfect formation. The rest were a shuffling rabble.

The last of Lord Gort's strong-points were closing up shop. They had kept the corridor open; now it was time to come in themselves—if they could. At the little French village of Ledringhem, fifteen miles south of Dunkirk, the remnants of the 5th Gloucesters collected in an orchard shortly after midnight, May 29. The sails of a nearby windmill were burning brightly, and it seemed impossible that these exhausted men, surrounded for two days, could get away undetected. But the Germans were tired too, and there was no enemy reaction as Lieutenant-Colonel G.A.H. Buxton led the party north along a stream bed.

They not only slipped through the German lines; they captured three prisoners along the way. At 6:30 a.m. they finally stumbled into Bambecque, once more in friendly country. The adjutant of the 8th Worcesters saw them coming: "They were dirty and weary and haggard, but unbeaten. . . . I ran towards Colonel Buxton, who was staggering along, obviously wounded. He croaked a greeting, and I saw the lumps of sleep in his bloodshot eyes. Our Commanding Officer came running out and told the 5th Gloucesters' second-in-command to rest the troops a minute. I took Colonel Buxton indoors, gave him a tumbler of stale wine, and eased him gently to the floor on to a blanket, assuring him again and again that his men were all right. In a few seconds he was asleep."

The men holding the strong-point at Cassel, 19 miles south

of Dunkirk, were also trying to get back to the sea. For three days they had held up the German advance while thousands of Allied troops swarmed up the escape corridor. Now they finally had orders to pull back themselves, but it was too late. The enemy had gradually seeped around the hill where the town stood. By the morning of May 29 it was cut off.

Brigadier Somerset, commanding the garrison, decided to try anyhow. But not during the day. There were too many Germans. The only chance would be after dark. Orders went out to assemble at 9:30 p.m.

At first all went well. The troops quietly slipped out of town, down the hill, and headed northeast over the fields. Somerset felt there was less chance of detection if they traveled cross-country.

It really didn't matter. The Germans were everywhere. With Somerset in the lead, the 4th Oxfordshire and Buckinghamshire Light Infantry were overwhelmed near Watou; the East Riding Yeomanry were virtually wiped out in a minefield; the 2nd Gloucesters were trapped in a thick woods called the Bois Saint Acaire.

"*Kamerad! Kamerad!*" shouted the German troopers swarming around the woods, trying to flush out the Gloucesters. Crouching in the brush, the Tommies lay low. A pause, and then a voice speaking good English over a loudspeaker: "Come out! Come out! Hitler is winning the war, you are beaten. Come out, or we will shell you out. Lay down your arms and come out running."

Second Lieutenant Julian Fane of B Company wasn't about to buy that. He had heard of another British battalion that listened to such a broadcast, threw down its arms, and came out . . . only to be machine-gunned down. He told the men near him, and they decided to fight it out.

Since the Germans had them targeted, the first step was to find a new position. Fane led his men in a wild dash to another wood 100 yards away. It did no good. The enemy quickly spotted them, and they spent the rest of the day huddling under a hale of artillery and mortar fire.

Darkness at last, and the little group continued north. They moved in single file, keeping as silent as possible, making use of every bit of cover. But if they had any delusion that they were traveling unseen, it was dispelled when a red Very light suddenly soared into the night. Instantly machine guns, mortars, rifles, every kind of weapon opened up on them. They had been ambushed.

Tracers criss-crossed the sky; a nearby haystack burst into flames, illuminating the group perfectly. Men were falling on all sides, and Fane himself was hit in the right arm and shoulder. He finally reached a ditch, where he was relatively safe as long as he kept an 18-inch profile. He gradually collected about a dozen other survivors. Together they crept off into the darkness, managing somehow to work their way around the German flank. He didn't know it, but his little band was all that remained of the 2nd Gloucesters.

One British soldier outside the perimeter was still very much in the fight. Private Edgar G. A. Rabbets had been just another Tommy in the 5th Northamptonshires until the great retreat. Then a German thrust almost caught the battalion near Brussels. A fire-fight developed, and at one point Rabbets raised his rifle and took a potshot at an enemy soldier about 200 yards away. The man dropped in his tracks.

"Can you do that again?" asked the company commander. Rabbets obligingly picked off another German.

Then and there Ted Rabbets was designated a sniper, and henceforth he acted entirely on his own. He had no previous training for his new work, but did enjoy one unusual advantage: he had once known a poacher who taught him a few tricks. Now he could move so quietly he could "catch a rabbit by the ears," and he could make himself so small he could "hide behind a blade of grass."

As a sniper, Rabbets soon developed a few trade secrets of his own: never snipe from tree tops—too easy to get trapped. Keep away from farmhouse attics—too easy to be spotted. Best vantage point—some hiding place where there's room to move around, like a grove of trees.

Following these rules, Rabbets managed to survive alone most of the way across Belgium. He tried to keep in occasional touch with his battalion, but usually he was deep in German-held territory—once even behind their artillery. From time to time he matched wits with his German counterparts. One of them once fired at him from a hole in some rooftop, missed by six inches. Rabbets fired back and had the satisfaction of seeing the man plunge out of the hole. Another time, while prowling a village street late at night, Rabbets rounded a corner and literally ran into a German sniper. This time Ted fired first and didn't miss.

Rabbets ultimately reached the coast near Nieuport and slowly worked his way west, dipping into the German lines on an occasional foray. On May 31 he finally rejoined the BEF at La Panne—still operating alone and perhaps the last fighting man to enter the perimeter.

All the way south, five divisions of General Prioux's French First Army fought on at Lille. It was still early on the morning of May 29 when a French truck convoy, approaching the city from Armentières, met some armored vehicles moving onto the road. The poilus sent up a great cheer, thinking that at last some British tanks were coming to help them. Only when the strangers began confiscating their arms did the Frenchmen realize that they had run into the 7th Panzer Division.

Cut off from the north, General Prioux surrendered during the afternoon at his headquarters in Steenwerck. He had gotten his wish: to remain with the bulk of his army rather than try to escape. Most of his troops holed up in Lille, continuing to tie down six enemy divisons.

By now it didn't matter very much. With the escape corridor closed, Rundstedt's Army Group A and Bock's Army Group B at last joined forces, and the Germans had all the troops they needed for the final push on Dunkirk.

But this May 29 saw an important change in the composition of the German forces. Once again the tanks were gone—pulled out this time on the urging of the panzer generals themselves. Guderian summed up the reasons in a report he submitted on the evening of the 28th after a personal tour of the front: the armored divisions were down to 50% of strength . . . time was needed to prepare for new operations . . . the marshy terrain was unsuitable for tanks . . . the Belgian surrender had released plenty of infantry—far more effective troops for this kind of country.

Added to these very practical arguments was perhaps an intangible factor. Guderian and the other panzer commanders were simply not temperamentally suited to the static warfare that was developing. Theirs was a world of slashing thrusts, breakthroughs, long rolling advances. Once the battle had turned into a siege, they lost interest. By the evening of the 28th Guderian was already poring over his maps of the lower Seine.

In any event, OKH agreed. At 10:00 a.m. on May 29 General Gustav von Wietersheim's motorized infantry took over from Guderian, and later in the day General Reinhardt's tanks were also pulled out. But this didn't mean that the battered Allied troops were home free. On the contrary, ten German divisions—mostly tough, experienced infantry—now pressed against the 35-mile Dunkirk perimeter.

At the western end, the 37th Panzer Engineers hoisted a swastika flag over Fort Philippe around noon, and the port of Gravelines fell soon afterward. All the way east the 56th Division was marching on Furnes. About 3:30 p.m. Bicycle Squadron 25 reached the east gate of the old walled town. Here they ran into a French column trying to get into the perimeter. After a brief fire-fight, Captain Neugart of the 25th forced the Frenchmen to surrender.

Then along came two French tanks, so unsuspecting that their turrets were open. Corporal Gruenvogel of the bicyclists jumped on one of them, pointed his pistol down through the open turret, and ordered the crew to surrender. They complied . . . as did the crew of the second tank, even without such urging.

Captain Neugart now sent a captured French major along with two of his own men into Furnes to demand that the whole town surrender. But audacity has its limits, and this time he got only a scornful reply from the Allied troops now barricading the streets.

On the beaches no one knew how long the troops manning the perimeter could keep the Germans out. At Bray-Dunes Commander Thomas Kerr half-expected to see them burst onto the sands any minute. He and Commander Richardson continued loading the troops into boats; but they arranged for a boat of their own to lie off Bray, ready to rescue the naval shore party, "just in case." This gave them some confidence, but talking quietly together that night, they agreed they'd probably end up in some German prison camp.

Dover and London knew even less. At one point on the 28th the Admiralty actually told Tennant to report "every hour" the number of people to be embarked—orders that could only have come from someone who hadn't the remotest picture of the situation. Tennant patiently replied, "Am doing my best to keep you informed, but shall be unable to report for hours."

But even at a distance one thing was clear: all too often the ships weren't where they were needed the most. Sometimes there were plenty of vessels at the mole, but no troops on hand. Other times there were troops but no ships. The same was true at the beaches. Someone was needed offshore to control the flow of shipping, the same way Captain Tennant was directing the flow of men between the mole and the beaches.

Rear-Admiral Frederic Wake-Walker got the nod. Fifty-two years old, Wake-Walker was known as an exceptionally keen organizer, and a good seaman too. His last command had been the battleship *Revenge*—a sure sign of talent, for the Royal Navy gave the battleships to only its most promising officers. At the moment, he held down a staff job at the Admiralty; he was readily available for temporary assignment.

Returning to his office from lunch on Wednesday, May 29, Wake-Walker learned that he was wanted by Rear-Admiral Sir Tom Phillips, the Vice-Chief of Naval Staff. Phillips asked him if he would like to go to Dunkirk and "try and get some organization into the embarkation there." Wake-Walker said that he'd be "delighted," and the appointment was worked out. It was important that he should not seem to be superseding Tennant. The Captain would still be SNO on shore; Wake-Walker in charge of everything afloat.

An hour later he was on his way by car to Dover. Arriving about 6:00 p.m., he went directly to Ramsay's casemate for a quick briefing. In the Dynamo Room he was shown a map, depicting the coast east of Dunkirk. The three beaches—Malo, Bray, and La Panne—had been optimistically numbered, with each beach in turn divided into three sections. The BEF would be coming down to these particular beaches, while certain others west of Malo were reserved for the French.

This neat map, with its careful delineations, little prepared him for the chaos he found when he arrived off Bray on the destroyer *Esk* at 4:00 the following morning, May 30. Transferring to the minesweeper *Hebe*, Wake-Walker soon learned about the "real war" from Captain Eric Bush, who had been filling in until he got there. At dawn Wake-Walker could see for himself the dark masses of men on the beaches, the long lines that curled into the sea, the men standing waist-deep in the water . . . waiting and waiting.

"The crux of the matter was boats, boat crews, and towage," the Admiral later recalled. At 6:30 a.m. he radioed Dover that small boats were urgently needed, and at 7:30 he asked for more ships, and again stressed the need for small boats.

It was a familiar refrain, growing in volume these past few hours. At 12:10 a.m. Brigadier Oliver Leese of Gort's staff had telephoned the War Office, stressing that the perimeter could only be held for a limited time. Send as many boats as possible—quickly. At 4:00 the War Office called back with the welcome word that Admiral Ramsay was "going to get as much small craft as possible across as soon as he can."

But nothing came. At 4:15 the destroyer *Vanquisher*, lying off Malo, radioed, "More ships and boats urgently required off west beach." At 6:40 the destroyer *Vivacious* echoed the plea: "Essential to have more ships and boats."

By 12:45 p.m. Brigadier Leese was on the phone again, this time with General Dill, Chief of the Imperial General Staff. No ships yet, he complained. Off La Panne, Admiral Wake-Walker was getting desperate. He now sent Captain Bush back to Dover in the *Hebe*, to explain in person the vital necessity of sending out boats and crews.

By 3:00 p.m. Gort himself was trying. He first phoned Admiral Pound, then General Dill, pointing out that there were still no ships. Every hour counted, he stressed.

Headquarters could at least complain to somebody. The troops waiting on the beaches didn't even have that satisfaction. After a restless night curled up in the sand, Captain John Dodd of the Royal Artillery looked out to sea in the first light of dawn and saw—nothing. "No ships in sight," he noted in his diary. "Something must have gone wrong."

At Bray-Dunes Sapper Joe Coles felt "terrible disappointment" and resigned himself to a day of troubled sleep in the Dunes. At Malo Chaplain Kenneth Meiklejohn couldn't understand it. There had been no air attacks, yet no one seemed to have embarked all night. A dreadful thought crossed his mind: "Has the Navy given us up?"

Plunging down from the sky, a German Stuka dive-bombs an Allied tank, as Hitler strikes west in May 1940. Together with the armored panzer division, the Stuka symbolized a new kind of lightning war—the *Blitzkrieg*—which the Allies were utterly unprepared to meet. German columns knifed through to the sea, trapping the British and French against the coast of Flanders. (Hergestellt im Bundesarchiv Bestand)

On the receiving end of the German onslaught were the Allied commanders, British General the Viscount Gort (left) and French General Maurice Gamelin. Within days Gamelin was fired and Gort was reeling back toward the French port of Dunkirk. Below, a file of British troops straggles into Dunkirk, hoping to escape by sea. (Top: Wide World Photos. Bottom: Hergestellt im Bundesarchiv Bestand)

Thousands of Allied soldiers soon crowded the beaches that stretched from Dunkirk to La Panne, a small Belgian resort ten miles to the east. Long lines of men curled out into the sea, patiently waiting to be picked up. (*Times*)

As the troops waited, German planes continued to pound them. For protection they dug foxholes in the dunes. Casualties were surprisingly light, since the sand tended to smother the exploding bombs. (Imperial War Museum)

Across the English Channel, a giant rescue operation was hastily organized under the command of Vice-Admiral Bertram H. Ramsay. Here Admiral Ramsay briefly relaxes on the balcony of his headquarters, carved out of the famous chalk cliffs of Dover. (Courtesy of Jane Evan-Thomas)

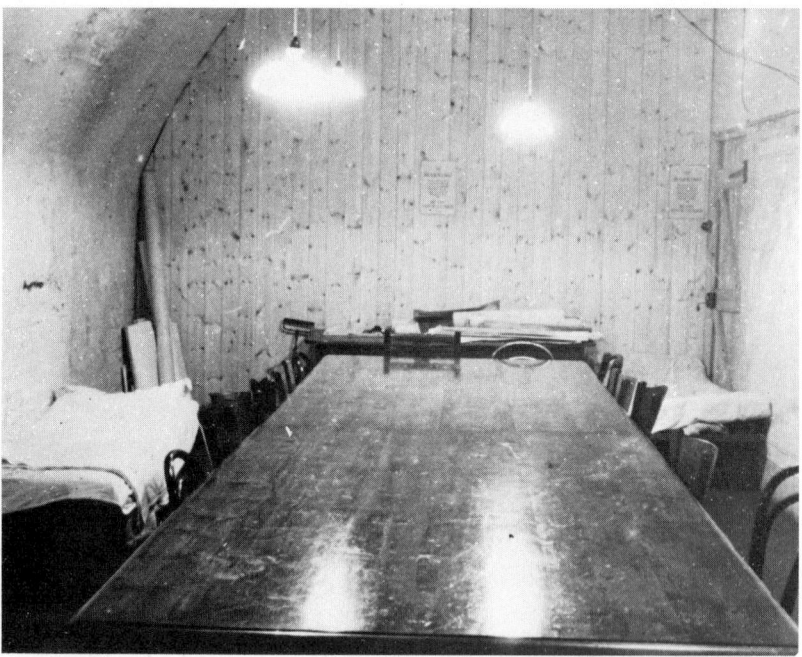

Command center for the evacuation was the austere "Dynamo Room," buried deep in the Dover cliffs. Here Ramsay's staff, using a battery of telephones, assembled and deployed a rescue fleet that ultimately totaled 861 ships. This photo, never before published, is believed to be the only picture ever taken of the room. (Courtesy of W. J. Matthews)

Every kind of vessel was used for the evacuation, ranging from warships to small pleasure craft. Above, a "G" Class destroyer races toward Dunkirk "with a bone in her teeth." This entire class was eventually knocked out. Below, the yacht *Sundowner* was luckier. She rescued 135 men and escaped without a scratch. Her owner-skipper, Commander C. H. Lightoller, had performed earlier heroics as Second Officer on the *Titanic*. (Top: Imperial War Museum. Bottom: courtesy of Patrick Stenson and Sharon Rutman)

Dunkirk was easy to find. A huge pall of smoke from burning oil tanks hung over the shattered port. The smoke seemed to symbolize defeat and disaster, but had the happy side effect of concealing the harbor from German bombers. (Courtesy of W. J. Matthews)

In contrast, La Panne, at the eastern end of the evacuation area, looked deceptively tranquil. Rescue ships can be seen here, picking up troops near the shore. Gort's headquarters was in one of the detached houses on the far right. (Courtesy of J. L. Aldridge)

Picking up troops direct from the beach seemed to take forever—"loading ships by the spoonful" was the way one embarkation officer described it. Above, a trawler and a coaster take aboard men wading out from the shore. At right, British Tommies are up to their shoulders in water, approaching a rescue ship. (Top: Wide World Photos. Bottom: The Granger Collection)

Captain William G. Tennant (left) was finally appointed by Admiral Ramsay to take charge at Dunkirk and speed up the evacuation. As Senior Naval Officer (SNO), Tennant discovered that the eastern mole of Dunkirk harbor was ideal for loading ships. Here a destroyer could lift 600 men in 20 minutes, while it took 12 hours along the beaches. For most of the next week the mole was packed with an endless line of troops (below) trudging out to the waiting ships. (Top: ILN Pic Lib. Bottom: *Times*)

Ingenuity triumphed on the beaches too. Abandoned lorries were strung together, to form improvised piers leading out into the water. Here one of these "lorry jetties" is visible in the background. (Courtesy of D.C.H. Shields)

Soon an unbroken line of crowded ships could be seen carrying the men across the Channel to safety. (Culver Pictures)

The Luftwaffe did not leave the rescue fleet alone. These two pictures show how suddenly disaster could strike. In the top photo an Allied ship has just blown up, while two others lie nearby still untouched. In the bottom photo, taken an instant later (note that the configuration of smoke is still the same), the two nearby ships have now disappeared, obliterated by the rain of bombs. Troops on the beach are futilely firing their rifles at the planes. (Top: Imperial War Museum. Bottom: Fox Photos Ltd.)

The French destroyer *Bourrasque* joins the growing list of Allied casualties. Packed with troops, she struck a German mine and went down with a loss of 150 lives. (Imperial War Museum)

A fleet of French fishing trawlers was a late addition to Ramsay's armada. They concentrated on the inner harbor of Dunkirk, where hundreds of poilus swarmed aboard. (Wide World Photos)

Bombs and mines were not the only perils faced by the rescue fleet. The *Schnellboote*, fast German motor torpedo boats, prowled the seas at night, sinking and damaging Ramsay's ships. (Hergestellt im Bundesarchiv Bestand)

German artillery added to the toll. Nothing was safe—neither the ships, the harbor, the mole, nor the men on the beaches. "Greetings to Tommy" is the message painted on this shell. (Hergestellt im Bundesarchiv Bestand)

German troops finally broke into La Panne on June 1 and began moving down the beach toward Dunkirk itself. Below, the fall of Dunkirk, June 4. Weary but triumphant, German troops of the 18th Infantry Division stack their arms and rest. (Hergestellt im Bundesarchiv Bestand)

The quarry was gone. In nine desperate days Ramsay's fleet brought back more than 338,000 Allied troops. Typical was this batch, disembarking from the minesweeper *Sandown*. Naval officer in the lower-left foreground is Lieutenant Wallis, the ship's First Lieutenant. (Courtesy J. D. Nunn)

Sometimes it seemed as if half the canine population of France had been evacuated too. Never was the Englishman's legendary fondness for dogs more ringingly affirmed. At least 170 dogs were landed in Dover alone. (Wide World Photos)

Disheveled but happy, the Tommies were sent by train to assembly areas all over Britain for rest and reorganization. At every station a relieved populace showered them with cigarettes, cakes, candy, and affection. (Wide World Photos)

At Dunkirk, the captured French rear guard heard no cheers. They would soon be marching off to POW camp, most for the duration of the war. (Hergestellt im Bundesarchiv Bestand)

1940. DUNKERQUE. LES ANGLAIS S'OPPOSENT A
L'EMBARQUEMENT DES DERNIERS FRANÇAIS
QUI VENAIENT DE PROTEGER LEUR RETRAITE

In another two weeks France was knocked out of the war. The new pro-
German Vichy government lost no time charging that the British had run
out, leaving the French holding the bag at Dunkirk. Actually, Ramsay's
rescue fleet saved over 123,000 French soldiers, 102,570 in British ships.
Despite the statistics, French bitterness continues, even today. (Musée des
Deux Guerres Mondiales—B.D.I.C., Universités de Paris)

9

The Little Ships

Lieutenant Ian Cox, First Lieutenant of the destroyer *Malcolm*, could hardly believe his eyes. There, coming over the horizon toward him, was a mass of dots that filled the sea. The *Malcolm* was bringing her third load of troops back to Dover. The dots were all heading the other way—toward Dunkirk. It was Thursday evening, the 30th of May.

As he watched, the dots materialized into vessels. Here and there were respectable steamers, like the Portsmouth–Isle of Wight car ferry, but mostly they were little ships of every conceivable type—fishing smacks . . . drifters . . . excursion boats . . . glittering white yachts . . . mud-spattered hoppers . . . open motor launches . . . tugs towing ship's lifeboats . . . Thames sailing barges with their distinctive brown sails . . . cabin cruisers, their bright work gleaming . . . dredges, trawlers, and rust-streaked scows . . . the Admiral Superintendent's barge from Portsmouth with its fancy tassels and rope-work.

Cox felt a sudden surge of pride. Being here was no longer just a duty; it was an honor and a privilege. Turning to a somewhat startled chief boatswain's mate standing beside him, he burst into the Saint Crispin's Day passage from Shakespeare's *Henry V*:

And Gentlemen in England, now abed
Shall think themselves accurs'd they were not here.

The efforts of the Small Vessels Pool and the Ministry of Shipping were at last paying off. The trickle of little ships that began in Tough's boatyard was turning into a deluge. There was still no public announcement of the evacuation, but England is a small place. In one way or another, the word reached those who were needed.

It was a midnight phone call from the Admiralty that alerted Basil A. Smith, a London accountant and owner of the 24-foot cabin cruiser *Constant Nymph*. Would Smith confirm that his boat was ready for sea and could sail on four hours' notice? Early next morning, May 27, the summons came: take her down to Sheerness at once.

Captain Lemon Webb was nursing the Ipswich spritsailing barge *Tollesbury* up the Thames on an ordinary cargo run. Then a motorboat eased alongside, and a naval officer ordered him to a nearby jetty. There a tug took her in tow, and *Tollesbury* was on her way to Sheerness, too.

The crew of the Margate lifeboat *Lord Southborough* were playing darts at their favorite pub when their turn came. A cryptic message said report to the boathouse at once. Within hours they were heading direct for Dunkirk—no stop at Sheerness for them. For Coxswain Edward D. Parker it was almost a family outing. His brother and nephew were in his crew; a son had already gone over with the Margate pilot boat; another son was one of Commander Clouston's men on the mole.

The cockle boat fleet of Leigh-on-Sea lay peacefully at anchor on May 30 when the call came for them. Bearing imposing names like *Defender, Endeavour, Resolute,* and *Renown,* they sounded like dreadnoughts; actually they were only 40 feet long with a 2½-foot draft. Normally they were engaged in the humblest of tasks—gathering in the cockle shellfish found in the mud flats of the Thames estuary. The crew were all civilians, but every man volunteered. Seventeen-year-old Ken Horner was considered too young and left behind, but he wasn't about to buy that. He ran home, got his mother's permission, and bicycled off in pursuit of the fleet. He caught up with his boat at Southend.

These vessels came with their crews, but that did not always happen. In the race against time, yachts were often commandeered before their owners could be located. Other weekend sailors just couldn't drop everything and sign up in the Navy for a month—the standard requirement. As the little ships converged on Sheerness and Ramsgate, the main staging points, Admiral Preston's Small Vessels Pool looked around for substitute crews.

Shipwright A. W. Elliott was working in Johnson & Jago's boatyard at Leigh-on-Sea when a bobby pedaled up on a bicycle. He announced that volunteers were needed to get "some chaps" off the French coast. Elliott needed no urging.

At Lowestoft on the east coast the Small Vessels Pool commandeered taxis to bring down a contingent of commercial fishermen. In London, Commander Garrett of the Pool spent three straight nights calling up various clubs . . . rounding up yachtsman members . . . packing them off in Admiralty cars to Sheerness and Ramsgate.

It was during these hectic days that Sub-Lieutenant Moran Caplat arrived in London for a few days' leave. An actor and yachtsman in peacetime, he was currently serving on a naval trawler in the North Sea, but the ship was being refitted, and for the moment he was free. He was aware that Dunkirk was coming to a boil, but felt it was no concern of his.

Going to the Royal Ocean Racing Club for breakfast, he was surprised to find nobody there. Even the steward was gone. He finally located the steward's wife, who explained that everyone had vanished after a call from the Admiralty a day or so ago. Mildly mystified, he settled down in a chair to relax alone.

The phone rang, and he answered. It was the Admiralty. A voice said they wanted "still more hands" and asked who he was. Caplat identified himself, and the voice said, "You're just what we need." He was then told to go to Sheerness immediately. Still baffled, he caught a train at Waterloo Station within an hour.

Five minutes' walk from the Royal Ocean Racing Club was the ship chandlers shop of Captain O. M. Watts on Albemarle Street. Downstairs the Captain cheerfully dispensed a hodgepodge of charts and nautical gear; upstairs he gave navigation lessons to young gentlemen who hoped for a commission in the

Royal Navy Volunteer Reserve. They were mostly professional men: solicitors, brokers, actors, bankers from the City, and such. Few knew much about the sea; some had never been out of sight of land.

John Fernald was a young American theatrical director attending the Captain's classes every Thursday evening. Usually the session was blackboard work, but not on Thursday, May 30. When he arrived with his friend David Homan, a scenery designer, Watts took them aside for a private chat. Quietly he explained there would be no regular class tonight; the Navy needed volunteers immediately for a "hazardous job."

Neither Fernald nor Homan liked the prospect of moving from navigational theory to practice so abruptly, but they couldn't see any graceful way out; so they volunteered. Captain Watts told them to grab what gear they could and report immediately to the Port of London Authority down by the Tower.

Fernald rushed back to his flat, picked up an old pea jacket, and hurried down to Tower Hill, as directed. Most of the others were already there. Some didn't even have time to change their clothes and were still wearing the cutaways and striped trousers of the City. Stockbroker Raphael de Sola, however, was resplendent in the jacket of the Royal London Yacht Club, blue trousers to match, a visored cap, and a greatcoat worthy of the First Sea Lord of the Admiralty.

Along with Captain Watts's scholars, there were a number of more obviously waterfront types: lightermen, dock workers, deckhands, barge men. High and low together, they milled around the lobby of the Port Authority building, still not knowing what they were to do.

Then a Royal Navy commander appeared and gave them a quick briefing. They were to man ship's lifeboats collected from vessels lying at the London docks. These would be towed down the river and across the Channel, where they would be used to help rescue the BEF.

A bus now took the group to Tilbury, where the lifeboats were waiting. The rule was four men to a boat; twelve boats to a tow. Fernald and Homan managed to stick together, and soon after midnight they were on their way. In the quiet of the night, broken only by the water rushing by and the throb of the tug up ahead, Fernald wondered at the incredible change in his life that had snatched him from a humdrum existence in London and put him in an open boat racing through the dark.

First stop was Sheerness. This bustling harbor on the Thames estuary had become the collecting point for all the little ships streaming down the river. Here they were sorted out and put into shape under the watchful eye of Commodore A. H. Taylor, a retired Rear-Admiral who could normally be found shuffling paper in the Economic Warfare Division of the Admiralty.

Engines were the big problem. Many of the boats had been laid up for the winter and were hard to get running again. Others had idiosyncrasies apparently known only to their absent owners. The Thames excursion steamers had boilers that couldn't use salt water. It was a miracle that Captain T. E. Docksey and his engineers managed to get more than 100 boats in good enough shape to cross the Channel.

Every ship also needed someone on board who could keep the engine running. By now there were plenty of weekend-sailor volunteers, but few of these bankers and shopkeepers really understood machinery. The Shipping Federation, an organization of operators, was asked to help and issued a call for volunteers. About 350 marine engineers responded.

From Sheerness most of the little ships moved on to Ramsgate. Here fuel tanks were topped off, provisions loaded, and convoys made up. Many of the craft had no compass, and some of the skippers had never been out of sight of land. Lieutenant-Commander Raymond Grundage, the Routing Officer, issued more than 1,000 charts, 600 with routes lined off for neophyte navigators.

Problems could be enormous—or exasperatingly minute. Robert Hilton, a physical education specialist, and Ted Shaw, a red-headed cinema manager, had teamed up to bring the motorboat *Ryegate II* down the river. They expected to pick up supplies at Ramsgate, but all they received were two cans of water. Otherwise the boat was bare—not even a tumbler for the water. The naval supply depot at Ramsgate seemed unable to cope; they finally went to a pub, had a drink, and pocketed the glasses.

Each little ship had its own tale of troubles, but at the start they all suffered from one common problem: none of them were armed. Lieutenant C. D. Richards carefully hoarded his stockpile of 105 Lewis machine guns, doling them out only to the tugs and escort vessels.

Later the crews would scavenge the beaches, gathering a plentiful supply of discarded Bren guns; and sometimes a BEF gunner might even attach himself to a vessel, but at first they were defenseless. It was enough to make a member of the crew feel a bit uneasy. "Even a record of the 1812 Overture would be better than nothing," observed one skipper.

It was 10:00 p.m., May 29, when the first convoy of little ships set out from Ramsgate on the long trip across the Channel. None of the eight launches in the group had any navigating instruments. Nevertheless, Lieutenant R. H. Irving, skipper of the escorting motorboat *Triton*, was confident. Unlike most, he knew these waters well. Waiting outside Ramsgate breakwater, he shouted to the other ships to close up and follow him. Three of the boats developed engine trouble and had to turn back, but the others stuck to *Triton* and arrived safely off La Panne at dawn.

At 1:00 a.m. on the 30th another convoy left Ramsgate—this time, nineteen launches led by the Belgian ferry *Yser*—and from then on the flow steadily increased. By late afternoon it was hard to tell where one convoy ended and the next began. All that night, and the 31st too, the little ships poured across the Channel.

Frequently they passed ships like the *Malcolm* heading back to England. Decks packed with troops, they were a sobering sight. For their part, the men on the returning vessels watched this armada of small craft with mounting excitement and pride. The very names seemed to say "England": *Swallow* . . . *Royal Thames* . . . *Moss Rose* . . . *Norwich Belle* . . . *Duchess of York* . . . *Blue Bird* . . . *Pride of Folkestone* . . . *Palmerston* . . . *Skylark* . . . *Nelson* . . . *Southend Britannia* . . . *Lady Haig* . . . *New Prince of Wales.*

Many of the names also had a personal quality, suggesting that this rescue effort was no mere naval operation; that it was really a family affair: *Grace Darling* . . . *Boy Bruce* . . . *Our Maggie* . . . *Our Lizzie* . . . *Girl Nancy* . . . *Handy Billie* . . . *Willie and Alice* . . . *Auntie Gus.*

Traveling in company, usually shepherded by an armed tug or skoot, the little ships moved across a smooth, gray carpet of sea. The English Channel has a reputation for nastiness, but it had behaved for four days now, and the calm continued on May 30. Best of all, there was a heavy mist, giving the Luftwaffe no chance to follow up the devastating raids of the 29th.

"Clouds so thick you can lean on them," noted a Luftwaffe war diarist, as the Stukas and Heinkels remained grounded. At Fliegerkorps VIII General Major von Richthofen couldn't believe it was that bad. At headquarters the sun was shining. He ordered Major Dinort, commanding the 2nd Stuka Squadron, to at least try an attack. Dinort took his planes up, but returned in ten minutes. Heavy fog over Dunkirk, he phoned headquarters. Exasperated, Richthofen countered that the day was certainly flyable where *he* was. If *Herr Generalmajor* didn't believe him, Dinort shot back, just call the weather service.

But cloudy weather didn't guarantee a safe passage for the little ships. Plenty of things could still go wrong. The Channel was full of nervous and inexperienced sailors.

"Periscope on the starboard bow," shouted the lookout of the 80-foot excursion steamer *New Prince of Wales*. It turned out to be the mast of a sunken ship, standing fifteen feet out of the water, complete with shrouds.

Next, *New Prince of Wales* was almost run down by a destroyer that mistook her for a German S-boat. The skipper, Sub-Lieutenant Peter Bennett, managed to flash a recognition signal just in time. A little later he ran alongside an anchored French cargo ship, hoping to get some directions. "*Où est l'armée britannique?*" he called. The reply was a revolver shot. These were dangerous days for strangers asking questions.

Uncorrected compasses were another source of trouble. It was easy to find the French coast, but the right spot was another matter. Sub-Lieutenant William Ronald Williams anchored his lighter a few hundred yards off an empty stretch of beach and had a boat row him ashore. Walking a quarter-mile inland in search of somebody in authority, he hailed a couple of soldiers he saw silhouetted against a distant blaze.

"*Lieber Gott!*" one of them cried, and they began shooting at him. Williams ducked behind a dune and shot back. Both Germans fell, but there were other voices now, and Williams raced back to the beach. In less than five minutes he had his lighter under weigh at her full six knots.

One way or another, most of the little ships eventually reached the right part of the coast and went to work. Essentially they were ferries, carrying or towing troops from the beaches to the larger vessels lying further out. Sometimes it was easy—just a matter of towing some rowboat or inflated raft; other times it was difficult and dangerous—especially when they had to pluck men directly from the sea.

"Well done, motorboat, wait for me," a voice hailed Lieutenant Irving, as he nursed *Triton* alongside a destroyer with one more load. An officer wearing a lambskin coat leapt aboard. It was Commodore Gilbert Owen Stephenson, a 62-year-old retired vice-admiral, who had been recruited for the crisis and put in charge of all offshore operations at La Panne. Hatless and wet through, he seemed oblivious to his own discomfort as he told Irving to carry on. He added that he might later have "one or two other jobs" for *Triton* to do.

Stephenson then threw himself into the rescue work too. Nothing was beneath him. He steered, passed lines, helped haul the exhausted troops aboard. Through it all he kept up a line of cheerful chatter. "Come on, the Army!" he would cry; or, to some half-drowned soldier, "Where have I seen you before? You're so good-looking I'm sure I know you."

Late in the afternoon Stephenson had *Triton* take him to a certain spot off the beach. Instructing Irving not to move, he explained he was going ashore to look for Lord Gort. If he brought back the General, Irving was to take him straight to England. With that, Stephenson plunged over the side and waded ashore through the surf, often up to his neck in water.

In an hour he was back, again wading through the surf, but there was no sign of Lord Gort. Stephenson offered no explanation, nor did Irving ask. They simply went back to their rescue work, the Commodore still hatless and soaked to the skin. Along with his words of cheer for the troops, he had plenty to say to Irving himself. Sometimes the lieutenant was a "good fellow"; other times, "a bloody fool." Irving didn't mind. He'd do anything for a senior officer like this.

Off Bray-Dunes to the west, the *Constant Nymph* was hard at work too. At first Basil Smith, her accountant-skipper, could find only French troops. These he ferried out to the skoot *Jutland*, which was serving as a "mother ship." Then a British army officer swam out to say there was a whole division of the BEF waiting a little farther west. Smith shifted his boat slightly and began picking them up.

It was never easy. On top of all the other problems, the Germans were now within artillery range, and began shelling the beach. East of La Panne an enemy observation balloon rode unmolested in the sky directing the fire. Smith was one of the few who didn't seem disturbed. As he later explained, he was deaf and had a lot to do.

Off Malo-les-Bains the *Ryegate II* was having less success. Coming over from Ramsgate, her engines broke down; then it turned out she drew too much water to get close to the beach; finally she fouled her propeller on some piece of wreckage. Disgusted, her skipper Sub-Lieutenant D. L. Satterfield tied up to the skoot *Horst* and assigned his crew to a couple of ship's boats.

Bob Hilton and Ted Shaw, the pair who had brought *Ryegate II* down the Thames, manned the *Horst*'s own lifeboat. As they pulled toward the shore, they could hear the skoot's radio blaring away. It was incongruously tuned into the BBC's "Children's Hour."

Coming through the surf, Hilton and Shaw were immediately mobbed and capsized. Gradually they learned the art of successful ferry-work. Basically, it consisted of getting close enough to pick up men, but not so close as to be swamped. For seventeen straight hours they rowed, side by side, carrying troops to the *Horst*.

Hour after hour the little ships worked the beaches, returning to Ramsgate only when they could find no more fuel, or when the crews were too tired to carry on. Then they discovered that the trip home could be perilous too. The motor launch *Silver Queen* had neither charts nor compass, but the crew felt they had a good idea where England was, and they headed that way.

Halfway over they found a soldier's compass, and this increased their confidence. Finally they sighted land, and then a friendly-looking harbor. Approaching the breakwater, they were greeted by a blast of gunfire. Hopelessly twisted around, they had stumbled into Calais by mistake.

Six batteries of German guns pounded away as *Silver Queen* frantically reversed course. One round crashed into her stern; another landed on the starboard bow. The Belgian launch *Yser*, traveling in company, was hit too. Someone on the *Yser* fired a Very pistol in a desperate call for help. Amazingly, a friendly destroyer did catch the signal, hurried over, and provided covering fire while the two strays crept out of range. Somehow *Silver Queen* limped back to Ramsgate, discharged a load of troops, and then quietly sank at her pier.

For most of the little ships, the time of greatest danger was not going over or coming back; it was at the beach itself. Even when the troops behaved perfectly, the boats were in constant danger of capsizing. The sea was still smooth, but the wind was veering to the east and the surf began rising. The loading went more slowly than ever.

At La Panne, Lieutenant Harold J. Dibbens of the Military Police had been puzzling over the loading problem ever since reaching the beach the previous afternoon. Unlike most of the BEF, Dibbens was thoroughly at home on the sea. He grew up on the Isle of Wight—always around boats—and even served a hitch in the Navy before settling into his career as a detective at Scotland Yard. When war came, his professional experience won him a direct commission in the Military Police, and until "the balloon went up" he spent most of his time fighting pilferage and chasing black marketeers. The great retreat ended all that, and now here he was, with the remnants of 102nd Provost Company, waiting on the beach like so many others.

Watching the confusion at the water's edge—some boats overturning, others drifting away untended—Dibbens decided that the biggest need at the moment was a pier or jetty stretching out to sea. Then the boats could come alongside and be loaded far more efficiently. But where to find the materials for such a jetty? His eye fell on the mass of abandoned trucks and lorries that littered the beach. Now all he needed was a little manpower.

"Want a sapper unit! Need a sapper unit!" Dibbens shouted, stalking through the dunes, where many of the troops were waiting. He was acting on his own initiative—had no authority at all—but it was a time when resourcefulness was what counted, and a colonel would listen to a corporal, if his idea was good enough.

Captain E. H. Sykes of the 250th Field Company, Royal Engineers, stepped forward. What was wanted? Dibbens couldn't order the Captain to do anything, but he suggested a deal: his own men would provide a supply of lorries, if Sykes's men would use them to build a jetty out into the sea. As a "sweetener" the sappers could be the first group to use the completed jetty.

Sykes agreed and detailed 2nd Lieutenant John S. W. Bennett's section to do the construction. These men threw themselves into the job with amazing enthusiasm, considering their mood until now. They had just completed a long march to the coast, and the last night had been hell. They had lost many of their officers somewhere in the dark, and most of the company just melted away. Normally 250 strong, they were down to 30 or 40 by the time they reached La Panne.

Lieutenant Bennett was one of the few officers who stuck with them all the way. He did his best, but in peacetime he was on the Faculty of Fine Art at Cambridge, and what they wanted right now was a professional soldier. There was a lot of grumbling, until in exasperation he finally told them, "If you want me to lead you, I'll lead you; if you want me to leave you, I'll leave you."

"Frankly, I don't give a damn what you do," someone called out from the ranks.

But the art professor was a better leader than they realized. The men were soon working flat-out. They lined up the lorries side by side, leading into the sea. They loaded them with sandbags and shot out the tires to keep them in place. They scavenged timber from a lumberyard for staging. They ripped decking from stranded ships for a plank walkway. They even added the touch of a rope railing.

When they began the tide was out, but now it came rolling in. Soon the men were up to their waists in the surf, lashing the lorries with cable. Sometimes they had to hold the jetty together by linking arms until a lashing could be made. Buffeted by the surf, they were soaked to the skin and covered with oil and grease.

The men of 102nd Provost Company had been good scavengers—sometimes too good. At one point an irate brigadier stormed up to Dibbens. Somebody had stolen four lorries he had earmarked for use as ambulances. Dibbens expressed appropriate dismay, said he couldn't imagine who could have done a thing like that, and quietly replaced the missing lorries with four others stolen from somebody else.

The "provost jetty," as it came to be called, was finished during the afternoon of May 30 and proved a huge success. All evening, and all the next day, a steady stream of men used it to board the growing fleet of small boats and launches engaged in ferry work. Ironically, Bennett's men were not among them. Corps headquarters decided that they had done such a splendid job, they now must maintain it. Down the drain went the promise that they would be the first "customers." Instead, they learned the hard way the old military maxim: never do a task too well, or you'll be stuck with it forever.

Later there would be considerable speculation over who first thought of the jetty. Besides Lieutenant Dibbens, credit has been given to Commodore Stephenson, Commander Richardson, and General Alexander, among others. Curiously, all these claims may be valid. It seems to have been one of those ideas "whose time had come," for examination of Luftwaffe photographs shows that no fewer than ten different lorry jetties were slapped together on May 30–31 between Malo-les-Bains and La Panne.

This in turn meant there were many builders besides the long-suffering 250th Field Company. One such unit was A Squadron of the 12th Lancers, who built a jetty about three miles west of La Panne. They were anything but experienced in this sort of work—they were an armored reconnaissance unit—but the perimeter was now fully manned, and all surplus fighting troops were being funneled to the beaches.

With the regulars moving in, there was a striking improvement in discipline. At Bray-Dunes Commanders Kerr and Richardson had their first easy night. As Kerr explained a little unkindly, they were at last dealing with "real officers."

The long shadow of tradition was now very much in evidence. When Colonel Lionel H. M. Westropp ordered the 8th King's Own Royal Regiment to head down the beach toward the mole, he first assembled his officers. He reminded them that they wore the badge of one of the oldest regiments of the line. "We therefore will represent the Regiment as we march down the beach this afternoon. We must not let it down, and we must set an example to the rabble on the beach."

The battalion set off in perfect step, arms swinging in unison, rifles correctly slung, officers and NCO's properly spaced. The "rabble on the beach" were suitably impressed.

Nineteen-year-old 2nd Lieutenant William Lawson of the Royal Artillery knew that appearances were important, but he felt he had a good excuse for looking a little scruffy. His artillery unit had been badly mauled on the Dyle, again at Arras, and had barely made it back to the perimeter—two rough weeks almost always on the run.

Now at last he was at La Panne, and it was the Navy's turn to worry. Wandering down the beach, he suddenly spied a familiar face. It was his own father, Brigadier the Honorable E. F. Lawson, temporarily serving on General Adam's staff. Young Lawson had no idea his father was even in northern France. He rushed up and saluted.

"What do you mean looking like that!" the old Brigadier thundered. "You're bringing dishonor to the family! Get a haircut and shave at once!"

The son pointed out that at the moment he couldn't possibly comply. Lawson brushed this aside, announcing that his own batman, a family servant in prewar days, would do the job. And so he did—a haircut and shave right on the sands of Dunkirk.

At the mole Commander Clouston had standards, too. Spotting one of the shore patrol with hair far longer than it could have grown in the last three or four days, he ordered the man to get it cut.

"All the barbers are shut, sir," came the unruffled reply. Clouston still insisted. Finally, the sailor drew his bayonet and hacked off a lock. "What do you want me to do with it now," he asked, "put it in a locket?"

Under the Commander's firm leadership, the mole continued

to operate all day, May 30. A steady stream of destroyers, mine-sweepers, Channel steamers, and trawlers pulled alongside, loaded up, and were off again. For one two-hour stretch, Clouston had the troops trotting out the walkway on the double. He embarked over 24,000 during the afternoon and evening.

Clouston's efforts got a big assist from a major policy reversal engineered in Dover. Early afternoon Admiral Ramsay phoned Admiral Pound in London, insisting that the modern destroyers be put back on the job. They were absolutely essential if he was to get everybody off in the time he had left. After a heated exchange, Pound finally relented. At 3:30 p.m. orders went out, sending the destroyers back to France.

German batteries were now firing on Dunkirk harbor from Gravelines, but the mole lay just out of range. German planes made occasional hit-and-run attacks on the shipping, but Kesselring's great fleets of bombers remained grounded. In sharp contrast to yesterday's fear and confusion, today the mood was cheerfully relaxed. While the *Malcolm* loaded some Cameron Highlanders, her navigator Lieutenant Mellis played his bagpipes on the foc'sle. As one party of Royal Dragoon Guards moved along the walkway, a big Royal Marine stood ladling out hot stew. One Dragoon officer had no cup, but he did produce a long-stemmed cocktail glass picked up somewhere. The Marine filled it with gravy, solemnly inquiring, "Can I put a cherry in it, sir?"

But the greatest change was on the beaches. Discipline continued to improve; the columns of waiting men were quiet and orderly; the ever-growing stream of little ships methodically ferried the troops to the larger vessels lying offshore. As Captain Arthur Marshall's twelve-man internal security unit patiently waited their turn, a colonel bustled over. Apparently worried that the unit had nothing to do, he ordered the men to "tidy up the beach a bit."

At first Marshall felt the colonel must be joking; but no, he was dead serious. The smaller the mess they left, he explained, the less likely the Germans would think that the BEF had left precipitously. The result would decrease the enemy's feeling of triumph, thereby helping the war effort.

Finally convinced that the colonel meant what he said, Marshall's party glumly went to work—piling abandoned overcoats here, stowing empty crates there, neatly coiling stray lengths of rope. They kept at it as long as the colonel was in sight.

Overall, May 30 proved a very good day. Thanks to better discipline, the lorry jetties, and above all, the surge of little ships, the number of men lifted from the beaches rose from 13,752 on the 29th to 29,512 on the 30th. A total of 53,823 men were evacuated on this gray, misty day—much the highest daily figure so far.

Casualties were mercifully light. Thanks to the heavy overcast, the rescue fleet streamed across the Channel unchallenged by the Stukas and Heinkels. First loss of the day came when the French destroyer *Bourrasque*, bound for Dover, struck a floating mine. Nearby ships saved all but 150 of her troops.

Later, during the night of May 30–31, another French destroyer, *Siroco*, was torpedoed by S-boats lurking off Kwinte Buoy. For a while her skipper, Gui de Toulouse-Lautrec (cousin of the painter), thought he might save his ship, but she let off a huge cloud of steam which attracted the attention of a passing German patrol bomber. A bomb crashed down on the vessel's stern, igniting her ready ammunition. A column of flame shot 200 feet into the sky, and *Siroco* was gone.

But most of the ships reached England safely, landing their ragged passengers in Dover and other southeast coast ports. Herded toward waiting trains, their ordeal was mirrored in their faces—unshaven, hollow-eyed, oil-streaked, infinitely weary. Many had lost their equipment; but some clutched odd, new possessions picked up along the way. A pair of wooden sabots dangled from Private Fred Louch's gas mask . . . a French poilu carried a live goose . . . Bombardier Arthur May still had 6,000 of his 10,000 cigarettes . . . 2nd Lieutenant R. C. Taylor's batman had somehow rescued the Lieutenant's portable gramophone. Along with the men, the inevitable dogs trooped ashore—170 in Dover alone.

Everything about this motley crowd said "evacuation," but until now there had been a news blackout. With the men pouring home, this was no longer possible; so on the evening of the 30th London finally issued a communiqué announcing the withdrawal. It was, the *Times* sniffed, "what so many people in this country have seen with their own eyes."

Among the thousands of soldiers brought back, a select few

had been carefully hand-picked. Whatever else happened, Lord Gort hoped to get enough good men home to form the nucleus of a new army that might some day return and even the score. General Pownall, Gort's Chief of Staff, left on the evening of May 29th, as did the Commander-in-Chief's personal aide, Lord Munster. Now, on the 30th, it was General Brooke's turn. After a lunch of *petit poussin* and asparagus, miraculously conjured up by his aide, Captain Barney Charlesworth, he paid a final visit to his division commanders.

It was not easy. Brooke was known as a brilliant but rather cold man; this afternoon he was all emotion. Saying good-bye to General Montgomery, who would take over the Corps, he broke into tears. Monty patted him on the back, said all the right things. Finally they shook hands, and Brooke trudged slowly away.

One man absolutely determined not to leave was Lord Gort. The General's decision became known in London on the morning of May 30, when Lord Munster arrived from the beaches. Winston Churchill was taking a bath at the time, but he could do business anywhere, and he summoned Munster for a tub-side chat. It was in this unlikely setting that Munster described Gort's decision to stay to the end. He would never leave without specific orders.

Churchill was appalled at the thought. Why give Hitler the propaganda coup of capturing and displaying the British Commander-in-Chief? After discussing the matter with Eden, Dill, and Pownall, he wrote out in his own hand an order that left Gort no choice:

> If we can still communicate we shall send you an order to return to England with such officers as you may choose at the moment when we deem your command so reduced that it can be handed over to a corps commander. You should now nominate this commander. If communications are broken, you are to hand over and return as specified when your effective fighting force does not exceed the equivalent of three divisions. This is in accordance with correct military procedure, and no personal discretion is left you in the matter.

Whoever Gort appointed was to fight on, "but when in his judgment no further organised evacuation is possible and no further proportionate damage can be inflicted on the enemy, he is authorised in consultation with the senior French commander to capitulate formally to avoid useless slaughter."

These instructions reached Gort during the afternoon, and he read them aloud at a final GHQ conference that assembled in his beachfront villa at 6:00 p.m. Besides General Barker, commanding I Corps, and Monty, now in charge of II Corps, the meeting included Brooke, who had not yet pushed off. The final plans for the evacuation were discussed: I Corps would be the last to go, and its commander, Barker, would take over from Gort as directed by London.

As the meeting broke up, Montgomery lingered behind and asked to see Gort privately for a moment. Once they were alone, Monty unburdened himself. It would be a dreadful mistake, he said, to leave Barker in charge at the end. The man was no longer fit to command. The proper course was to send Barker home and appoint instead the 1st Division commander, Major-General Harold Alexander. He had just the calm, clear mind needed for this crisis. With luck, he might even get the rear guard back safely to England.

Gort listened but didn't commit himself.

Down on the beach General Brooke prepared to go. Usually a rather snappy dresser, he had discarded his new Huntsman breeches and Norwegian boots for a pair of old slacks and shoes. More practical, in case he had to go swimming. But he didn't have to swim at all. Instead he rode piggy-back out to a rowboat on the broad shoulders of the faithful Charlesworth. By 7:20 he was on his way to a waiting destroyer.

Around 8:00 a new visitor turned up at GHQ. Admiral Wake-Walker had come to see Lord Gort. With the small craft starting to pour in, he wanted to work out better coordination with the army. During the past few days, all too often the available ships weren't where the troops were, and vice versa.

Gort greeted him warmly. The Commander-in-Chief and his staff were about to have dinner; Wake-Walker must join them. They moved into a longish dining room with French windows opening on the sea. The conversation was mostly small talk, and as he sat there sharing the General's last bottle of champagne, Wake-Walker found it a remarkable experience. They were on the brink of the greatest military disaster in British history, yet here they sat, chatting idly and sipping champagne as though it were just another social evening at the seashore. Only one thing seemed out of the ordinary: his trousers were soaking wet from wading ashore.

Gort was charm itself, cheerful and unperturbed. He assured the Admiral that just by being here he would have a great stabilizing effect. Wake-Walker found it hard to believe that the mere presence of a desk-bound sailor like himself could prove so inspirational.

After a final dish of fruit salad, they got down to business. It soon became clear to Wake-Walker that Gort and his staff felt that their part of the job was done. They had gotten the BEF to the coast more or less intact; now it was up to the Royal Navy to get them home—and so far, the Navy hadn't tried very hard.

Wake-Walker said any lack of success was not through want of trying. He stressed the difficulty of lifting large numbers of men off the beaches and urged that more troops be shifted down to Dunkirk, where they could use the mole. Brigadier Leese remained unconvinced. The Army had marched enough. The ships should go where the men were. It should be perfectly possible to take men off the beaches . . . except for the "ineptitude of the Navy."

Wake-Walker bristled. He told Leese he had no business or justification to talk that way.

The discussion turned to getting the rear guard off. No matter how the others were evacuated, this was going to be a tight squeak. The Germans were pressing Nieuport and Furnes hard, and it didn't seem possible to hold the eastern end of the perimeter beyond the night of May 31–June 1. It was hoped to get everybody else off during the day, then quickly pull the rear guard back to the beaches at midnight. Ramsay had promised to make a supreme effort and was sending a whole new armada of small craft to lie off the coast. With luck they would be where needed, and the rear guard would swarm aboard before the enemy could interfere.

It was a very demanding timetable. Apart from the rear

guard, estimated at 5,000, there were tens of thousands of other troops to come off beforehand. Wake-Walker's heart sank at the prospect. The thought of that last-minute rush for the boats in the dark, with the enemy in hot pursuit, was not a pleasant picture.

By 10:00 p.m. they had talked themselves out. Wake-Walker headed back for the destroyer *Worcester*, which he was using at the moment as a flagship. Going down to the beach, he found a large inflated rubber boat, and recruited eight soldiers to paddle him out. As Tennant and Leese watched from the shore, they started off, but the boat was too crowded and began to swamp. They all jumped out and waded back to the beach for a new try with fewer paddlers. "Another example of naval ineptitude," Wake-Walker dryly told Leese.

Back at GHQ the staff prepared a situation report for the War Office, which went off at 11:20 p.m. It reported that the six remaining divisions in the beachhead were being thinned out tonight, and the eastern end of the perimeter should be completely clear some time tomorrow night, May 31–June 1. Evacuation of the rest of the BEF was proceeding satisfactorily. The report didn't say, but at the present pace, the lift should be complete by the end of June 1.

Thirty-nine minutes later, at 11:59, the Chief of the Imperial General Staff, General Dill, phoned from London. Gort assured him that the night was quiet . . . that all was going well on the beaches. Dill brushed this aside and got to the real purpose of his call. The Prime Minister wanted him to get off as many French as possible—not just a "fair" number, but an *equal* number. Winston Churchill himself came on the phone and confirmed the order.

It was an astonishing development. Instead of winding up the evacuation with a last-minute lift of a small rear guard on June 1, the whole French Army was now involved. Nobody—absolutely nobody—knew how many that meant, but it was clear that all the careful calculations and timetables worked out during the day were now meaningless.

10

"Bras-Dessus, Bras-Dessous!"

"Let's help the Froggies, too," Bob Hilton suggested to Ted Shaw as they began their seventeen-hour stint, rowing troops from the beach to the ships lying off Malo-les-Bains. Shaw agreed, and from then on, they never worried whether a soldier was French or English. Both were on the same side. It seemed simple enough.

Higher up, it wasn't that easy. When the evacuation began, the Admiralty simply assumed that British troops would be taken off in British ships, French troops in French ships. That was the way everything else had been done. Each of the Allies had conducted its own retreat to the coast, then manned its own part of the perimeter. In the same spirit the British had made their own decision to evacuate. Reynaud had been informed, and now it was up to the French to do the same.

As for the French, at this point they weren't even thinking evacuation. On May 19, the day Weygand took over, Admiral Darlan told Supreme Headquarters that such a step could lead only to "disaster." Darlan preferred to hold on to the beach-head, turn it into a continuing threat to the German flank. It was with this thought in mind that Captain Auphan began rounding up hundreds of French trawlers. They were to supply the beachhead, not evacuate it. In Dunkirk Admiral Abrial faithfully reflected the same point of view.

The French finally faced reality on May 27, when Auphan, Admiral Leclerc, and Admiral Odend'hal met with Ramsay at Dover Castle. They had come to discuss supplying Dunkirk, only to discover that the British were already leaving. Now the French would have to catch up. Auphan's trawlers could be used, but they weren't remotely enough. Few French warships were available; most were stationed in the Mediterranean by arrangement with the Royal Navy.

An agreement was hastily hammered out between the French officers and Admiral Ramsay. Paragraph 5 declared that "all naval means for evacuation shall be shared between Dover and Dunkerque." This was admittedly vague, but to the French it seemed to promise at least some access to British shipping.

They soon learned what "sharing" could mean. When Belgium surrendered on May 28, General Champon, head of the French mission to King Leopold, made his way to La Panne. With him came the mission staff, numbering 100 to 150 men. They were a hand-picked lot, and the Allied area commander General Georges ordered "immediate evacuation." Champon asked Lord Gort for space on some British ship.

Gort fired off a telegram to the War Office asking confirmation from Brigadier Swayne, British liaison officer at French Supreme Headquarters. "Swayne should point out," Gort added helpfully, "every Frenchman embarked is a loss of one Englishman." Why this argument would be persuasive at French headquarters, Gort didn't say. But he did offer a final suggestion: "Why not send a French destroyer, using own boats?"

The next day—Wednesday, the 29th—found Champon and his staff still stranded at La Panne. General Georges again urged Gort to act, and Brigadier Swayne followed up with a telephone call to General Pownall, Gort's Chief of Staff. Pownall reported that orders had been issued covering Champon and "some of his officers," then asked rather pointedly if this mission was meant to have top priority, "thus displacing an equal number of British troops?"

No, said Swayne, he was certain that wasn't what Georges meant. The General just wanted to make sure that the Champon mission had equal status with the British.

The problem dragged on. Thirty-six more hours would pass before Champon finally got off at 8:00 p.m., May 30.

If it was that hard to make room for 100 hand-picked men, the prospects weren't bright for the thousands of ordinary poilus now pouring into the perimeter. From the south came remnants of the French First Army . . . from the east, the badly mauled 60th Division . . . from the west, the 68th Division retiring from Gravelines—all converging on the beaches at once. They were in for a long wait: on May 29 over 47,000 men were evacuated, but only 655 were French.

Winston Churchill understood both the arithmetic and the political ramifications. On the 29th he addressed a memo to Anthony Eden and to Generals Dill and Ismay:

> It is essential that the French should share in such evacuations from Dunkirk as may be possible. Nor must they be dependent only upon their own shipping resources. Arrangements must be concerted at once . . . so that no reproaches, or as few as possible, may arise.

Meanwhile General Georges appealed again to Lord Gort. This time his message concerned not just the Champon mission, but all the troops now gathering on the beaches. As relayed over the telephone by the accommodating Brigadier Swayne, Georges urged that the evacuation be carried out by the British and the French "with mutual co-operation and support."

"I am quite prepared to cooperate," Gort wired General Dill in London, "but support—by which is implied resources—is all on our side. Strongly urge that the French should take their full share in providing naval facilities."

This of course ignored the fact that the French had very little in the way of "naval facilities," with their fleet down in the Mediterranean. Pointing out that he had already evacuated "small parties of French," Gort once again reminded London: "Every Frenchman embarked is at the cost of one Englishman." His instructions said that the safety of the BEF came first. In light of that, he asked, what *was* the government's policy toward the French?

General Dill wrestled with this for some hours, finally wired Gort a little lamely that the safety of the BEF still came first, but he should try to evacuate "a proportion" of French troops.

In London that night, Churchill remained uneasy. Despite his directive, there was little evidence that the French were sharing in the evacuation. At 11:45 p.m. he shot off another telegram, this time for Reynaud, Weygand, and Georges:

> We wish French troops to share in evacuation to fullest possible extent, and Admiralty have been instructed to aid French Marine as required. We do not know how many will be forced to capitulate, but we must share this loss together as best we can, and, above all, bear it without reproaches arising from inevitable confusion, stresses, and strains.

At this moment Admiral Wake-Walker, crossing the Channel to take charge offshore, had a very different view of Admiralty policy. Before leaving, he had been briefed by Admiral Pound, the First Sea Lord. Pound had told him that the French were not thought to be pulling their weight; he was to "refuse them embarkation, if British troops were ready to embark."

Next morning, May 30, Churchill summoned the three Service Ministers and the Chiefs of Staff to a meeting in the Admiralty War Room. An important guest was General Pownall, just back from La Panne. Once again the Prime Minister stressed the importance of getting off more French troops.

Pownall spoke up, defending the present figures. As usual, he trotted out the familiar argument: so long as the French did not produce ships of their own, "every Frenchman embarked meant one more Englishman lost."

Pownall felt that he had forced Churchill to face an "inconvenient truth," but the Prime Minister had been hearing this argument for two days now, and if he showed displeasure, it more likely stemmed from exasperation.

More phone talks with Gort followed during the day. At 4:20 p.m. General Dill confirmed that Gort's first consideration was the safety of the BEF, but he must also do his best to send off a "fair proportion" of the French. At 8:10 p.m. the War Office again notified Brigadier Swayne that French troops were to share in the evacuation "to fullest possible extent."

Then came Admiral Ramsay's figures for the total number rescued during the day: British 45,207; French 8,616.

Clearly phrases such as "fair share," "fullest possible extent," and "fair proportion" could mean what anybody wanted them to mean—thousands of troops, or just one soldier. If the French were really to share the British ships, the orders would have to be far more precise. It was almost midnight, May 30, when Churchill finally faced the matter squarely.

"British and French troops must now evacuate in approximately equal numbers," General Dill stressed in his telephone call to Gort, relaying the Prime Minister's new orders. Lest there be any misunderstanding, Dill repeated the instructions three different times in the conversation. When Churchill himself came on the wire, the Prime Minister emphasized that the whole future of the alliance was at stake.

He was right. Paris was full of rumors and recriminations these days, mostly to the effect that the British were running home, leaving the French holding the bag. Hoping to clear up any misunderstandings, Churchill flew to Paris the following morning, May 31, for a meeting of the Allied Supreme War Council. Accompanied by General Dill and a few top aides, he was met at the airport by his personal representative to Reynaud, Major-General Sir Edward Spears, who had been bearing the brunt of the French complaints these past few days.

At 2:00 p.m. the British and French leaders met at the Ministry of War on the rue Saint-Dominique. Joining the group for the first time was Marshal Pétain, an ancient gloomy figure in civilian clothes. General Weygand was there too, wearing a huge pair of riding boots that made him look, General Spears felt, like Puss in Boots. The French sat on one side of a large baize-covered table; the British on the other. Through the tall, open windows lay a garden basking in the sunshine. It was another of those glorious spring days—so many this year—that seemed to mock these grim statesmen and generals trying to ward off disaster.

Churchill opened the meeting on a cheerful note. The evacuation, he reported, was going far better than anyone had dared hope. As of noon this day, 165,000 men had been lifted off.

"But how many French?" Weygand asked sharply. The Prime Minister dodged a direct answer for the moment: "We are companions in misfortune. There is nothing to be gained from recrimination over our common miseries."

But the question wouldn't go away. After a brief survey of the Norwegian campaign, the discussion came back to Dunkirk, and it turned out that of the 165,000 evacuated, only 15,000 were French. Churchill did his best to explain this awkward disparity: many of the British were rear area troops already stationed near Dunkirk . . . the French had farther to come . . . if just the fighting divisions were counted, the disparity wasn't so bad.

Reynaud broke in. Whatever the reasons, the hard facts remained: of 220,000 British, 150,000 had been rescued: of 200,000 French, the number saved was only 15,000. He couldn't face public opinion at home with figures like these. Something had to be done to evacuate more French.

Churchill agreed and explained the new "equal numbers" directive. He also stressed that three British divisions still at Dunkirk would stand by the French until the evacuation was complete.

Darlan then drafted a telegram to Admiral Abrial in Bastion 32, describing the decisions taken by the Council. It mentioned that when the perimeter closed down, the British forces would embark first.

Churchill leapt to this feet. *"Non!"* he cried. *"Partage—bras-dessus, bras-dessous!"* His atrocious French accent was a legend, but this time there was no mistaking him. With dramatic gestures he vividly acted out an arm-in-arm departure.

Nor did he stop there. Emotionally carried away, he announced that the remaining British troops would form the rear guard. "So few French have got out so far," he declared, "I will not accept further sacrifices by the French."

This was a lot more than arm-in-arm, and to General Spears it was going too far. After more discussion, the final draft simply said that the British troops would act as rear guard "as long as possible." It also said that Abrial would be in overall command.

It was just as well that Lord Gort did not know of the Prime Minister's outburst. It was difficult enough to swallow the policy of "equal numbers." At least it wasn't retroactive. London agreed that the rule only applied *from now on*. Still, it could be costly. The War Office had instructed him to hang on longer, so that as many French as possible could be evacuated. But how long? This morning, May 31, everything pointed to a heavy German attack on Furnes. If he hung on too long just to save more Frenchmen, he might lose the whole Guard's Brigade.

He was still mulling over this problem when General Alexander—the calm, capable commander of the 1st Division—visited GHQ at 8:30 a.m. Gort glumly told him to thin out his division, since it looked as if he would have to surrender most of his men alongside the French. At least that was what the War Office's instructions seemed to mean.

At 9:00 a.m. Anthony Eden came on the phone with an interpretation of these orders that must have greatly eased Gort's mind. As Eden explained to Brigadier Leese:

> The instructions sent the previous night to hold on so as to enable the maximum number of Allied troops to be evacuated must be interpreted to mean that [Gort] should only do so as long as he was satisfied that he could continue to hold his position with the forces at his disposal, but he should not prejudice the safety of the remainder of his force by trying to hold his position beyond that time.

In other words, hanging on for the sake of evacuating an equal number of Frenchmen was desirable—as long as it was safe.

Enlightened, Gort now drove down to Dunkirk to meet with Admiral Abrial at 10:00 a.m. The Admiral was, as usual, in Bastion 32. Besides his staff of naval officers, he had with him General Fagalde, commander of the French military forces in the perimeter, and General de la Laurencie, who had just arrived with the only French troops to escape from the German trap at Lille.

Gort's sessions with Abrial were often strained. Tucked away

in Bastion 32, the man never seemed to know what was going
on. Today, all was cordial. Gort relayed the "equal numbers"
policy, stated that he had already promised to evacuate 5,000 of
de la Laurencie's men. Abrial said that Weygand preferred to
use the space for some mechanized cavalry units, and de la
Laurencie made no objection. Gort also offered the French
equal access to the eastern mole. If it seemed a little odd for the
British to be offering the French free use of a French facility in a
French port, Abrial was tactful enough to keep silent.

Gort and Fagalde now exchanged full information on each
other's positions along the perimeter—apparently the first time
this had been done—and Gort announced that he had been ordered home. At this point General Blanchard turned up. Nomi-
nally the Army Group commander, these days he was virtually
unemployed. Gort invited him and General de la Laurencie to
accompany his own party to England. Both politely declined. As
de la Laurencie put it: "My flag will remain planted on the
Dunes, until the last of my men have embarked."

There were farewell toasts. Everyone promised to meet in
France soon again.

Returning to La Panne, Gort summoned General Alexander
to the seaside villa that served as GHQ. The Commander-in-
Chief had reached a major decision: Alexander, not Barker,
would take over after Gort's own departure for England. He
never explained the switch. Perhaps he was impressed by Montgomery's fervent protest the previous evening, but the stolid
Gort was not known to be easily influenced by the mercurial
Monty.

In any case the orders were cut and waiting when Alexander
arrived around 12:30 p.m. Technically, he would relieve Barker
as Commanding Officer of I Corps, consisting of three rather
depleted divisions. His orders were to "assist our French Allies
in the defence of Dunkirk."

He would be serving under Abrial, as decided in Paris, but
with an important escape clause added: "Should any order
which he may issue to you be likely, in your opinion, to imperil
the safety of your command, you should make an immediate appeal to His Majesty's Government."

That was all, as Gort originally dictated the orders to Colonel

Bridgeman, still acting as the General's Operations Officer. Yet there was an important omission. Gort had left out the War Office's instruction authorizing surrender "to avoid useless slaughter." Bridgeman felt it should be included, but didn't dare say so to his chief. Finally, he got a copy of London's original telegram, pointed to the passage in question, and asked whether he wanted it included, too. Gort said yes, and it was done. To the end they managed to avoid actually saying the dreaded word, "surrender."

Technically, Gort's orders would not take effect until 6:00 p.m., when GHQ was scheduled to close down. As a practical matter, they became operational almost right away. After a quick lunch, Alexander drove back to his headquarters and turned his division over to one of his brigadiers. Then he drove down to Dunkirk, accompanied by his Chief of Staff Colonel William Morgan and the ubiquitous Captain Tennant. At 2:00 p.m. they entered the candle-lit gloom of Bastion 32 for Alexander's first meeting with Admiral Abrial and General Fagalde.

It did not go well. Abrial planned to hold a reduced beachhead, running as far east as the Belgian border, with French troops on the right and a mixed French-British force under Alexander on the left. This force would act as a rear guard, holding the beachhead indefinitely while the rest of the Allied troops embarked. Then, presumably, the rear guard itself would scurry to safety at the last minute.

Alexander felt it would never work. Protracted resistance was impossible. The troops were in no condition to fight indefinitely. The proposed perimeter was too near the harbor and the beaches. Enemy artillery fire at short range would soon stop the evacuation completely. Instead, he proposed to wind up the evacuation as fast as possible, with the last troops pulling back to the beach the following night, June 1–2.

Abrial was unimpressed. If the British insisted on leaving anyhow, he added, "I am afraid the port will be closed."

Alexander decided it was time to invoke the escape clause in his orders. He announced that he would have to refer the matter to London. Then he drove back to La Panne, relieved to find that the telephone line was still open.

At 7:15 p.m. he managed to get through to Anthony Eden

and quickly explained the problem. An hour later Eden called back with new and welcome instructions from the Cabinet:

> You should withdraw your force as rapidly as possible on a 50–50 basis with the French Army, aiming at completion by night of 1st/2nd June. You should inform the French of this definite instruction.

The phrase "on a 50–50 basis with the French Army," Eden explained, did not require Alexander to make up for any past discrepancies; it simply meant that equal numbers of French and British troops must be withdrawn from now on. Supported by the Cabinet, Alexander hurried back to Bastion 32.

Meanwhile, Abrial, too, had gone to his superiors. Wiring Weygand, he protested that Alexander—who had been placed under him—was refusing to follow instructions to fight on. Instead, the British commander planned to embark on the night of June 1–2, whatever happened, "thus abandoning the defence of Dunkirk."

Weygand could do little but buck the complaint to London. At 9:00 p.m. he radioed Dill, Chief of the Imperial General Staff, reminding him of the decisions reached by the Supreme War Council that very afternoon. Paragraph 4 had specifically put Abrial in charge.

The Admiral was still waiting for some word from Weygand, when Alexander arrived back in Bastion 32 with the British Cabinet's instructions. He announced that he would hold his sector of the perimeter until 11:59 p.m., June 1—tomorrow night—then would withdraw to the beaches under cover of darkness. The French were welcome to come along and share the British shipping, but whatever they did, he was pulling out.

Faced with no alternative, Abrial agreed.

It was now after 11:00 p.m. Alexander had shifted his headquarters to the outskirts of Dunkirk, but the roads were strange and full of craters. It seemed safer to stay in Bastion 32 overnight, so he and Colonel Morgan curled up on the concrete floor—as hard and as cold as relations were getting to be between the two great Allies.

Completely oblivious to all this high-level wrangling, an old soldier sat in his quarters at La Panne on the afternoon of May 31, snipping medal and campaign ribbons from a uniform blouse. General Gort was getting ready to go home. The evacuation was Alexander's headache now, and at the moment Gort's main concern was to see that no German soldier made a souvenir out of anything he had to leave behind.

He was to go at 6:00 p.m. Two separate plans had been made for his embarkation, and it was typical of these trying days that neither group of planners knew of the other's existence. Under one of these plans—developed by the Navy liaison at GHQ—four motor torpedo boats would dash over from Dover to pluck Gort and his staff off the beach. The orders were very vague. The commander of the little flotilla only knew that he was to pick up "a party." When he arrived, he checked with Admiral Wake-Walker, in charge offshore, for further directions.

Wake-Walker knew even less. No one had briefed him, and it never occurred to him that these motor torpedo boats had been sent to pick up the Commander-in-Chief. He thought that was *his* responsibility. He assigned the MTB's to courier chores and continued his own planning. Gort would leave his villa shortly after 6:00, going to a designated spot on the beach two miles west of La Panne. Here he and his staff would be met by a launch and taken out to the destroyer *Keith* lying offshore. The *Keith* would then run the party back to Dover. Commodore Stephenson would be in direct charge, with Wake-Walker himself supervising.

As planned, Gort's party left his villa at 6:00 p.m., but that was as far as they followed the script. For some reason the two staff cars carrying the group did not go to the designated rendezvous, but to a spot much closer to La Panne. This meant no small boats were waiting, and the departure from the beach became a very ragged affair. Ultimately Gort's staff wound up on the *Keith*, he himself on the minesweeper *Hebe*, and his batman, driver, and luggage all on the motor yacht *Thele*.

Safely aboard the *Hebe*, Gort went to the bridge to greet the skipper, Lieutenant-Commander J. S. Wemple. There was time for only the briefest exchange of niceties; then the sea, the sky, the ships all seemed to erupt with explosions. The weather had cleared, and the Luftwaffe was back—ten separate raids this evening. As the *Hebe's* crew rushed to their gun stations, Gort learned how useless his role had at last become. He settled quietly in a corner of the bridge, raised his binoculars, and gazed absently around.

"Won't you go below and take cover, sir?" suggested Captain Eric Bush, one of Ramsay's coordinators working with Tennant and Wake-Walker.

"No, thank you, I'm quite happy where I am," the General replied politely. Finally the raid tapered off, and Gort—unruffled as ever—went below for a bite to eat.

The *Hebe* still did not head for England with her distinguished passenger. By now hundreds of ordinary soldiers were swarming aboard, delivered from the beaches by the ever-growing swarm of little ships. Wake-Walker decided to wait until she had a full load before sending her back.

Dover and London grew restless, then frantic. Seven hours had passed since the Admiralty had dispatched the four MTB's to pick up Gort, and still there was no sign of him. Those boats could do 40 knots; they should have been back long ago. Worse, the latest radio traffic indicated that the MTB's hadn't even been used to get the General. What had happened to him anyhow?

"Report immediately why MTB's sent for Commander-in-Chief were diverted to other duties," Admiral Phillips, the Vice-Chief of Naval Staff, radioed Wake-Walker at 11:36 p.m. "Take immediate action to embark Commander-in-Chief and report steps taken."

On the *Keith*, Wake-Walker sent one of the MTB's to the *Hebe* to get Gort, but he was no longer there. He had taken a launch, hoping to reach the *Keith*. A half-hour passed, and still no sign of the launch.

Now it was Wake-Walker's turn to agonize. The night was black; no lights showing. Had the launch missed the *Keith*? Was Gort out there somewhere drifting in the dark? Wake-Walker had visions of the disgrace that would be his if he botched this job and lost the Commander-in-Chief of the BEF.

It was after midnight, the opening minutes of June 1, when the launch finally loomed out of the dark. Gort climbed aboard the *Keith*, reunited at last with his staff.

But only briefly. He and Brigadier Leese quickly transferred to the speedboat *MA/SB 6* and headed for Dover. At 6:20 a.m. they landed at the Admiralty Pier, where Gort gulped a cup of tea and caught the next train to London.

Anthony Eden and members of the War Cabinet were on hand to greet him, but the little group passed almost unnoticed amid the crowds swirling around Victoria Station. By now bedraggled soldiers were tumbling off every train from the south coast into the waiting arms of friends and relatives. Gort seemed to be just one more of them. He was already a fading figure of the past.

Far more important than the escape of a discredited chieftain was the rescue on May 31 of 53,140 more men who could help form the nucleus of a new British Army.

Thousands of them used the lorry jetties that had been improvised at Bray-Dunes and La Panne. Despite the ingenuity of the builders, these were rickety affairs that heaved alarmingly in the surf and changing tides. Still, a steady stream of soldiers clambered out along the duck boards, dropping into the rowboats and launches that came alongside.

"Well, my lucky lad, can you row?" a sailor greeted Private Percy Yorke of the 145th Field Ambulance, as he tumbled into a boat. "No? Well, now's your time to bloody well learn." Yorke learned by doing, and managed to reach the excursion steamer *Princess Elizabeth*.

Major E. R. Nanney Wynn, 3rd Division Signals, reached the end of a jetty and peered down at a waiting motor whaler. Manning it, improbably, was a ship's steward immaculate in his short white jacket. It was almost like going Cunard.

Other troops made use of the growing mountain of debris that littered the beaches. Private C. N. Bennett of the 5th Northamptonshires came across a discarded army boat made of canvas. It was designed to carry six men across a river; now ten men jumped into it and headed across the sea. Using their rifles as paddles, they hoped to get to England. It was just as well that a motor launch soon spotted them and took them to the destroyer *Ivanhoe*.

Brigadier John G. Smyth, commanding the 127th Infantry Brigade, rallied nineteen men around a big ship's lifeboat stranded well up on the beach. A heavy, bulky thing, it required all their strength to shove it down to the water. Even then their troubles weren't over: it was a sixteen-oared boat, and not one of Smyth's recruits could row.

They shoved off anyhow, with Smyth at the tiller and the men at the oars. After a few strokes the "crew" began falling over backwards; the oars were tangled up; and the boat was turning in crazy circles. As he later recalled, "We must have looked like an intoxicated centipede."

There couldn't have been a worse time to give a lesson in basic rowing. The Luftwaffe chose this moment to stage one of its raids, and the Brigadier's instructions were punctuated by gunfire, exploding bombs, and geysers of water. The men tried again, this time with Smyth shouting out the stroke, "One-two, in-out!" The crew caught on, and the boat moved steadily toward a waiting destroyer. They even made a real race out of it, beating an overloaded motor launch carrying their division commander.

Farther along the beach, Private Bill Stratton of the RASC helped haul an abandoned lifeboat to the water's edge, then watched a stampede of men jump in and take it over. Determined not to let all his hard work go for nothing, Stratton made a flying leap and landed on top of the crowd. Predictably, the boat soon swamped. Stratton was a good swimmer, but his greatcoat dragged him down. He was about to go under when a navy launch appeared. Someone pulled him over the side and flung him down on the bottom, "like a fish."

Inevitably there were confrontations. Near Malo-les-Bains a column of wading men retrieved two small rowboats lying offshore. Suddenly a voice called, "Halt, or I fire!" It was a Scots colonel heading up an adjoining column, and he clearly felt his men had first call on the boats. Finally, a compromise was worked out allowing both columns to use them.

Near La Panne, Yeoman Eric Goodbody set out in a whaler with eight naval signalmen from GHQ. As they shoved off, an officer on shore ordered him to bring back four soldiers who had also piled in. Goodbody refused—he was in charge of the whaler and everybody in her, he declared. The officer pulled a gun ... Goodbody drew his ... and for a moment the two stood face to face, aiming their pistols at each other. At this point the four soldiers quietly volunteered to go back, and another crisis was passed.

At Bray-Dunes Sapper Joe Coles was aroused by a friend who had found a large rowboat swamped and stranded on the beach. They bailed it out, then were hurled aside by a mob of soldiers piling in. About to swamp again, it was emptied by a Military Policeman at pistol point.

Order restored, Coles and his friend tried again. This time they shoved off safely and took a load of troops to a skoot, then headed back for another load. Dozens of men were swimming out to meet them, when they were hailed by an officer floating nearby on a raft. Brandishing his revolver, the officer ordered them to take him first. Coles felt the swimmers should have priority—the raft was in no trouble—but that pistol was very persuasive. The officer had his way.

One reason for frayed nerves was the state of the sea. For the first time since the evacuation began, the wind was blowing onshore, building up a nasty surf throughout the morning of May 31. The loading went more slowly than ever, and at Bray-Dunes Commander Richardson finally decided that nothing more could be done. He ordered the troops on the beach to head for Dunkirk: then he, Commander Kerr, and the naval shore party salvaged a stranded whaler, rounded up some oars, and began pulling for England.

They didn't realize how tired they were. Every stroke hurt. Soon they were barely moving, and they probably would have broached to and swamped; but the Margate lifeboat spotted them in time. It hurried over and picked them up.

At 10:35 a.m. Admiral Wake-Walker radioed the situation to Ramsay at Dover.

> Majority of pulling boats are broached to and have no crews: Conditions on beach very bad owing to freshening onshore wind. Only small numbers are being embarked even in daylight. Consider only hope of embarking any number is at Dunkirk. . . .

By "Dunkirk" he of course meant the eastern mole. For Tennant and his aides, the mole was more and more the answer to everything. They were constantly trying to concentrate the boat traffic in that direction. Ramsay knew its importance too, but he also guessed that there were still thousands to be evacuated, and everything had to be used—including the beaches, even though the going was slow.

At 11:05 a.m. Wake-Walker tried again. "Dunkirk our only real hope," he telegraphed Ramsay. "Can guns shelling pier from westward be bombed and silenced?"

This was a new problem. Until May 31, the German guns had been a nuisance, but that was all. Their aim was haphazard; the shells usually fell short. Now, batteries had been planted this side of Gravelines; and the result was soon apparent.

At 6:17 a.m. the minesweeper *Glen Gower* lay alongside the mole, ready to receive her first troops of the day. As the skipper Commander M.A.O. Biddneph waited on the bridge, he suddenly heard a whistling noise . . . then a bang, quickly followed by several more bangs. A mass of black fragments leapt up on the foredeck, just where the gunnery officer, Sub-Lieutenant Williams, was standing. At first Biddneph thought it must be a stick of bombs, but there wasn't a plane in the sky. Then he realized it was a salvo of shells, one of them piercing the deck exactly between Williams's feet. Miraculously, the gunnery officer wasn't touched, but twelve men were killed or wounded in the explosion below.

The mole itself continued to lead a charmed life. Since its discovery by the Luftwaffe on May 29 it had been bombed by Stukas, pounded by artillery, and battered by rescue ships coming alongside too heavily. Rammed by the minesweeper *King Orry*, the seaward tip was now cut off completely. Yet for most of its length, it remained usable. Here and there gaps appeared, but they were bridged with boards, doors, and ships' gangplanks. The loading went on.

Still, the dash to the waiting vessels was always unnerving. None felt it more than Private Alfred Baldwin of the Royal Artillery. He was carrying on his shoulders his friend Private Paddy Boydd, who had smashed a foot. Stumbling along the walkway, Baldwin came to a gaping hole, bridged by a single plank. Two sailors standing by said, "Take a run at it, mate," adding, "don't look down." Baldwin followed their advice, except that he did look down. Dark water swirled around the piles twenty feet below. Somehow he kept his balance, and another pair of sailors grabbed him at the far end, cheering him on: "Well done, keep going!"

He struggled on, panting and stumbling, until he ran into two more sailors, who helped him maneuver Boydd up the gang-plank to a waiting ship. She turned out to be the Channel packet *Maid of Orleans*, the very same vessel that had brought him to France at the start of the war.

Baldwin made his dash when the tide was high. At low tide the mole could be even more trying. Corporal Reginald Lock-erby reached the destroyer *Venomous*, only to find there was a fifteen-foot drop to the ship's deck. Several telegraph poles leaned against the side of the mole, and the troops were expect-ed to slide down them to get aboard. Trouble was, neither ship nor poles had been made fast. Both were unpredictably swaying and heaving up and down. One slip meant falling into the sea and being crushed between boat and dock.

"I can't do it, Ern," Lockerby gasped to his friend Private Er-nest Heming.

"Get down there, you silly sod, or I'll throw you down!" shouted Heming. "I'll hold the top of the pole for you."

Somehow Lockerby mustered the strength and courage. He slid down the pole, then held it from the bottom as Heming fol-lowed.

No French troops were yet using the mole, but starting May 31, the new policy of equal numbers was very much in evidence along the beaches. When the motor yacht *Marsayru* arrived from Sheerness about 4:00 p.m., her first assignment was to help lift a large number of French waiting at Malo-les-Bains. The yacht's civilian skipper G. D. Olivier sent in his whaler, but it was stormed by about 50 poilus, and immediately capsized. He edged farther east, "where the French troops appeared to be a little calmer," and tried again. This time no problem, and over the next 48 hours he lifted more than 400 French soldiers.

Nearby a small flotilla of Royal Navy minesweeping craft was doing its bit. The *Three Kings* picked up 200 Frenchmen . . . the *Jackeve*, 60 . . . the *Rig*, another 60. The same sort of thing was happening at Bray-Dunes and La Panne.

How many French troops remained to be evacuated under

this policy of equal numbers? Neither Paris nor Admiral Abrial in Bastion 32 seemed to have any idea. To the weary organizers of the rescue fleet in London and Dover, it didn't make much difference. They were already sending everything that could float. . . .

In all her working years the 78-foot *Massey Shaw* had never been to sea. She was a Thames fire boat—or "fire float," as Londoners preferred to say—and until now her longest voyage had been down the river to fight a blaze at Ridham. She had no compass, and her crew were professional firemen, not sailors.

But the *Massey Shaw* drew only 3.9 feet, and to the Admiralty this was irresistible. There was also a vague notion that she might come in handy fighting the fires sweeping Dunkirk harbor, an idea that conveys less about her effectiveness than it does about the innocence still prevailing in some quarters at the Admiralty.

A call for volunteers went out on the afternoon of May 30. Thirteen men were picked, with Sub-Officer A. J. May in charge, and in two hours the *Massey Shaw* was on her way. There had barely been time to buy a small marine compass. On the trip down the river, the crew busied themselves boarding up the cabin windows and dabbing gray paint on the various brass fittings and hose nozzles. The situation must be serious indeed: the *Massey Shaw*'s bright work had always been sacred.

At Ramsgate she picked up water and a young Royal Navy sub-lieutenant with a chart. Then across the Channel with the additional help of a pocket tide table that somebody found. Arriving off Bray-Dunes late in the afternoon of May 31, the crew studied the beach with fascination. At first glance it looked like any bank holiday weekend—swarms of people moving about or sitting in little knots on the sand. But there was one big difference: instead of the bright colors of summer, everybody was dressed in khaki. And what first appeared to be "breakwaters" running down into the surf turned out to be columns of men, also dressed in khaki.

The *Massey Shaw* sent in a rowboat toward one of the columns. It was promptly swamped and sunk by the troops piling in. Then a stranded RAF speedboat was salvaged in the hope it might be used, but 50 men crowded aboard, putting it out of action too. Toward 11:00 p.m. still another boat was found. A line was now strung between the *Massey Shaw* and the beach, and the new boat was pulled back and forth along this line, rather like a sea-going trolley car. The boat carried only six men at a time, but back and forth it went, ferrying load after load.

Finally the *Massey Shaw* could hold no more. There were now 30 men packed in the cabin, which had seemed crowded with six the night before. Dozens more sprawled on the deck; there didn't seem to be a square foot of empty space.

It was dark when the *Massey Shaw* finally weighed anchor and started back for Ramsgate. So far, she had led a charmed life. The Luftwaffe was constantly overhead, but not a plane had attacked. Now, as she got under weigh, her screws kicked up a phosphorescent wake that caught the attention of some sharp-eyed enemy pilot. He swooped down and dropped a single bomb. It was close, but a miss. The *Massey Shaw* continued safely on her way, bringing home another 65 men.

Like the *Massey Shaw*, the Tilbury Dredging Company's steam hopper dredge *Lady Southborough* had never been to sea. Plucked from rust-streaked obscurity in Portsmouth harbor, she checked in at Ramsgate, then set out for Dunkirk with three other Tilbury hoppers early on the morning of May 31. Arriving at 12:30 p.m., *Lady Southborough* anchored off Malo-les-Bains, lowered her port lifeboat with three hands, and began lifting troops off the beach.

As the *Lady Southborough* hovered several hundred yards offshore, a German plane dropped a stick of four bombs. No hits, but they lifted the ship's lifeboat clear out of the water and whacked it down again, springing every plank. Nobody was hurt, but the boat was finished. Seeing that it was ebb tide, skipper Anthony Poole now drove *Lady Southborough* head-first onto the beach, so that he could pick up the troops directly from the water. They swarmed out, and one Frenchman—who evidently had not heard of the new British policy of equal numbers—offered to pay acting Second Mate John Tarry to get aboard.

Nearby, another Tilbury hopper dredge, *Foremost 101*, lay at anchor. The usual signs of disorder were everywhere: boats swamped by the surf . . . others sinking under the weight of too

many men . . . others drifting about without oars or oarsmen.
Amid this chaos was a single note of serenity. A petty officer
had found a small child's canoe in some boating pond ashore.
Now he was ferrying soldiers one by one out to the waiting
ships. As he threaded his way through the debris, none of the
swimmers ever bothered him. By common consent he seemed
to have a *laissez-passer* to work in peace, without interference.

Going home in the dark was the hardest part. As *Lady Southborough* groped uncertainly through the night, a destroyer
loomed up, flashing a signal. None of the dredge's crew could
read Morse; so there was no answer. The destroyer flashed
again; still no answer. Finally one of the soldiers on board said
he was a signalman: could he help? Some more flashes, and the
soldier announced that the destroyer had now demanded their
identity three times; if they didn't answer at once, she would
blow them out of the water. Watching the signalman flash back
the ship's name, Second Mate Tarry cursed the day she had
been christened *Lady Southborough*. Those sixteen letters
seemed to take forever. But at last the destroyer was satisfied,
and *Lady Southborough* crawled on to Ramsgate.

Meanwhile the cascade of little ships continued in all its variety—the stylish yacht *Quicksilver*, which could make twenty
knots . . . the cockle fleet from Leigh-on-Sea . . . the Chris Craft
Bonnie Heather, with its polished mahogany hull . . . the Dutch
eel boat *Johanna*, which came complete with three Dutch owners
who couldn't speak a word of English . . . to name just a few.
Countless other boats, which Admiral Ramsay called "free
lances," were now heading out of south coast ports like Folkestone, Eastbourne, Newhaven, and Brighton. Most never bothered to check with Dover; no one would ever record their
names.

The French and Belgian fishing vessels requisitioned by Captain Auphan were beginning to turn up too, adding an interna-
tional flavor to the rescue effort. Names like *Pierre et Marie*,
Reine des Flots, and *Ingénieur Cardin* joined *Handy Billie*, *Girl
Nancy*, and at least nine *Skylarks*. The French mailboat *Côte d'Argent* began using the east mole like any British steamer.

Most of the French crews were from Brittany and as unfamiliar with these waters as the cockle boatmen from the Thames
estuary, but there was the inevitable exception. Fernand

Schneider, assistant engineer on the minesweeping trawler *St. Cyr*, came from Dunkirk itself. Now he had the agony of watching his hometown crumble into ruins, but at the same time the comfort of visiting his own house from time to time.

Knowing the area, Schneider also knew where food was to be had, and the *St. Cyr*'s skipper occasionally sent him on foraging expeditions to bolster the trawler's meager rations. He was on one of these forays on May 28 when he decided to check his house on the rue de la Toute Verte. It was still standing, and better yet, his father Augustin Schneider was there. Augustin had come in from the family refuge in the country, also to see how the house was faring. They embraced with special fervor, for the occasion was more than a family reunion, more than a celebration that the house was intact—it was Fernand's 21st birthday.

The old man went down in the cellar and brought up a bottle of Vouvray. Then for an hour the two forgot about the war while they joyfully killed the bottle. Parting at last, father and son would not see each other again for five years.

Fernand Schneider was the only sailor at Dunkirk who celebrated his birthday at home, but the rescue fleet was full of improbable characters. Lieutenant Lodo van Hamel was a dashing Dutch naval officer, always conspicuous because he flew the only Dutch flag in the whole armada. Lieutenant-Colonel Robin Hutchens was an old Grenadier Guardsman, mired in a dull liaison job at the Admiralty. An experienced weekend sailor, he headed for Dover on his day off; now he was in charge of the War Department launch *Swallow*. Captain R. P. Pim normally presided over Winston Churchill's map room; today he wallowed across the Channel commanding a Dutch skoot. Samuel Palmer served on the Plymouth City Patrol, but he was an old navy "stripey," and that was good enough. In charge of the seven-ton *Naiad Errant*, a cranky motor yacht that was always breaking down, he split up the cabin door and told the soldiers on board to start paddling.

Robert Harling was a typographical designer, but as a student in Captain Watts's navigation class, he had volunteered with the rest. Now he found himself one of four men assigned to a ship's lifeboat stripped from some liner at Tilbury docks. His companions turned out to be an advertising executive, a garage propri-

etor, and a solicitor. They had practically nothing in common—
yet everything, joined as they were in an open boat on this
strange adventure.

The boat was one of twelve being towed across the Channel
by the tug *Sun IV*, skippered at the moment by the managing
director of the tugboat company. The afternoon was beautiful,
and the war seemed very far away. For a long time there was little to do but shoot the breeze. As they neared the French coast,
marked by the pillar of black smoke over Dunkirk, the conversation fell off, and the mood in Harling's boat became tense.

"There they are, the bastards!" someone suddenly called,
pointing up at the sky. Harling looked, and soon made out
more than 50 planes approaching with stately precision. They
were perhaps 15,000 feet up, and at this distance everything
seemed to happen in slow motion. Gradually the planes drew
closer . . . then were directly overhead. Fascinated, he watched
the bombs fall lazily toward the earth. Then suddenly they were
rushing down at breakneck speed, crashing into the sea, just
missing two nearby destroyers.

Soon some RAF fighters appeared, tearing into the German
formation. Harling was mildly surprised that the Hurricanes
and Spitfires really did rout the enemy—just as the communi-
qués said. But that wasn't the end of it. In a last gesture of defiance, one of the German fighters swooped down, strafing the
Sun IV and her tow. Watching it come, Harling felt mesmer-
ized—he couldn't even duck in time—then in a second it was
over. The bullets ripped the empty sea; the plane zoomed up
and out of sight. *Sun IV* and her charges steamed on untouched.

The sky was not the only source of danger. After a night of
ferry work, the six cockle boats started back for Ramsgate at
3:00 a.m., June 1. Most had fared very well, but *Letitia* had now
broken down and was being towed by the drifter *Ben and Lucy*.
Then *Renown*'s engine went, and she latched onto *Letitia*. The
three vessels limped along, with *Renown* yawing wide at the end
of the tow.

It was about 3:30 when *Renown* brushed a German mine,
freshly laid by some bomber or S-Boat. There was a blinding
flash, and every trace of *Renown* and her crew of four vanished
completely.

The methodical German shelling continued taking its toll

too—often with frightening suddenness. As the pleasure steamer *New Prince of Wales* lay off Bray-Dunes on the 31st, Sub-Lieutenant Bennett left the bridge to help start a balky engine. He
had just reached the deck when there was a shrieking, tearing
sound, coming at him straight from above. There was a shattering explosion . . . a momentary glimpse of gray streamers of
smoke laced with bits of shell . . . pain in his left foot, left thigh,
and the left side of his face . . . and he found himself lying on
deck. As he lost consciousness, he decided this must be the end.
He had seen enough war movies showing men dying with blood
running out of their mouths. That was the way they always
went, and that was what was happening to him.

He came to a few minutes later, happy to find he was still
alive. But two of his men were killed, and the *New Prince of Wales*
was a write-off. The motor boat *Triton* was nearby, and Lieutenant Irving eased her over to take off the survivors. By now Bennett was on his feet again and even feeling belligerent. His face
was a bloody mess, but his mind was clear, and he took over as
coxswain for Lieutenant Irving.

They weren't all heroes. Off Bray-Dunes one Dutch skoot lay
motionless for hours, doing little or nothing. The skipper was
tipsy, and the second in command seemed less than enthusiastic. Troops rowed out to her anyhow, and finally she was rea-
sonably full. At this point Corporal Harold Meredith of the
RASC heard the skipper explain, "I'm supposed to take you out
to the destroyers, which are lying farther offshore, but I've had
a very rough day, and tonight I am Nelson. I've unfortunately
put my telescope to my blind eye, and I cannot see any destroyers; so I'm taking you all the way home."

One way or another, 68,014 Allied troops were evacuated this
May 31. As usual, the most dramatic incidents occurred off the
beaches, but the most effective work was again done on the east
mole. The destroyer *Malcolm* showed what one ship could do—
1,000 men lifted at 2:15 a.m. . . . another 1,000 at 2:30 p.m. . . .
still another 1,000 lifted in the early hours of June 1. Her efficiency made the job look easy, yet it was anything but that. Warrant Engineer Arthur George Scoggins nursed his machinery in
a steam-filled engine room where the temperature hit 140° to
150°.

For the first time British ships were carrying a really respectable number of Frenchmen—10,842 were rescued this day. Not enough to satisfy Premier Reynaud, but it was a start. And the difficulties were more than the critics in Paris could ever realize. Usually the poilus wanted to bring all their equipment. Many refused to be separated from their units. They seemed unable to comprehend that if too many people got into a small boat at once, it might capsize or run aground. The British crews were inclined to think that the French were just naturally landlubbers, in contrast to "our island race." The evidence suggests that much of the trouble stemmed from the language barrier.

"*En avant mes héros! Courage mes enfants!*" Sub-Lieutenant A. Carew Hunt summoned up his limited store of French, trying to tempt some hesitant soldiers to wade out to his boat. Minutes later he was waving his revolver at them to stop the rush.

"*Débarquez!* You bloody fools, get out! Get out! *Nous sommes ensables!*" shouted one of Captain Watts's scholars as his boat grounded under the weight of too many Frenchmen. Nobody understood, and nobody moved. Finally a French NCO caught on, reworked the language, and the order was obeyed.

Sub-Lieutenant Michael Solomon, who knew French well, never had any trouble during a brief stint as interpreter for Commander Clouston on the eastern mole. English officers shouting "*Allez!*" got nowhere—that was insulting—but the right words, plus a little tact, could work wonders. ·

So the loading went on, and one more crisis was passed. The equal numbers rule did not upset Ramsay's timetable after all. Thanks to Clouston's organizing ability, far more men were evacuating from the mole than anyone had dared hope. The surge of little ships across the Channel helped too. By now there were enough boats for everyone—both French and British.

But already a new crisis was at hand. All day May 31, German shells had been falling on the beach and shipping at La Panne. Now, as dusk settled over the battered town, the bombardment grew worse than ever. It suggested that all was far from well along the eastern end of the perimeter. If it collapsed, Bock's seasoned troops could break into the beachhead and end the evacuation for good.

11

Holding the Perimeter

German shells screeched overhead as Captain P. J. Jeffries of the 6th Durham Light Infantry leaned over and plucked a small flower in the garden of the chateau at Moeres, a Belgian village toward the eastern end of the perimeter. Jeffries didn't know what this flower was—sort of a cross between an azalea and a rhododendron—but he vowed to find out and plant some in his own garden . . . if he ever got home again.

At the moment his chances didn't look too good. Jeffries was second in command of the 6th DLI, one of the units assigned to hold off the Germans while the rest of the BEF and the French escaped to England. For two days enemy pressure had been growing on the Durhams' section of the canal defense line, and now on the morning of May 31 German shells began landing uncomfortably close to battalion headquarters.

The first actual penetration came not at Moeres, but still farther east near Nieuport, the coastal town that served as the perimeter's eastern anchor. Here at 5:00 a.m. German infantry crossed the canal in rubber boats and stormed the brickworks held by the 1st/6th East Surreys. By noon they were in danger of being outflanked. Their "sister" battalion, the 1st East Surreys, rushed to the rescue just in time. Together they managed to stop the enemy, but it took every man. At one point the two battalion commanders manned a Bren gun together. One colonel fired the gun, while the other acted as "No. 2," feeding it with ammunition.

Next, an even closer squeak. While the Surreys were clinging to their brickyard, a new German attack hit the British 8th Brigade three miles to the west. At 12:20 p.m. a hysterical sapper stumbled into Furnes, the main town in the area, blurting that the front had been broken and the Germans were pouring across the canal unopposed.

No time to lose. Reinforcements from the crack 2nd Grenadier Guards were rushed to the scene under a quick-thinking 2nd lieutenant named Jones. He found two battalions of the brigade about to retire without orders. If this happened, a gaping hole would open up in the perimeter, allowing the Germans to pour in behind the defenders. The few remaining officers were trying to rally their men, but nobody would listen.

Jones took more drastic measures. He found it necessary to shoot some of the panic-stricken soldiers, and others were turned around at bayonet-point. He then reported back to headquarters that the brigade was once again stabilized but in desperate need of experienced officers and ammunition. Lieutenant J. Trotter of the 2nd Grenadier Guards was then sent to help him, along with 14,000 rounds of ammunition. By 3:00 p.m. the men were all back in position and morale was high—proving once again the importance of that elusive quality, leadership, in shaping the fortunes of war.

During the afternoon the Germans shifted their efforts to the area southwest of Furnes, but with no better results. They managed to storm across the canal at Bulscamp, but soon bogged down on the other side. Flooded terrain and a spirited defense blocked any further advance. In such a predicament the standard remedy was to soften resistance with artillery, and shells were soon raining on the Durham Light Infantry's chateau at Moeres. Toward evening the DLI abandoned the place with few regrets. This country was meant to be an epicure's delight, but for three days they had lived on a diet of tinned pilchards in tomato sauce.

Evening, and the target was Nieuport again. It's doubtful

whether the exhausted East Surreys could have stood up to any serious attack. Fortunately, just as the German columns massed, help came from an unexpected direction. Eighteen RAF bombers, supported by six planes from the Fleet Air Arm, swept in from the sea, smashing and scattering the enemy force. The British troops forgot their weariness; leapt and waved and shouted with excitement. Until now they thought that only the Germans could pull off this sort of stunt.

While the British brigades to the east desperately parried the German thrusts, the Allied troops to the west had a relatively quiet day. The line from Fort Mardyck to the ancient walled town of Bergues was a French responsibility; General Beaufrère's 68th Infantry Division lay waiting behind a patchwork of ditches. A mixed garrison of French and British held Bergues itself. Some long-range guns were shelling the place, but the medieval walls stood up to modern artillery amazingly well.

It was the Bergues-Furnes Canal Line to the east of town that seemed most exposed. While the flat fields were bound to reveal an advancing enemy, they also gave away the defenders. There was no cover, except for an occasional tree or farmhouse.

The 2nd Coldstream Guards eyed uneasily the 2,200 yards assigned to them. Lieutenant Jimmy Langley of No. 3 Company moved his platoon into a small brick cottage directly north of the canal. He was anything but a picture-book guardsman—he stood only five feet eight—but he was lively and immensely resourceful. He lost no time converting the cottage into a miniature Gibraltar.

From scores of trucks and lorries abandoned along the canal bank, Langley's men brought back a vast haul of booty. The weapons alone were impressive—12 Bren guns, 3 Lewis machine guns, 1 Boyes antitank rifle, 30,000 rounds of ammunition, and 22 hand grenades. Considering there were only 37 men left in the company, this was fire power indeed.

Nor was food neglected. Stacks of bully beef, canned vegetables, and tinned milk were piled in the kitchen. And since Langley was especially partial to marmalade and Wiltshire bacon, there was a liberal supply of these too. They might, he decided, be there a long time; so they should be prepared for the good life as well—he added two cases of wine and two crates of beer.

During the afternoon the company commander, Major Angus McCorquodale, dropped by and made his contribution too: a bottle of whiskey and two bottles of sherry. McCorquodale was one of those throwbacks to a glorious earlier age in British military history. Gleaming with polished brass and leather, he scorned the new battle dress. "I don't mind dying for my country," he declared, "but I'm not going to die dressed like a third-rate chauffeur."

He liked Langley's set-up so much he decided to make the cottage the Company's forward headquarters, and the two of them bedded down in a small back room for some rest. They were up before dawn, June 1, removing roof tiles and turning the attic into a machine-gun nest. Neither the roof nor the end walls were really strong enough, but it was too late to worry about that now. Langley settled down to wait for Jerry with a pair of binoculars and two buckets of cold water by his side. The buckets were for cooling the wine, or the beer, or the Bren-gun barrels—whichever seemed to need it most.

There was no night of quiet waiting at Furnes. Shells poured down on the old Flemish town, as they had all day. The 1st Grenadier Guards huddled under an avalanche of falling slate and masonry from the seventeenth-century buildings that ringed the marketplace. The churchyard of venerable Saint Walburge was so thick with shrapnel that walking on the grass was like tramping over a carpet of jagged glass.

In the roomy cellar that served as battalion headquarters, Signalman George W. Jones hunched over a portable radio listening to the BBC evening news. It was the first voice he had heard from the outside world in three weeks. It assured him that two-thirds of the troops trapped at Dunkirk were now evacuated and safely back in England.

Jones felt anything but assured. Here he was, stuck with the rear guard in a collapsing town miles from home, and now he heard that the best part of the army was safely back in England. It was a very lonely feeling.

Lance Sergeant John Bridges, also of the 1st Grenadier Guards, was sure they would never get away. He had originally joined the regiment as a drummer boy, hoping to see the world, play a little football, and ultimately become a writer. But now the dream was buried in the rubble of Furnes. His company commander, Major Dickie Herbert, showed him how to dig a round foxhole, so he could shoot in any direction. That could only mean they were about to be surrounded.

Then an unexpected reprieve. Toward evening Major Herbert returned from a brigade conference and immediately called a meeting of his own officers and NCO's. He lost no time getting to the point: his first words were, "We're going home." A map was produced, and a staff lieutenant lined off the route to the beaches. There were no histrionics, no exhortations. It was all so matter-of-fact that to Bridges it seemed rather like planning a family outing.

At 10:00 p.m. the battalion began "thinning out"—first the headquarters personnel, the signalers, the quartermaster units; then the infantry companies, one by one; and finally certain hand-picked parties from No. 2 and No. 4 Companies, especially skilled in rear-guard work. Everything went very smoothly. After all, they had been doing it since Brussels.

The premium was on silence. The enemy must not find out. The rear-guard parties wrapped sandbags around their boots to deaden the sound on the cobblestone streets. Still, there were heart-stopping moments as the columns, tramping single file, noisily scrambled over piles of rubble, bricks, broken glass, and tangled telephone wire. How could the Germans miss hearing them?

Yet there was no sound of unusual activity in the sections of town now occupied by the enemy. Only the steady pounding of shells that had gone on for two days. By 2:30 a.m., June 1, the last Grenadier Guard had pulled out.

For Sergeant Bridges the march to La Panne was a three-mile nightmare. He especially hated mortar fire, and tonight every mortar in the German Army seemed concentrated on him. Most of the shells landed ahead of the column, which meant few casualties but gave the terrifying impression that the battalion was always marching straight into hell. At one point Bridges's rifle got caught in a tangle of telephone wire, and the more he tried to get it loose, the more he himself became enmeshed in the tangle. On the verge of panic, he was finally freed by his sergeant major, who also brought him to his senses with a good slap.

Adding to the confusion, hundreds of abandoned cattle, sheep, pigs, and chickens were loose and running among the stumbling men. They reminded Bridges of the stories he had heard about wild animals fleeing before a great forest fire.

All along the eastern end of the perimeter—the II Corps area—the battalions were thinning out and falling back on La Panne. As with the 1st Grenadier Guards, the process usually began about 10:00 p.m. and continued to around 2:30 a.m., when the last rear-guard parties retired. Probably the last unit of all to pull out was the carrier platoon of the 1st Coldstream, which hung around Furnes till 2:50 a.m., covering the withdrawal of the battalion's infantry.

As always, silence was the rule—which could fool a friend as well as foe. Private F. R. Farley was on sentry duty that night in a lonely copse east of Furnes. He knew his battalion, the 1st/7th Middlesex, would be withdrawing, and he was to be called in when the time came. Hours passed, and nothing happened. From time to time he heard faint sounds: a car starting, a muffled word of command. Then complete silence. He listened—a sentry did not leave his post lightly—then decided to slip back, and see what was happening.

Everyone had gone. The NCO had forgotten to call him in. Desperately he sprinted through the copse to the main road. He was just in time to leap onto the last truck of the last column of the battalion, as it started down the coastal road for La Panne.

The convoy stopped on the edge of town; the men piled out; and the trucks were disabled in the usual way—a bullet in the radiator, the engine left running until it seized. Moving into La Panne, Farley joined a flood of troops converging on the place from every direction. The whole eastern end of the perimeter was being abandoned; all had instructions to make for La Panne.

Beyond that, there seemed to be no orders. Some men slumped in doorways; others lay exhausted on the *pavé*; others wandered aimlessly about, as officers and NCO's called out unit numbers and rallying cries, trying to keep their men together.

The shelling had unaccountably stopped, and for the moment all was relatively quiet. As the men waited to be told what to do, a thousand cigarettes glowed in the darkness.

Eventually there was a stirring, but instead of moving onto

the beach, the troops were ordered back a couple of streets. They were now further from the sea, but much better dispersed. It was just as well, for at this moment a spotter plane droned overhead, dropping flares that brilliantly lit up the whole scene. Then came the thump of distant guns, followed by the shriek of falling shells.

There was a shattering crash as the first salvo landed at the intersection near the beach. The hotels and shops in the area were mostly built in the "modern" style of the 30's, full of chrome and plate glass. Now the glass came cascading down, adding to the general din.

"Into the shops! Off the streets!" The cry went up, and the troops needed no further urging. Rifle butts went to work on the doors and windows remaining, and the men swarmed in, just as a second salvo was landing.

Farley and several others from the 1st/7th Middlesex broke into a large corner shop, and once inside were thankful to find stairs leading down to a basement. Here they crouched in comparative safety as the shelling swept methodically up and down the streets salvo after salvo, turning the town into a dust-choked ruin. Flames began to lick through upper windows as fires took hold.

It was important not to go entirely underground. There was always the danger of missing some important order. The men took turns keeping watch at the door—very unpleasant duty with the town collapsing around them. Farley found the knack was to leap back to the stairs whenever a salvo seemed likely to be close. He got very good at it.

After an hour and a half, Captain Johnson of Headquarters Company slipped in with the latest orders: listen for some whistle blasts as soon as there is a lull in the shelling . . . then clear out and run for the beach at the double . . . turn left at the bandstand and keep going for half a mile. That would be where the battalion would reassemble and embark.

No one was to stop for anything. Casualties to be left where they fell. The medical orderlies would take care of these. The essential thing was to clear the streets without delay at the first feasible moment.

Just before 2:45 a.m. Private Farley heard the whistle loud

and clear. His group raced up the cellar steps and out into the street. Other units were pouring out of other buildings, too. Jumbled together, they all surged toward the beachfront. The flames from the burning buildings lit their way; the crash of bursting shells spurred them on. The "lull," it turned out, meant only a shift in targets. But the most unforgettable sound—a din that drowned out even the gunfire—was the steady crunch of thousands of boots on millions of fragments of broken glass.

Soon they were by the bandstand . . . across the esplanade . . . onto the beach—and suddenly they were in a different world. Gone was the harsh, grating clatter; now there was only the squish of feet running on wet sand. The glare of the fire-lit streets gave way to the blackness of the dunes at night. The smoke and choking dust vanished, replaced by the clean, damp air of the seaside . . . the smell of salt and seaweed.

Then the shelling shifted again, aimed this time right at the beach where the men were running. Private Farley of the Middlesex saw a flash, felt the blast, but (oddly enough) heard no "bang" as a close one landed just ahead. He was untouched, but the four men running with him all went down. Three lay motionless on the sand; the fourth, propped up on one hand, pleaded, "Help me, help me."

Farley ran on. After all, those were the orders. But he knew in his heart that the real reason he didn't stop was self-preservation. The memory of that voice pleading for help would still haunt his conscience forty years later.

Half a mile down the beach was the point where the Middlesex had been ordered to reassemble for embarkation. Private Farley had imagined what it would be like. He pictured a well-organized area where senior NCO's would stand at the head of gangway ladders taking name, rank, and serial number as the troops filed aboard the waiting ships. Actually, there was no embarkation staff, no waiting ships, no organization whatsoever.

Nobody seemed to be in charge. The 2nd Royal Ulster Rifles had been told that reception camps would be waiting for them when they got to the beach, that a Division Control Staff would take over from there and guide them to the ships. They found no trace of either the camps or the Control Staff, and of course no sign of the ships.

The 1st Grenadier Guards reached the beach intact, but with no further orders, the battalion soon broke up. Some men headed for Dunkirk; others joined the columns hopefully waiting at the water's edge; Sergeant Bridges led a small group of six or eight into the dunes to wait for dawn. Maybe daylight would show them what to do.

But would they last that long? At one point Bridges heard an ominous rumble coming toward them. It sounded like the whole German Army, and he crouched in the sand, awaiting that final confrontation. It turned out to be only horses, abandoned by some French artillery unit, galloping aimlessly up and down the sand.

But the next big noise might always be the enemy, and still there was no sign of any ships. To Lieutenant-Commander J. N. McClelland, the senior naval officer remaining at La Panne, the situation was turning into a hideous exercise in arithmetic. It was now 1:00 a.m.; the British couldn't expect to hold La Panne beyond dawn at 4:00. Some 6,000 troops were pouring onto the beach; they had lifted off only 150 since nightfall. At this rate, nearly the whole force would be lost.

He conferred briefly with Major-General G. D. Johnson, the senior army officer on the beach at this point. Yes, McClelland assured the General, he had made a personal reconnaissance both above and below the position. No, there weren't any ships. Yes, they were meant to be there. No, he didn't think they would come now—something must have gone wrong. To McClelland the Royal Navy's absence was almost a matter of personal shame. He formally apologized to Johnson for the nonarrival of the boats.

They decided that the only course left was to march the bulk of the troops down the beach toward Dunkirk and try to embark from there. Or perhaps they would run across some ships at Bray-Dunes along the way.

A few men—mostly wounded and exhausted stragglers—were not fit to march. These would be left behind, and McClelland headed down to the lorry jetties to look after them, on the chance that some ships might still turn up.

More German guns were ranged on the beach now, and McClelland was twice knocked down by shell bursts. One smashed his signal lamp; the second wounded his left ankle. As often happens, it didn't hurt much at first—just a numb feeling—and he hobbled on down the beach.

At the embarkation point it was the same old story: no boats for over half an hour. McClelland now ordered the remaining troops to join the trek to Dunkirk. Even if they couldn't keep up with the main body, they must try. He himself rounded up all the stragglers he could find and sent them on their way. Then he limped off after the rest.

About two miles toward Bray-Dunes he suddenly saw what he had been searching for all night—ships! Three vessels lay at anchor not far from the shore. A small party of soldiers stood at the water's edge firing shots, trying to attract attention. There was no response from the ships. They just sat there, dark and silent.

McClelland looked farther down the beach. The night was filled with explosions, and in the flashes he could make out swarms of troops, but no trace of any other boat. These three anchored ships were the only chance. Somehow they must be told that the troops were moving steadily westward toward Dunkirk. Once these ships knew, they could alert the others, and the rescue fleet could finally assemble at the right place.

He plunged into the sea and began swimming. He was dead tired; his ankle began acting up; but he kept on. As he thrashed alongside the nearest ship, somebody threw him a line and he was hauled aboard. She turned out to be HMS *Gossamer*, one of Ramsay's hard-working minesweepers. Taken before the captain, Commander Richard Ross, McClelland managed to pant out his message: La Panne abandoned; all shipping should concentrate much farther west. Then he collapsed.

For Commander Ross, it was the first piece of solid intelligence to come his way since leaving Dover at 6:00 p.m. The *Gossamer* was one of the group of vessels earmarked for lifting the rear guard at the eastern end of the perimeter, amounting to some 4,000 men. The plan called for three big batches of ships' lifeboats to be towed by tugs across the Channel and stationed at three carefully designated points off La Panne. The rear guard would be instructed where to go, and at 1:30 a.m. the lifeboats would start ferrying the men to minesweepers waiting at each of the three points. Escorting destroyers would provide covering fire if the enemy tried to interfere. ("All tanks hostile," the orders reminded the destroyers.) The final directives were issued at 4:00 a.m., May 31, and the "special tows," as Ramsay called them, began leaving Ramsgate at 1:00 p.m.

Every possible contingency had been covered—except the fortunes of war. German pressure on the perimeter was too great. The covering position could no longer be held by the 4,000-man rear guard. Under heavy enemy shelling the troops were pulling back sooner than expected, and farther west than planned. The special tows must be alerted to go to a different place at a different time.

But Dover no longer had any direct communication with the special tows. Ramsay could only radio the accompanying minesweepers, hoping that the change in plans would be passed along to the tugs and their tows. He did this, but predictably his message never got through.

The armada chugged on to the originally designated spots, but now, of course, there was no one there. With no further directions, they groped along the coast, hoping somehow to make contact. *Gossamer* had, in fact, just stumbled on a sizable contingent when McClelland swam out, gasping his advice to look farther west.

The alert radio interception unit at General Georg von Kuechler's Eighteenth Army headquarters knew more than the BEF about the special tows and where they could be found. At 7:55 p.m. on the 31st, Captain Essmann of Headquarters phoned XXVI and IX Corps command posts, giving the latest information along with some instructions on what should be done.

Beginning at twilight, a heavy harassing fire was to be concentrated on the approach roads leading to the supposed embarkation points. . . . Armored reconnaissance patrols were to check whether the enemy had managed to evacuate. . . . If so, an immediate thrust was to be made to the coast.

Not exactly an inspiring blueprint for an army closing in for the kill. A lackadaisical mood, in fact, seemed to permeate most German military thinking these past two days. To Colonel Rolf Wuthmann, Operations Officer of General von Kluge's Fourth Army at the western end of the perimeter, it was a cause for alarm. "There is an impression here that nothing is happening today, that no one is any longer interested in Dunkirk," he complained to General von Kleist's Chief of Staff on May 30.

Quite true. All eyes were now on the south. *"Fall Rot"*—Operation "Red"—the great campaign designed to knock France out of the war, would jump off from the Somme in just six days. Its immense scope and dazzling possibilities easily diverted attention from Dunkirk. Guderian and the other panzer generals—once so exasperated by Hitler's halt order—now wanted only to pull out their tanks, rest their men, prepare for the great new adventure. Rundstedt, commanding Army Group A, had already shifted his entire attention to the Somme. On the 31st Bock, commanding Army Group B, received a fat bundle of papers from OKH regrouping his forces too. At OKH, General Halder, the Chief of Staff, spent most of the day far behind the lines, checking communications, the flow of supplies, the status of Army Group C—all for the great new offensive.

As for Dunkirk, it was hard to escape the feeling that it was really all over. Some ten German infantry divisions now pressed a few thousand disorganized Allied soldiers against the sea. Kluge's Chief of Staff Kurt Brennecke might scold, "We do not want to find these men, freshly equipped, in front of us again later," but no German command was more thoroughly preoccupied with the coming drive south than Brennecke's own Fourth Army. General Halder might complain, "Now we must stand by and watch countless thousands of the enemy get away to England right under our noses," but he didn't stand by and watch very much himself. He too was busy getting ready for the big new push.

It always seemed that one more try would finish up Dunkirk, but no one was quite in the position to do it. With the closing of the trap, there were too many overlapping commands and too little coordination. Finally, in an effort to centralize responsibility, General von Kuechler's Eighteenth Army was put in complete charge. On May 31, at 2:00 a.m., all the various divisions along the entire 35-mile length of the perimeter passed under his control.

It wasn't long before Kuechler was getting advice. The following evening General Mieth of OKH telephoned a few "personal suggestions" from the highest levels. General von Brauchitsch suggested the landing of troop units from the sea in the rear of the British forces . . . also, the withdrawal of German units from the Canal Line so as to open up opportunities for the Luftwaffe without endangering friendly troops. And finally, an idea from Adolf Hitler himself: Kuechler might consider the possibility of using antiaircraft shells with time fuses to compensate for the reduced effectiveness of ordinary artillery fire on the beaches, where the sand tended to smother the explosions. Like many shakers and movers of the earth, the Fuehrer occasionally liked to tinker.

For the moment, these intriguing ideas were put aside. Kuechler had already made his plan, and it called for nothing as offbeat as a landing behind the British forces, even if that were possible. Instead, he simply planned an attack by all his forces at once along the entire length of the perimeter on June 1.

First, his artillery would soften the enemy up with harassing fire, starting immediately and continuing the whole night. The attacking troops would jump off at 11:00 a.m., June 1, closely supported by General Alfred Keller's Fliegerkorps IV.

Everything was to be saved for the main blow. During the afternoon of the 31st, Eighteenth Army issued a special directive warning the troops not to engage in any unnecessary action that day. Rather, their time should be spent moving the artillery into position, gathering intelligence, conducting reconnaissance, and making other preparations for the "systematic attack" tomorrow.

All very sound, but this inflexibility also suggests why so little use was made of the radio intercept about Ramsay's special tows. It clearly indicated that the British were abandoning the eastern end of the perimeter this very night—leaving themselves wide open in the process—yet the German plans were frozen, and nothing was done.

If anybody at Eighteenth Army headquarters sensed a lost

opportunity on the evening of May 31, there's no evidence of it. Preparations went steadily ahead for the unified attack tomorrow. The artillery pumped out shells at a rate the British Tommies would never forget, and the Luftwaffe joined in the softening-up process.

Special emphasis had been placed on the Luftwaffe's role, and for the duration of the attack Eighteenth Army was virtually given control of its operations. General Kesselring's Air Fleet 2 was simply told to attack Dunkirk continuously until the Eighteenth told it to stop.

Making use of his authority, around noon on the 31st Kuechler requested special strikes every fifteen minutes on the dunes west of Nieuport, where the British artillery was giving his 256th Infantry Division a hard time. Kesselring promised to follow through, but later reported that ground fog was keeping some of the planes from taking off.

Bad weather was a familiar story. It had scrubbed almost all missions on the 30th, and curbed operations on the 31st. It was, then, good news indeed when June 1 turned out to be bright and clear.

12

"I Have Never Prayed So Hard Before"

As the growl of approaching planes grew louder, veteran Seaman Bill Barris carefully removed his false teeth and put them in his handkerchief pocket—always a sure sign to the men on the destroyer *Windsor* that hard fighting lay ahead. It was 5:30 a.m., June 1, and the early morning mist was already burning off, promising a hot sunny day.

In seconds the planes were in sight, Me 109's sweeping in low from the east. Gun muzzles twinkling, some strafed the eastern mole, where the *Windsor* lay loading; others hit the beaches . . . the rescue fleet . . . even individual soldiers wading and swimming out to the ships. Normally the German fighters did little strafing. Their orders were to remain "upstairs," flying cover for the Stukas and Heinkels. Today's tactics suggested something special.

Tucked away in the dunes west of La Panne, Sergeant John Bridges of the 1st Grenadier Guards safely weathered the storm. Around him clustered six to eight other Grenadier Guards, the little group he had formed when the battalion dissolved during the night. At that time nobody knew what to do, and it seemed best to wait till dawn.

Now it was getting light, and the choice was no easier. Joining the trek to Dunkirk looked too dangerous. Bridges could see nothing but gun flashes and towering smoke in that direction. On the other hand, joining one of the columns waiting on the beach below looked futile. There were so few boats and so many men. In the end, Bridges opted for the beach; perhaps the group could find some shorter queue where the wait would be reasonable.

A pistol shot ended that experiment. An officer accused the group of queue-jumping and fired a warning blast in the general direction of Bridges's feet. Undaunted, the Sergeant turned his mind to the possibility of getting off the beach without queueing up at all. Noticing an apparently empty lifeboat drifting about 100 yards off shore, he suggested they swim out and get it. Nobody could swim.

He decided to go and bring it back himself. Stripping off his clothes, he swam out to the boat, only to find it was not empty after all. Two bedraggled figures in khaki were already in it, trying to unlash the oars. They were glad to have Bridges join them, but not his friends. They weren't about to return to shore for anybody. Bridges hopped out and swam back to the beach.

But now the group had vanished, scattered by an air raid. Only Corporal Martin was left, faithfully guarding Bridges's gear. Looking to sea, they saw yet another lifeboat and decided to make for that. Martin, of course, couldn't swim, but Bridges—ever an optimist—felt that somehow he could push and pull the Corporal along.

It would have been easier if Bridges had been traveling light. But he was dressed again, carrying his pack and gas cape, and there was much on his mind besides Corporal Martin. While in Furnes, their unit had been stationed in a cellar under a jewelry and fur shop. There was much talk about not leaving anything for the Germans to loot, and first thing Bridges knew, he had turned looter himself. Now his pack and gas cape were filled with wristwatches, bracelets, and a twelve-pelt silver fox cape.

The two men waded into the sea, Bridges trying to help Martin and hang onto his riches at the same time. Somehow they reached the lifeboat, which turned out to be in the charge of a white-haired, fatherly-looking brigadier, still wearing all his ribbons and red trim. He was skillfully maneuvering the boat about, picking up strays here and there. Martin was hauled aboard, and Bridges prepared to follow.

"You'll have to drop your kit, Sergeant," the brigadier sang out. Every inch of space was needed for people. With a lack of hesitation that surprised even himself, Bridges let it all go— bracelets, watches, jewelry, furs, and perhaps most important, the load on his conscience.

Pulled aboard, he took an oar, and with the brigadier steering, they gradually approached a destroyer lying not far away. Planes began strafing, and the man rowing next to Bridges was hit. They crawled on, and were almost there when an officer on the ship called out to stay clear. She was stuck on a sandbar, running her screws full speed ahead to get free.

The brigadier tried, but whether it was tide, current, suction, or plain inexperience, they were relentlessly drawn to the side of the ship. A rising swell caught Bridges's oar against the hull, and through some play of physics he could never hope to understand, he was catapulted upward, clear out of the boat. He caught hold of a grid, which served as a ship's ladder, and willing hands hauled him on board.

Next instant the lifeboat plunged down again and was caught under the racing screws. The boat, the brigadier, Martin, and everyone else were chewed to bits. Bridges looked back in time to catch a brief, last glimpse of Martin's startled face as it disappeared beneath the sea.

He sank to the deck, leaning against the bulkhead. The destroyer turned out to be the *Ivanhoe*, and as Bridges began stripping off his wet clothes, a sailor brought him a blanket and a pack of cigarettes. He did not have much time to enjoy them. Once again the sound of aircraft engines warned of new danger from the skies.

The German bombers had arrived. Luckily, the *Ivanhoe* had at last wriggled free of the sandbar, and Commander P. H. Hadow was able to dodge the first attacks, delivered by level-bombing Heinkels. No such luck with the Stukas. At 7:41 a.m. two near misses bracketed the ship, and a third bomb crashed into the base of the forward funnel.

Down in the boiler room Private J. B. Claridge, who had been plucked from the sea at La Panne, was drying out his uniform when the ship gave a violent shudder, the lights went out, and a shower of burning embers fell about him. He was standing near a ladder to the deck, and he raced up through a cloud of swirling steam. He and another man were the only two to get out alive.

Sergeant Bridges watched from his resting place against the bulkhead. He was still stunned by his own ordeal, but he was alert enough to note that the *Ivanhoe*'s crew were beginning to take off their shoes. That could only mean they thought the ship was sinking.

He needed no better proof. Slipping off his blanket, he went over the side, naked except for his helmet, which he always managed to keep. He swam slowly away from the ship, using a sort of combination breast-and-side stroke that he especially favored. He could keep it up forever—or at least until some ship appeared that looked like a better bet than the *Ivanhoe*.

But the *Ivanhoe* was not finished. The fires were contained; the foremost magazine flooded; and the damaged boilers sealed off. Then the destroyer *Havant* and the minesweeper *Speedwell* eased alongside and removed most of the troops. As *Speedwell* pulled away, she picked up one more survivor swimming alone in the sea. It was Sergeant Bridges.

On the *Ivanhoe* the engineering officer Lieutenant Mahoney coaxed some steam out of his one remaining boiler, as the ship started back to England. Creeping along at seven knots, assisted by a tug, she made an ideal target and was twice attacked by the Heinkels. Each time, Commander Hadow waited until the first bombs fell, then lit smoke floats inside various hatches to simulate hits. The ruse worked: both times the planes flew off, apparently convinced that the destroyer was finished.

On the *Havant*, the troops transferred from the *Ivanhoe* barely had time to settle down before the Stukas pounced again. Two bombs wrecked the engine room, and a third landed just ahead of the ship, exploding as she passed over it.

The lights went out, and once again hundreds of soldiers thrashed about in the dark, trying to get topside. *Havant* took a heavy list, compounding the confusion. But once again help lay close at hand. The minesweeper *Saltash* came alongside, taking off some troops. Others transferred to a small pleasure steamer, the *Narcissa*, which used to make holiday cruises around Margate.

The crew of the *Havant* stayed on for a while, but for her there was no clever escape. The hull was ruptured, the engine room blown to bits. At 10:15 a.m. *Havant* vanished into the sea.

"A destroyer has blown up off Dunkirk," someone laconically observed on the bridge of the destroyer *Keith* lying off Bray-Dunes. Admiral Wake-Walker looked and saw a ship enveloped in smoke just off Dunkirk harbor, six miles to the west. At the time he didn't know it was the *Ivanhoe*—or that she would survive. He only knew that the German bombers were back on the job, and might be coming his way next. It would be hard to miss the concentration of ships working with the *Keith* off Bray: the destroyer *Basilisk*, minesweepers *Skipjack* and *Salamander*, tugs *St. Abbs* and *Vincia*, and the skoot *Hilda*.

Sure enough, a compact formation of 30 to 40 Stukas appeared from the southwest. Every gun in the fleet opened up, and a curtain of fire seemed to break up the formation. But not for long. Shortly before 8:00 a.m. three Stukas came hurtling down, right at the *Keith*.

The ship heeled wildly. In the wheelhouse everyone was crouching down, with the helmsman steering by the bottom spokes of the wheel. Teacups skidded across the deck. Then three loud explosions, the nearest just ten yards astern. It jammed the helm, and the *Keith* began steering in circles.

Captain Berthon switched to manual steering, and things were beginning to get back to normal, when three more planes dived. This time Wake-Walker saw the bombs released and watched them fall, right at the ship. It was an odd sensation waiting for the explosion and knowing that he could do nothing. Then the crash ... the teeth-rattling jolt ... a rush of smoke and steam boiling up somewhere aft.

Surprisingly, he could see no sign of damage. It turned out that one of the bombs had gone right down the second funnel, bursting in the No. 2 boiler room far below. Power gone, plates sprung, *Keith* listed sharply to port.

Not far away, Lieutenant Christopher Dreyer watched the hit from his motor torpedo boat *MTB 102*; he hurried over to help. Wake-Walker decided he was doing no good on the crippled

Keith, and quickly shifted to Dreyer's boat. It was the Admiral's eighth flagship in twenty-four hours.

On the *Keith*, now wallowing low in the water, Captain Berthon gave the order to abandon ship. Scores of men went over the side, including most of General Gort's staff. Colonel Bridgeman was sure of only one thing: he didn't want to swim back to La Panne. He splashed about, finally joined two sailors clinging to a piece of timber. Eventually they were picked up by the tug *Vincia* and taken to Ramsgate.

The Stukas were far from finished. About 8:20 they staged a third attack on the *Keith*, hitting her again in the engine room, and this time they saved something for the other ships nearby. The minesweeper *Salamander* escaped untouched, but her sistership *Skipjack* was a different story. The leader of the German flight scored two hits; then a second Stuka came roaring down. On the range-finder platform Leading Seaman Murdo MacLeod trained his Lewis gun on the plane and kept firing even after it released its bombs. The Stuka never came out of its dive, plunging straight into the sea.

But the damage was done—three more hits. *Skipjack* lurched heavily to port, and the order came to abandon ship. It was none too soon. In two more minutes *Skipjack* turned turtle, trapping most of the 250 to 300 troops aboard. She floated bottom-up for another twenty minutes, then finally sank.

The *Keith* lingered on, attended by a typically mixed assortment of small craft picking up survivors. After a fourth visit from the Stukas, the Admiralty tug *St. Abbs* came alongside around 8:40 and took off Captain Berthon and the last of the crew. Before leaving, Berthon signaled *Salamander* and *Basilisk* to sink the ship, lest she fall into enemy hands.

Both vessels replied that they were out of control and needed help themselves. Concentrating on his own ship, Berthon apparently didn't see the Stukas pounding the other two. *Basilisk* especially was in a bad way. A French trawler took her in tow, but she grounded on a sandbar and had to be abandoned around noon. The destroyer *Whitehall* picked up most of her crew, then finished her off with a couple of torpedoes.

Meanwhile the Stukas staged still another attack on the abandoned *Keith*—the fifth of the morning—and at 9:15 they finally sank her. The sea was now covered with fuel from sunken ships, and the surviving swimmers were a pathetic sight—coated black with oil, half-blind, choking and vomiting as they tried to stay afloat.

The tug *St. Abbs* poked about picking them up, twisting and turning, using every trick in the book to shake off the Stukas. Besides survivors from the sunken ships, she took aboard Major R.B.R. Colvin and a boatload of Grenadier Guards trying to row back to England. About 130 men jammed the tug's deck— some dreadfully wounded, others unhurt but sobbing with fright. An army doctor and chaplain passed among them, dispensing first aid and comfort. As the bombs continued to rain down, the padre told Major Colvin, "I have never prayed so hard before."

Eventually the Stukas moved off, and *St. Abbs* steamed briefly in peace. Then at 9:30 a single level-bomber passed overhead, dropping a stick of four delayed-action bombs right in the tug's path. They went off as she passed over them, tearing her bottom out.

Knocked down by the blast, Major Colvin tried to get up, but one leg was useless. Then the ship heeled over, and everything came crashing down. He felt he was falling into a bottomless pit, pushed along by rushing water, surrounded by falling coal. Next thing he knew, he was swimming in the sea some 50 yards from a lot of wreckage. *St. Abbs* was gone, sunk in just 30 seconds.

There were only a few survivors. Most had originally been on the *Keith* or *Skipjack*; this was their second sinking of the morning. This time they found themselves struggling against a strong tide that carried them along the coast, almost due east. They would soon be in German-held waters, but there seemed nothing they could do about it. Suddenly they saw a chance. A wrecked steamer lay directly in the way. The more agile swimmers managed to get over to her.

Passing under the stern, Major Colvin grabbed a gangway hanging in the water, and despite his bad leg, he pulled himself aboard. The wreck turned out to be the cargo liner *Clan Mac-Alister*, bombed and abandoned on May 29. She now lay partially sunk and hard aground about two miles off La Panne.

Some fifteen other survivors of *St. Abbs* also reached the hulk. Climbing aboard, they found themselves in a setting worthy of the legendary *Mary Celeste*. In the deserted deckhouse everything was still in place. Some sailors helped Major Colvin into a bunk, found him a couple of blankets and a set of dry clothes.

Midshipman H. B. Poustie of the *Keith* did even better. Covered with oil, he wandered into the captain's cabin and found the perfect uniform for an eighteen-year-old midshipman: the captain's dress blues, resplendent with four gold rings around the sleeves.

There was food too. Exploring the galley, someone came up with a light luncheon of canned pears and biscuits. To the tired and hungry survivors, it seemed like a feast.

The big question was: What next? Clearly they couldn't stay here much longer. It was ebb tide, and the *Clan MacAlister* now stood high out of the water on an even keel. From the air she looked undamaged, and the planes bombed her vigorously. Soon, the enemy artillery would be in La Panne, a stone's throw away.

One of the ship's boats still hung in the davits, and Captain Berthon—late of the *Keith* and senior officer present—ordered it loaded with provisions and lowered. With luck, they could row to England.

They were just about to start when a Thames lighter hove into view. She looked like a far better bet, and the castaways attracted her attention with yells and pistol shots. The lighter transferred them to a cement carrier so lowly she had no name—just Sheerness Yard Craft No. 63. She was, however, staunch enough to get them home.

On the beach west of La Panne, the 1st Suffolks had a grandstand view of the Stuka attack on the *Basilisk*. Still farther west, on a dune near Zuydcoote, the staff of the 3rd Grenadier Guards watched the *Keith*'s ordeal. All the way west, the sailors on the mole saw another swarm of Stukas sink the French destroyer *Foudroyant* in less than a minute. Captain Tennant himself watched the assault on the *Ivanhoe* and *Havant*.

There was something distant and unreal about it all—especially the battles in the sky that erupted from time to time. Any number of separate vignettes were frozen in the men's minds, like snapshots in an album: the thunderclap of a fighter and bomber colliding . . . a plane's wing fluttering to earth . . . the flash of flame as a Heinkel caught fire . . . the power drive of an Me 109, right into the sea . . . parachutes floating down . . . tracers ripping into the parachutes. It was hard to believe that all this was actually happening, and not just the familiar scenes from some old war film.

To Squadron Leader Brian Lane and the fighter pilots of No. 19 Squadron it was very real indeed. On June 1 their working day began at 3:15 a.m. at Hornchurch, a small field east of London. Still half-asleep, they gulped down tea and biscuits and hurried out onto the tarmac, where the Spitfires were already warming up. The roar of the engines rose and fell as the mechanics made final adjustments, and the exhaust flames still burned bright blue in the first light of the new day.

Lane climbed aboard his plane, checked his radio and oxygen, made sure that the others were ready, and waved his hand over his head—the signal to take off. Once airborne, he listened for the double thump that meant his wheels were up, and cast a practiced eye over the various dials and gauges that made up his instrument panel. It looked as though he had been doing this all his life; actually he had been a civilian making electric light bulbs until a short time before the war.

In fifteen minutes he was crossing the English coast, heading out over the North Sea. A glance at his mirror showed the other planes of the squadron, properly spaced behind him, and behind them were three more squadrons—48 Spitfires altogether—roaring eastward toward the sunrise and Dunkirk.

Ten more minutes, and they were over the beaches, bearing left toward Nieuport, the eastern limit of the patrol. It was 5:00 a.m. now, light enough to see the crowds waiting on the sand, the variety of vessels lying offshore. From 5,000 feet it looked like Blackpool on a bank holiday.

Suddenly the Spitfires no longer had the sky to themselves. Ahead and slightly to the right, flying toward Nieuport on a converging course, twelve twin-engine planes appeared. Lane flicked on his radio: "Twelve Me 110's straight ahead."

The Germans saw them coming. On both sides the neatly spaced formations vanished, replaced by the general melee that so reminded the men on the ground of something concocted by Hollywood. Lane got on the tail of a Messerschmitt, watched it drift into his sights, and pressed the firing button that controlled his eight machine guns. Eight streams of tracer homed in on the 110. Its port engine stopped. Then, as it turned to get away, he got in another burst, this time knocking out the starboard engine. He hung around long enough to watch it crash.

That job done, Lane searched for more targets, but could find nothing. His tanks only had enough petrol for 40 minutes over the beaches, and now he was getting low. Flying close to the water, he headed back across the Channel and home to Hornchurch. One by one the other members of the squadron came in too, until finally all were present and accounted for.

As they excitedly swapped experiences on the tarmac, the squadron intelligence officer toted up the score—7 Me 110's claimed; also 3 Me 109's, which had apparently turned up at some point during the free-for-all. Slowly the pilots drifted into the mess. It was hard to believe, but it was still only 7:00 a.m. and they hadn't even had breakfast yet.

It's worth noting that this aerial battle did not follow the standard script. Usually a very few British fighters took on a very great number of German planes, but this time the Spitfires actually outnumbered the Me 110's, four to one.

This was no coincidence. It was part of a tactical gamble. Originally Fighter Command had tried to provide continuous cover over the beaches, but the few planes available were spread so thin, the result was virtually no protection at all. On May 27, for instance, 22 patrols were flown, but the average strength was only eight planes. The Luftwaffe easily smothered this effort and devastated the port of Dunkirk.

After that disaster the RAF flew fewer patrols, but those flown were much stronger. There was also extra emphasis on the hours when the beachhead seemed most vulnerable—dawn and dusk. Hence the 48-plane patrol led by Brian Lane, and he in turn was followed by another patrol of similar strength.

But the total number of planes always remained the same—Air Marshal Dowding wouldn't give an inch on that, for he was already thinking ahead to the defense of Britain herself. As a result, there were inevitably certain periods when there was no protection at all, and on June 1 the first of these periods ran from 7:30 a.m. to 8:50 a.m.—that harrowing hour and twenty minutes when the *Keith* and her consorts were lost.

By 9:00 a new patrol was on the line, and the German attacks tapered off, but there were four more periods during the day when the RAF could provide no fighter cover, and the Luftwaffe cashed in on them all. Around 10:30 a.m. bombs crippled the big railway steamer *Prague* and turned the picturesque river gunboat *Mosquito* into a blazing wreck.

Then it was the Channel packet *Scotia*'s turn. As she slowly capsized, 2,000 French troops managed to climb the deck against the roll, ending up perched on her hull. The destroyer *Esk* plucked most of them to safety. No such luck with the French destroyer *Foudroyant*. Hit during another gap in fighter protection, she turned over and sank in seconds.

The carnage continued. During the afternoon a 500-pound bomb landed on the deck of the minesweeper *Brighton Queen*, killing some 300 French and Algerian troops—about half the number aboard. Later the destroyer *Worcester* and the minesweeper *Westward Ho* were badly damaged but managed to get home. *Westward Ho* had 900 French troops aboard, including a general and his staff. When she finally reached Margate, the general was so overjoyed, he decorated two members of the crew with the Croix de Guerre on the spot.

Seventeen ships sunk or knocked out of action. That was the Luftwaffe's score this June 1. All day the human residue—the hollow-eyed survivors, the pale wounded on stretchers, the ragged bundles that turned out to be bodies—were landed on the quays of Dover, Ramsgate, and other southeast coast towns. The effect was predictable on the men whose ships happened to be in port.

At Folkestone the crew of the railway steamer *Malines* were especially shaken by the ordeal of the *Prague*. The two vessels belonged to the same line, and there was a close association between the crews. Some of the *Malines*'s men were already survivors of a ship sunk at Rotterdam, and *Malines* herself had been heavily bombed there. After two hard trips to Dunkirk she was now at Folkestone waiting for coal, when nerves began to crack. The ship's doctor certified that three engineers, the wireless operator, the purser, a seaman, and several engine room hands were all unfit for duty.

Malines was ordered to Dunkirk again on the evening of June 1, but with the crew on the edge of revolt, her captain refused to go. He was supported by the masters of two other steamers also at Folkestone, the Isle of Man packets *Ben-My-Chree* and *Tynwald*. They too refused to go, and when the local naval commander sent a written inquiry asking whether *Ben-My-Chree* would sail, her skipper simply wrote back, "I beg to state that after our experience in Dunkirk yesterday, my answer is 'No.' "

Trouble had been brewing for some time, particularly among the larger packets and passenger steamers. They were still manned by their regular crews and managed by their peacetime operators. These men had no naval training whatsoever, nor much of that special *élan* that the weekend sailors and other volunteers brought to the job.

As early as May 28 the steamer *Canterbury* refused to sail. She had been there twice, and that was enough. The Dynamo Room finally put a naval party aboard to stiffen the crew. This worked, and a hurried call was made to Chatham Barracks for 220 seamen and stokers. They would form a pool of disciplined hands, ready for duty on any ship where the crew seemed to be wavering.

When the *St. Seiriol* refused to sail on the 29th, an officer, armed guard, and seven stokers went on board at 10:00 a.m., and the ship left at 11:00. On the packet *Ngaroma* the engineers were the problem. They were quickly replaced by two Royal Navy stokers, and an armed party of six hands was added for good measure. *Ngaroma* went back to work.

But these were individual cases. The dismaying thing about *Malines*, *Tynwald*, and *Ben-My-Chree* was that the three ships seemed to be acting in concert. A hurried call was sent to Dover for relief crews and armed guards, but it would be some hours before they arrived. All through the night of June 1–2 the three ships—each able to lift 1,000 to 2,000 men—lay idle.

Other men were losing heart too. When the tug *Contest* was commandeered at Ramsgate for a trip to Dunkirk, the crew deliberately ran her aground. Refloated, the engineer refused to put to sea, claiming his filters would be blocked by sand.

Off Bray-Dunes, Admiral Wake-Walker signaled another tug to help a stranded minesweeper. The skipper paid no attention, wanted only to get away. Wake-Walker finally had to train a gun on him and send a navy sub-lieutenant to take charge.

There was also trouble with the vessels of the Royal National Lifeboat Institution. The boat from Hythe flatly refused to go at all. The coxswain argued that he had been asked to run his boat onto the beach, and once aground he could never get off. He would not try at Dunkirk what he could not do at Hythe—apparently ignoring the fact that at Dunkirk the tide would do it for him.

He managed to talk the Walmer and Dungeness boats out of going too. In disgust the Navy then took over the whole RNLI fleet, except the Ramsgate and Margate craft. They had already sailed for Dunkirk with their own crews.

These lifeboat crews were no sniveling cowards. The coxswain of the Hythe boat had been risking his life in the service for 37 years, 20 of them in charge of the boat. He had won the Institution's silver medal for gallantry. Yet there was something different about Dunkirk—the continuing danger, the inability to control events, the reality of being under fire. Such factors could undermine the resolve of even the staunchest men.

Nor was the Royal Navy immune. There was a tendency to feel that "it can't happen here," that naval training and discipline somehow insulated a man from the fear and uncertainty that beset civilian hearts. Yet this was not necessarily so. Morale on the destroyer *Verity*, shaky since May 27, seemed to collapse after a trip to Dunkirk on the 30th. Twelve men broke out of the ship, with six still absent on the 31st. Those who returned simply explained they couldn't "stand it" any longer. *Verity* was ordered to remain in Dover harbor.

Acute fear could be like a disease—both physical and highly contagious. The minesweeper *Hebe* was hit perhaps worst of all. She had been a sort of command ship off Bray-Dunes; few of the crew slept for five days. On the evening of May 31 the ship's sub-lieutenant collapsed, going into fits and convulsions. Next day, 27 members of the crew came down the same way. Finally, as *Hebe* returned to Dover on the morning of June 1, the ship's surgeon collapsed too, mumbling that he could not face another trip to Dunkirk.

Rest was the answer, but rest was a luxury they couldn't have. After especially grueling trips the *Malcolm* and the *Windsor* did get a day off, but usually the ships just kept going. The main hope for relief came from the steady stream of new vessels and fresh hands that kept pouring in.

The Navy continued to comb its lists, searching for officers who could be borrowed from other duties. Commander Edward K. Le Mesurier was assigned to the aircraft carrier *Formidable*, building at Belfast. Important, but he could be spared for a week. He arrived at Ramsgate at noon, June 1, and by 5:30 he was on his way to Dunkirk. He found he had exchanged carrier duty for command of a tug, a launch, and five rowboats.

Sub-Lieutenant Michael Anthony Chodzko was a young reserve officer attending navigational school at Plymouth. Buried in his books, he didn't even know there was serious trouble until he was yanked out of class on May 31 and sent by train to Dover. Then, as the train ran along the chalk cliffs just before the station, he glanced out the car window and saw gunfire across the Channel. It was his first inkling of what lay ahead. Next morning, June 1, he was heading for Dunkirk with his first command—a small cabin cruiser called the *Aura*.

David Divine wasn't in the Navy at all. He was a free-lance writer and amateur sailor who naturally gravitated to Dover at the end of May, because that's where the big story was. Like the other journalists in town, he would stand in the grass that crowned the white cliffs and focus his binoculars on the incredible procession of vessels pouring across the Channel. But unlike the others, the sea ran in his blood, and the more he watched, the more he wanted to be part of this show.

It wasn't hard to join. Through his naval writing he had plenty of contacts at the Admiralty, and by May 31 he had the necessary papers that put him in the Navy for 30 days. He went to Ramsgate, looked over the mass of small craft now piling up in the harbor, and picked out for himself a small motor sailor called the *Little Ann*. With no formal assignment whatsoever, he jumped aboard and began getting her ready for sea. He was soon joined by a kindred soul—Divine never learned his name—and the two of them, with a couple of others, set out for Dunkirk early on June 1.

Charles Herbert Lightoller was another man who liked to do

things his own way. No stranger to danger, he had been Second Officer on the *Titanic*, where his coolness helped save countless lives that famous night. Now he was 66, retired from the sea, raising chickens in Hertfordshire, but he still had that combination of courage and good humor that served him so well in 1912.

And he still enjoyed life afloat. His 58-foot power cruiser *Sundowner* had been carefully designed to his exact specifications, and he liked nothing better than an occasional jaunt up and down the Thames with a party of friends. Once he even had 21 people aboard.

It was 5 p.m. on May 31 when Lightoller got a cryptic phone call from a friend at the Admiralty, requesting a meeting at 7:00 that evening. It turned out that the Navy needed *Sundowner* at once. Could he get her from the yacht basin at Chiswick down to Ramsgate, where a Navy crew would take over and sail her to Dunkirk?

Whoever had that idea, Lightoller bristled, had another guess coming. "If anybody is going to take her over, my eldest son and I will."

They set out from Ramsgate at 10 on the morning of the 1st. Besides Lightoller and his son Roger, they also had aboard an eighteen-year-old Sea Scout, taken along as a deck hand. Halfway across they encountered three German fighters, but the destroyer *Worcester* was near and drove them away. It was just as well, because *Sundowner* was completely unarmed, not even a tin hat aboard.

Midafternoon, they were off Dunkirk. It was ebb tide, and as he drew alongside the eastern mole, Lightoller realized that the drop was too great from the walkway to *Sundowner*'s deck. The troops would never be able to manage it. Instead, he berthed alongside a destroyer that was already loading, and his troops crossed over from her. He loaded *Sundowner* from the bottom up, with Roger in charge below decks.

No one ever tackled such an unglamorous assignment with more verve than Roger. To lower the center of gravity, he made the men lie down whenever possible. Then he filled every inch of space, even the bath and the "head."

"How are you getting on?" Lightoller called below, as the tally passed 50.

"Oh, plenty of room yet," Roger airily replied. At 75 he finally conceded he had enough.

Lightoller now shifted his efforts to the open deck. Again, the
troops were told to lie down and stay down, to keep the ship
more stable. Even so, by the time 50 more were aboard, Lightoller could feel *Sundowner* getting tender. He called it a day and
started for home.

The entire Luftwaffe seemed to be waiting for him. Bombing
and strafing, the enemy planes made pass after pass. Fortunately *Sundowner* could turn on a sixpence, and Lightoller had
learned a few tricks from an expert. His youngest son, killed in
the first days of the war, had been a bomber pilot and often
talked about evasion tactics. The father now put his lost son's
theories to work. The secret was to wait until the last instant,
when the enemy plane was already committed, then hard rudder before the pilot could readjust. Squirming and dodging his
way across the Channel, Lightoller managed to get *Sundowner*
back to England without a scratch.

Gliding into Ramsgate at 10 that night, he tied up to a trawler
lying next to the quay. The usual group of waterfront onlookers
drifted over to watch. All assumed that the 50 men on deck
would be *Sundowner*'s full load—an impressive achievement in
itself. But troops continued to pour out of hatches and compan-
ionways until a grand total of 130 men were landed. Turning to
Lightoller, an astonished bystander could only ask, "God's
truth, mate! Where did you put them?"

So the evacuation went on. Despite bombs and frayed nerves,
64,429 men were returned this June 1. They ranged from the
peppery General Montgomery to Private Bill Hersey, who also
managed to embark his French bride, Augusta, now thinly disguised in British battle dress. The number lifted off the beaches
fell as the troops pulled back from La Panne, but a record
47,081 were rescued from Dunkirk itself. The eastern mole continued to survive the battering it took from bombs, shells, and
inept shiphandling.

At 3:40 p.m. the small minesweeper *Mare* edged toward the
mole, hoping to pick up one more load of British soldiers waiting on the long wooden walkway. Nothing unusual about that,
but then something happened that was completely unprece-
dented. The captain of a British destroyer lying nearby ordered

Mare to proceed instead to the western mole and embark French and Belgian troops. For the first time a British ship was specifically diverted from British to Allied personnel.

Mare crossed the harbor and found a Portsmouth steam hopper and drifter already working the western mole. Three more minesweepers joined in, and between them the six ships lifted 1,200 poilus in little more than an hour.

Such endeavors helped produce statistics that were far more significant than any single incident: on June 1 a total of 35,013 French were embarked, as against 29,416 British. At last Winston Churchill had some figures he could take to Paris without embarrassment. For the Royal Navy, *bras-dessus, bras-dessous* had become an accomplished fact.

All morning the top command at London, Dover, and Dunkirk watched the pounding of the rescue fleet with growing alarm. Around noon Admiral Drax of The Nore Command at Chatham called the Admiralty's attention to the mounting destroyer losses. The time had come, he suggested, to stop using them during daylight. Ramsay reluctantly agreed, and at 1:45 p.m. flashed the message, "All destroyers are to return to harbour forthwith."

The *Malcolm* was just starting out on one more trip across the Channel. No ship had better morale, but even Lieutenant Mellis's bagpipes were no longer enough to lift the men's spirits. The air was full of stories about sinking ships, and the general feeling was that *Malcolm* would get it next. Then, as she cleared the breakwater, Ramsay's message arrived, ordering her back. Mellis felt he now knew how a reprieved prisoner feels.

The *Worcester* was just entering Dunkirk harbor, and her skipper, Commander Allison, decided it didn't make sense to return without picking up one more load at the mole. Packed with troops, she finally pulled out at 5:00 p.m. and immediately came under attack. Wave after wave of Stukas dived on her— three or four squadrons of about nine each—dropping more than 100 bombs. They pressed their attacks home, too, diving as low as 200 to 300 feet. Miraculously, there were no direct hits, but near misses sent giant columns of water over the ship, and bomb splinters riddled her thin steel plates. By the time the attacks tapered off, 46 men lay dead, 180 wounded.

Watching *Worcester*'s ordeal from his command post at the foot of the mole, Captain Tennant decided this was enough. At 6:00 p.m. he radioed Ramsay:

> Things are getting very hot for ships; over 100 bombers on ships here since 0530, many casualties. Have directed that no ships sail during daylight. Evacuation by transports therefore ceases at 0300. . . . If perimeter holds, will complete evacuation tomorrow, Sunday night, including most French. . . .

But *could* the perimeter hold another day? London had its doubts. "Every effort must be made to complete the evacuation tonight," General Dill had wired Weygand at 2:10 p.m. At 4 o'clock Winston Churchill warned Reynaud by telephone that the evacuation might be stretched out a day longer, but "by waiting too long, we run the risk of losing everything." As late as 8:00 p.m. Ramsay sent a ringing appeal to his whole rescue fleet, calling for "one last effort."

At Dunkirk General Alexander originally felt the same way, but by now he wanted more time. He was determined to get the rest of the BEF home, yet on the morning of June 1 there were still 39,000 British troops in the perimeter, plus 100,000 French. Applying the equal numbers policy, that meant lifting at least 78,000 men in the next 24 hours—obviously impossible.

At 8:00 a.m. he dropped by Bastion 32 with a new withdrawal plan, extending the evacuation through the night of June 2–3. Admiral Abrial gladly went along: the French had always had greater confidence than the British in holding the perimeter. Toward evening Captain Tennant agreed too. There was no alternative once he made the decision to end daylight operations.

London still had its doubts, but in the end the chairborne warriors at the Admiralty and War Office had to face an unpleasant truth: they just didn't know enough to make the decision. At 6:41 General Dill wired Alexander:

> We do not order any fixed moment for evacuation. You are to hold on as long as possible in order that the maximum number of French and British may be

evacuated. Impossible from here to judge local situation. In close cooperation with Admiral Abrial you must act in this matter on your own judgment.

So Alexander now had a green light. The evacuation would continue through the night of June 2–3, as he and Captain Tennant proposed. But success still depended on Tennant's precondition: "*if* the perimeter holds." This was a very big "if" and the answer lay beyond the control of the leaders in London, Dover, or Dunkirk itself.

13

"BEF Evacuated"

On the 2nd Coldstream Guards' segment of the defense line along the Bergues-Furnes Canal, Lieutenant Jimmy Langley waited in the cottage he had so carefully fortified and stocked with provisions. He had no idea when the British planned to pull out—company officers weren't privy to such things—but his men were ready for a long siege. In the first light of the new day, June 1, Langley looked through the peephole he had made in the roof, but could see nothing. A thick mist hung over the canal and the flat meadows to the south.

Sunrise. The mist burned off, and there—600 yards away on the other side of the canal—stood a working party of German troops. There were perhaps 100 of them, armed only with spades, and what their assignment was, Langley never knew. A blaze of gunfire from the cottage mowed them down—the last "easy" Germans he would meet that day.

The firing steadily increased as the enemy troops joined in. At one point they wheeled up an antitank gun, and Langley watched with interest as they pointed it right at his cottage. A few seconds later an antitank shell came crashing through the roof, ricocheting wildly about the attic. The Coldstreamers tumbled down the stairs and out the front door as four more shells arrived. The enemy fire slackened off, and Langley's men reoccupied their fortress.

The big danger lay to the right. At 11:00 a.m. General von Kuechler launched his "systematic attack," and around noon the enemy stormed across the canal just east of Bergues. The 1st East Lancashires were forced back and might have been overrun completely but for the prodigious valor of a company commander, Captain Ervine-Andrews. Gathering a handful of volunteers, he climbed to the thatched roof of a barn and held off the Germans with a Bren gun.

Just to the left of the East Lancs were the 5th Borderers. Now across the canal in strength, the enemy smashed at them too. If they collapsed, the 2nd Coldstream, to their left, would be hit next. An officer from the Borderers hurried over to Major McCorquodale's command post to warn that his battalion was exhausted and about to withdraw.

"I order you to stay put and fight it out," the Major answered.

"You cannot do that. I have overriding orders from my colonel to withdraw when I think fit."

McCorquodale saw no point in arguing: "You see that big poplar tree on the road with the white milestone beside it? The moment you or any of your men go back beyond that tree, we will shoot you."

The officer again protested, but the Major had had enough. "Get back or I will shoot you now and send one of my officers to take command."

The Borderer officer went off, and McCorquodale turned to Langley, standing nearby: "Get a rifle. Sights at 250. You will shoot to kill the moment he passes that tree. Are you clear?"

McCorquodale picked up a rifle himself, and the two Cold-streamers sat waiting, guns trained on the tree. Soon the Borderer officer reappeared near the tree with two of his men. They paused, then the officer moved on past McCorquodale's deadline. Two rifles cracked at the same instant. The officer fell, and Langley never knew which one of them got him.

Such measures weren't enough. The 5th Borderers fell back, leaving the Coldstream's flank wide open. Jimmy Langley's fortified cottage soon came under fire. The afternoon turned into a jumble of disconnected incidents: knocking out a German gun with the much-despised Boyes antitank rifle . . . washing down a delicious chicken stew with white wine . . . using the Bren guns in the attic to set three German lorries on fire, blocking the canal road for precious minutes. At one point an old lady appeared from nowhere, begging for shelter. Langley told her to go to hell; then, overcome by remorse, he put her in a back room where he thought she might be safe.

Another time he went to the battalion command post to see how McCorquodale was getting along. The Major was lying beside his trench, apparently hit. "I am tired, so very tired," he told Langley. Then, "Get back to the cottage, and carry on."

By now the Germans had occupied a house across the canal from Langley's place, and the firing grew more intense than ever. In the attic one of the Bren guns conked out, and Langley ordered the other downstairs. It would be more useful there, if the enemy tried to swim the canal and rush the cottage. Langley himself stayed in the attic, sniping with a rifle.

Suddenly a crash . . . a shower of tiles and beams . . . a blast of heat that bowled Langley over. In the choking dust he heard a small voice say, "I've been hit"—then realized that the voice was his own.

It didn't hurt yet, but his left arm was useless. A medical orderly appeared, slapped on a dressing, and began bandaging his head. So that had been hit too. He was gently carried down from the attic, put into a wheelbarrow, and trundled to the rear—one of the few Coldstreamers small enough to make an exit this way.

By now it was dark, and the battle tapered off. Firmly established across the canal, Kuechler's infantry settled down for the night. Resumption of the "systematic attack" could wait until morning. The British began quietly pulling back to the sea. It was all very precise: each battalion took along its Bren guns and Boyes antitank rifles. The 2nd Hampshires marched by their commander, closed up in three's, rifles at the slope. Most positions were abandoned by 10:00 p.m.

As the gunners of the 53rd Field Regiment marched cross-country toward Dunkirk, a sharp challenge broke the silence of the night, followed by a blaze of rifle fire. French troops, moving into defensive positions along the network of waterways that laced the area, had mistaken them for Germans.

No one was hit; the mix-up was soon straightened out; and the British gunners continued on their way, but with new respect for their ally. These Frenchmen were all business. Part of the 32nd Infantry Division, they had escaped with their corps commander, the feisty General de la Laurencie, from the German trap at Lille. Together with the local garrison troops of the *Secteur Fortifié des Flandres*, they were now taking over the center of the perimeter from the retiring BEF.

At the same time, the French 12th Division, which had also escaped from Lille, was moving into the old fortifications that lined the Belgian frontier. Dug in here, they would cover the eastern flank of the new shortened defense line. Since General Beaufrère's 68th Division had always defended the west flank, the entire perimeter was now manned by the French.

It was hard to believe that only yesterday, May 31, Winston Churchill had emotionally told the Allied Supreme War Council that the remaining British divisions would form the rear guard so that the French could escape. Since then there had been, bit by bit, a complete turn-around. Instead of the British acting as rear guard for the French, the French were now acting as rear guard for the British.

Later the French would charge that the switch was yet another trick by "perfidious Albion." Actually, the British weren't all that pleased by the arrangement. They had little faith left in their ally. As the 5th Green Howards pulled back through the French guarding the new defense line along the Belgian border, Lieutenant-Colonel W. E. Bush collected his company officers and paid a courtesy call on the local French commander. The real purpose was not to cement Allied unity, but to see whether the French were up to the job. They turned out to be first-rate troops under a first-rate officer.

These French had their first test on the afternoon of the 1st, as Kuechler's "systematic attack" cautiously approached from the east. General Janssen's 12th Division stopped the Germans cold.

All the way west it was the same story. The Germans had some armor here—the only tanks that hadn't gone south—but General Beaufrère's artillery, firing over open sights, managed to hold the line.

Covered by the French, the remaining British units converged on Dunkirk all through the night of June 1–2. As the 6th Durham Light Infantry trudged through the ruined suburb of Rosendaël, the steady crunch of the men's boots on broken glass reminded Captain John Austin of marching over hard ice crystals on a cold winter's day. It was a black, moonless night, but the way was lit by burning buildings and the flash of exploding shells. The German infantry might be taking the night off, but not their artillery. The DLI's hunched low, as against a storm, their steel helmets gleaming from the light of the flames.

Admiral Ramsay's ships were already waiting for them. Lifting operations were to run from 9:00 p.m. to 3:00 a.m. but when the first destroyer reached the mole, few of the troops had arrived from the perimeter. Those who came down from Bray-Dunes were mostly huddled in the houses and hotels along the beach promenade, seeking cover from the rain of shells.

Commander E. R. Condor couldn't see anybody at all when he brought the destroyer *Whitshed* alongside the mole soon after dark. Just smoke, flames, and a few dogs sniffing around. Spotting a bicycle lying on the walkway, Condor mounted it and pedaled toward shore looking for somebody to rescue. Eventually he found some poilus, and then some Tommies near the base of the mole. He sent them all out, along with a few other troops who now began to appear.

At 10:30 p.m. Major Allan Adair led out the 3rd Grenadier Guards, still carrying their Bren guns; they boarded the Channel steamer *Newhaven* . . . at 11:00 hundreds of French joined the crowd, and for a while the troops moved out four abreast— unconsciously symbolizing the troubled alliance . . . at 12:00 the gunners of the 99th Field Regiment marched out to the destroyer *Winchelsea*. Occasional shells prodded them along. "I've been hit," the man next to Sergeant E. C. Webb quietly remarked, dropping out of line.

"Hand out the wounded". . . "Lay out the dead". . . "Wounded to the front" . . . "Watch the hole." The sailors of the shore party kept up a running stream of orders and directions as they guided the troops along. An effort was made to keep a lane open for the stretcher bearers, but there was no time for the dead. They were simply pushed off the mole onto the pilings below.

It was after midnight when the 1st/6th East Surreys finally

reached the mole. There was a long queue now, and the wait stretched into hours. The mole itself was so packed that the line barely moved, and the East Surreys were still inching forward when word came at 2:00 a.m. that the last two ships of the night were alongside—a big paddle steamer, and just ahead of her a destroyer. It was almost 3:00 by the time the East Surreys reached the paddle steamer. Deciding there was no time to lose, the battalion commander Colonel Armstrong quickly divided his men in two, sent the first half up ahead to the destroyer, and ordered the rear-guard half to go aboard the steamer. A few East Surreys were still waiting to embark, when the cry went up, "No more!" Armstrong emphatically pushed the last men down the gangway, then slid down himself as the vessel cast off.

The 5th Green Howards were halfway down the mole at 3:00. They had spent most of the night coming down from Bray-Dunes. It was only six miles, but the sand, the darkness, their utter weariness all slowed them down, and they took nearly five hours to make the march. Now, mixed in with other British units and a great horde of French, they slowly moved along the walkway, with frequent stops that nobody could explain. It was during one of these halts when the word came down, "No more boats tonight. Clear the mole!"

Bitterly disappointed, the Green Howards turned back, only to run headlong into other troops who hadn't gotten the word yet. For a while there was much pushing and shoving, and all movement came to a standstill. At this point a salvo of German shells landed squarely on the base of the mole, mowing down scores of men.

If Commander Clouston had been on hand, things might have gone more smoothly, but he had returned to Dover for the night. He had served as pier master for five days and nights without a break—had sent off over 100,000 men—now he wanted to confer with Ramsay about the last, climactic stage of the evacuation, and perhaps get a good night's sleep.

While the destroyers and Channel steamers lifted troops off the mole, Ramsay's plan called for the minesweepers and smaller paddle-wheelers to work the beach just to the east, going as far as Malo-les-Bains. Thousands of British and French soldiers stood in three or four queues curling into the sea as far as a man could wade. Gunner F. Noon of the 53rd Field Regiment waited for two full hours, while the water crept over his ankles . . . his knees . . . his waist . . . and up to his neck. Then, as the first trace of dawn streaked the eastern sky, somebody shouted, "No more! The ships will return tonight!"

The 2nd Coldstream Guards was another unit to reach the harbor late. After their long stand on the canal, the men were bone-tired, but they still had their Brens. As they moved down the paved promenade at Malo-les-Bains, they marched in perfect step, arms swinging. Most of the waiting troops watched in awe and admiration, but not all. "I'll bet that's the bloody Guards," called a caustic voice in the dark. "Try marching on tiptoes!"

One Coldstreamer who wasn't late was Lieutenant Jimmy Langley. Groggy from his wounds, he was vaguely aware of being trundled from the battlefield by wheelbarrow and loaded into an ambulance. The ride was one of those stop-and-go affairs that seem to take forever. He still felt no pain, but he was thirsty and dreadfully uncomfortable. Blood kept dripping onto his face from the man above him.

At last the ambulance stopped, and Langley's stretcher was lifted out. "This way," somebody said. "The beach is 200 yards ahead of you."

The stretcher party reached the water's edge. A ship's lifeboat lay waiting, rubbing gently against the sand. An officer in a naval greatcoat came over and asked Langley, "Can you get off your stretcher?"

"No, I don't think so."

"Well, I'm very sorry, we cannot take you. Your stretcher would occupy the places of four men. Orders are, only those who can stand or sit up."

Langley said nothing. It was hard to be turned back after coming so close, but he understood. The stretcher bearers picked him up and carried him, still silent, back to the ambulance.

About this time another Coldstreamer, Sergeant L.H.T. Court, joined one of the queues on the beach. Attached to 1st Guards Brigade HQ, he was carrying the brigade war diary, an imposing volume inscribed on a stack of Army Forms C 2118.

As he slowly moved forward into the sea, Court found his mind absorbed by three things: his bride of less than a year; his brother, just killed in Belgium; and the mountain of Forms C 2118 he was trying to save.

As the water reached his chest, he once again thought about his young wife. They had no children yet, and if he didn't return she'd have nothing to remember him by. This lugubrious thought was interrupted by his sudden discovery that some of the Forms C 2118 were floating away. A good headquarters man to the end, he put aside all else, and frantically splashed around retrieving his files.

Eventually Court neared the front of the queue, where a naval launch was ferrying men to a larger vessel further out. Then, at 3:00 a.m. a voice called out from the launch that this was the last trip, but added that there would be another boat later on. Court continued waiting, but no other boat ever came. Some of the men turned back toward the shore, but Court and a few others waded over to a grounded fishing smack lying nearby. He was hauled aboard, still clutching the brigade war diary.

The tide was coming in, and around 4:30 the boat began to move. By now some 90 to 100 men were aboard, most of them packed in the hold where the fish were normally put. A few knowledgeable hands hoisted the sails, and a course was set for England. But there was no wind, and nearly twelve hours later they were still only a mile and a half from Dunkirk. At this point a passing destroyer picked them up, including Court and the lovingly preserved papers.

There were others, too, who weren't inclined to wait eighteen hours for the Royal Navy to come back the following night. Thirty-six men of the 1st Duke of Wellington's Regiment took over a sailing barge appropriately called the *Iron Duke*. Colonel L. C. Griffith-Williams salvaged another stranded barge, loaded it with artillerymen, and set off for Britain. He knew nothing about navigation, but he found a child's atlas and a toy compass aboard. That would be enough. When a patrol boat later intercepted them, they were heading for Germany.

While the more adventuresome improvised ways to escape, most of the troops trudged back to the shore to wait out the eighteen hours. They passed the time in a variety of ways. It was now Sunday, June 2, and some men joined a chaplain celebrating Holy Communion on the beach at Malo-les-Bains. Ted Harvey, a fisherman stranded when his motor launch conked out, joined an impromptu soccer game. The 4th/7th Royal Dragoon Guards enjoyed motorcycle races in the sand and bet on which waterfront building would be hit by the next German shell.

But the most important game was to stay alive. Most of the waiting troops crowded into any place that seemed to offer the faintest hope of shelter. One group settled down in the shattered hulk of the French destroyer *l'Adroit*, lying just off Malo. Wrecked though she was, her twisted steel seemed to offer a measure of security. Others picked an old watchtower left over from Napoleon's time; its thick stone walls also seemed to promise safety.

Others packed the cellars of nearby buildings. The remnants of the 53rd Field Regiment chose the Café des Fleurs—flimsy, but it was right on the *plage*. Headquarters of the 5th Green Howards was established at 22 rue Gambetta, a comfortable house about a block from the beach. Here the battalion also adopted a stray poilu, who made right for the kitchen. True to the great tradition of his country, he soon produced a superb stew of beef and wine. Promptly christened "Alphonse," he was made an honorary member of the battalion and from now on sported a British tin hat.

The 5th Green Howards offered something very rare at Dunkirk: a sizable body of organized troops, complete with their own officers and accustomed to working together. Recalling the chaos at the mole when the loading stopped the previous dawn, the battalion commander Lieutenant-Colonel W. E. Bush decided the Green Howards had a useful role to play during the coming night, June 2–3. They would form a cordon to control the traffic and insure an orderly flow of men to the ships as they arrived. Four officers and 100 men should be enough to do the job. Those selected would, of course, be last off and might very well be left behind. The officers drew lots for the honor.

Plans for the evening were moving ahead at Dover too. Early in the morning Admiral Wake-Walker came over by MTB from Dunkirk. After a couple hours' rest, he attended a joint naval and military conference in the Dynamo Room. No one knew how many troops were left to be evacuated, but Wake-Walker gave an educated guess of 5,000 British and anywhere from 30,000 to 40,000 French.

Fortunately there were plenty of ships on hand. The suspension of daylight evacuation made it possible to collect virtually the whole fleet at Dover and the other southeast ports. Ramsay planned to use this vast concentration for what he called a "massed descent" on Dunkirk harbor. All troops to leave from Dunkirk itself; no more lifting from the beaches. Embarkation to start at 9:00 p.m. and continue until 3:00 a.m. Staggered sailings to insure a steady flow of ships. Three or four vessels to be alongside the mole continuously. Slow vessels to start first; fast ones later, to keep the flow even.

Captain Denny argued that the plan was too complicated—it would only result in confusion. It would be better simply to send everything over, and let the men on the spot work the details out. But most of the staff felt the scheme was worth trying.

As finally worked out, the plan provided for enough large ships to lift 37,000 men, plus whatever number might be picked up by the small craft that continued to ply across the Channel. In addition, the French would be using their own ships to lift troops from the beach just east of the mole, and from the west pier in the outer harbor. That should finish the job, and at 10:52 a.m., June 2, Ramsay signaled his whole command:

> The final evacuation is staged for tonight, and the Nation looks to the Navy to see this through. I want every ship to report as soon as possible whether she is fit and ready to meet the call which has been made on our courage and endurance.

"Ready and anxious to carry out your order" ... "Fit and ready"—the replies were bravely Nelsonian. But beneath the surface, most of the rescuers felt like Sub-Lieutenant Rutherford Crosby on the paddle-sweeper *Oriole*. His heart sank when he heard they were going back again. He thought the evacuation was all over. Ramsay had said as much yesterday, when he called for "one last effort."

But, like Crosby, most of the others soon resigned themselves to facing another desperate night. "We were going," he later wrote, "and that was all there was to it."

Not everyone agreed. The three passenger steamers at Folkestone—*Ben-My-Chree, Malines,* and *Tynwald*—continued to give trouble. Most of the day they were kept anchored in the harbor, but at 6:50 p.m. *Ben-My-Chree* came alongside the jetty to be readied for the night's work. The crew lined the rails, demonstrating and shouting that they were going to leave the ship. When they tried to go ashore a couple of minutes later, they were turned back by an armed naval guard advancing up the gangplank with fixed bayonets. A relief crew quickly took over, and *Ben-My-Chree* finally sailed at 7:05. Only the chief officer, three gunners, and the wireless operator remained from the original crew.

Then it was *Tynwald*'s turn. Her crew didn't try to leave, but as she docked at 7:10 p.m., they hooted and shouted down at the naval sentries. At 7:30 she was still sitting at the pier.

Meanwhile, nobody had paid any attention to the *Malines*. At 4:30 p.m she quietly weighed anchor, and without any authorization whatsoever, stood off for Southampton. Her master later explained, "It seemed in the best interests of all concerned."

There was, in fact, good reason for the civilian crews on these Channel steamers to be afraid. They were virtually unarmed and presented the biggest targets at Dunkirk. If any further proof were needed, it was supplied by a series of incidents that began at 10:30 on the morning of June 2. At this time the Dynamo Room received an urgent message from Captain Tennant in Dunkirk:

> Wounded situation acute. Hospital ship should enter during the day. Geneva Convention will be honourably observed. It is felt that the enemy will refrain from attack.

The plight of the wounded had been growing steadily worse for several days, aggravated by the decision to lift only fit men in the regular transports. Now Tennant was trying to ease the situation with this special appeal for hospital ships. He had, of course, no way of knowing whether the enemy would respect the Red Cross, but he sent the message in clear, hoping that the Germans would intercept it and order the Luftwaffe to lay off.

The Dynamo Room swung into action right away, and at 1:30 p.m. the hospital ship *Worthing* started across the Channel. Gleaming white and with standard Red Cross markings, it was impossible to mistake her for a regular transport. But that didn't help her today. Two-thirds of the way across, *Worthing* was attacked by a dozen Ju 88's. No hits, but nine bombs fell close enough to damage the engine room and force her back to Dover.

At 5:00 p.m. the hospital ship *Paris* sailed. She got about as far as the *Worthing*, when three planes tore into her. Again no hits, but near misses started leaks and burst the pipes in the engine room. As *Paris* drifted out of control, Captain Biles swung out his boats and fired several distress rockets. These attracted fifteen more German planes.

The Dynamo Room sent tugs to the rescue and continued preparing for the coming night's "massed descent." With so many vessels involved, it was essential to have the best men possible controlling traffic and directing the flow of ships and men. Fortunately the best was once again available. Commander Clouston, fresh from a night's rest, would once more be pier master on the mole. To help him, Captain Denny assigned an augmented naval berthing party of 30 men. Sub-Lieutenant Michael Solomon, whose fluent French had been a godsend to Clouston since the 31st, would again serve as interpreter and liaison officer.

The Clouston party left Dover at 3:30 p.m. in two RAF crash boats: *No. 243*, with the Commander himself in charge, and *No. 270*, commanded by Sub-Lieutenant Roger Wake, an aggressive young Royal Navy regular. They were going well ahead of the other ships in order to get Dunkirk organized for the night's work.

It was a calm, lazy afternoon, and as the two boats droned across an empty Channel, the war seemed far away. Then suddenly Lieutenant Wake heard "a roar, a rattle, and a bang." Startled, he looked up in time to see a Stuka diving on Clouston's boat about 200 yards ahead. It dropped a bomb—missed—then opened up with its machine guns.

No time to see what happened next. Seven more Stukas were

plunging on the two motor boats, machine guns blazing. Wake ordered his helm hard to port, and for the next ten minutes played a desperate dodging game, as the Stukas took turns bombing and strafing him. In an open cockpit all the way aft, Lieutenant de Vasseau Roux, a French liaison officer, crouched behind the Lewis machine gun, hammering away at the German planes. He never budged an inch—not even when a bullet took the sight off his gun six inches from his nose. One of the Stukas fell, and the others finally broke off.

Now at last Wake had a moment to see how Clouston's boat had weathered the storm. Only the bow was visible, and the whole crew were in the water. Wake hurried over to pick up the survivors, but Clouston waved him off . . . told him to get on to Dunkirk, as ordered. Wake wanted at least to pick up Clouston as senior officer, but the Commander refused to leave his men. There was no choice; Wake turned again for Dunkirk.

Clouston and his men continued swimming, clustered around the shattered bow of their boat. A French liaison officer clinging to the wreck reported an empty lifeboat floating in the sea a mile or so away. Sub-Lieutenant Solomon asked permission to swim over and try to bring it back for the survivors. Clouston not only approved; he decided to come along. This was their best chance of rescue, and Solomon alone might not be enough.

Clouston was a splendid athlete, a good swimmer, and confident of his strength. Perhaps that was the trouble. He didn't realize how tired he was. After a short while, he was exhausted and had to swim back to the others clinging to the wreck. Hours passed, but Solomon never returned with the empty boat. As the men waited, they sang and discussed old times together, while Clouston tried to encourage them with white lies about the nearness of rescue. One by one they disappeared, victims of exposure, until finally Clouston too was gone, and only Aircraftsman Carmaham remained to be picked up alive by a passing destroyer.

Meanwhile Sub-Lieutenant Solomon had indeed reached the empty boat. He too was exhausted, but after a long struggle managed to climb aboard. He did his best to row back to the wreck, but there was only one oar. After an hour he gave up: the boat was too large, the distance too far; and it was already dark.

He drifted all night and was picked up just before dawn by the French fishing smack *Stella Maria*. Wined, rested, and wearing a dry French sailor's uniform, he was brought back to Dover and transferred to the French control ship *Savorgnan de Brazza*. His story sounded so far-fetched he was briefly held on suspicion of being a German spy. Nor did his fluent French help him any. *"Il prétend de 'être anglais,"* the French commander observed, *"mais moi je crois qu'il est allemand parce qu'il parle français trop bien."* In short, he spoke French too well to be an Englishman.

An hour and a half after Clouston's advance party left Dover on the afternoon of June 2, Ramsay's evacuation fleet began its "massed descent" on Dunkirk. As planned, the slowest ships led the way, leaving at 5 p.m. They were mostly small fishing boats—like the Belgian trawler *Cor Jésu*, the French *Jeanne Antoine*, and the brightly painted little *Ciel de France*.

Next came six skoots ... then the whole array of coasters, tugs, yachts, cabin cruisers, excursion steamers, and ferries that by now were such a familiar sight streaming across the Channel ... then the big packets and mail steamers, the minesweepers and French torpedo boats ... and finally, kicking up great bow waves as they knifed through the sea, the last eleven British destroyers of a collection that originally totaled 40.

The Southern Railway's car ferry *Autocarrier* was a new addition. Lumbering along, she attracted a lot of attention, for in 1940 a car ferry was still a novelty in the cross-Channel service. The Isle of Man steamer *Tynwald* wasn't new, but in her own way she was conspicuous too. At Folkestone her crew had balked at making another trip. Now here she was, steaming along as though nothing had happened.

It hadn't been easy. Learning of the trouble, Ramsay sent over Commander William Bushell, one of his best troubleshooters. The Commander arrived to find *Tynwald* tied up at the quay, her crew in rebellion. Dover's instructions were a masterpiece of practical psychology: Bushell was on no account to consider himself in command of the ship, but was to make whatever changes were necessary to get her to Dunkirk. The chief officer relieved the master ... the second relieved the chief ... a new second was found ... other substitutes were rushed down from London by bus ... naval and military gun crews were added. At 9:15 p.m. *Tynwald* was on her way.

More than ever the ships were manned by a crazy hodge-podge of whoever was available. The crew of the War Department launch *Marlborough* consisted of four sub-lieutenants, four stokers, two RAF sergeants, and two solicitors from the Treasury who had come down on their day off. David Divine, the sea-going journalist, left the *Little Ann* stranded on a sand bar, hitched a ride home, shopped around Ramsgate for another boat, found a spot on the 30-foot motor launch *White Wing*.

"Where do you think you're going?" a very formal, professional-looking naval officer asked, as *White Wing* prepared to shove off.

"To Dunkirk," Divine replied.

"No you're not," said the officer, as Divine wondered whether he had broken some regulation. After all, he was new at this sort of thing. But the explanation had nothing to do with Divine. *White Wing*, of all unlikely vessels, had been selected as flagship for an admiral.

Rear-Admiral A. H. Taylor, the Maintenance Officer at Sheerness Dockyard, had now serviced, manned and dispatched over 100 small craft for "Dynamo." He was a retired officer holding down a good desk job in London; he had every reason to go back feeling he had done his bit—so he went to Ramsgate and wangled his way across the Channel.

There was a rumor that British troops were still at Malo-les-Bains, somewhat blocked off from the mole. Taylor quickly persuaded Ramsay that he should lead a separate group of skoots and slow motor boats over to Malo and get them. He picked *White Wing* for himself; so it was that almost by accident David Divine became an "instant flag lieutenant" for a genuine admiral.

At 9:30 p.m. Captain Tennant's chief assistant, Commander Guy Maund, positioned himself with a loudhailer at the seaward end of the eastern mole. As the ships began arriving, he became a sort of "traffic cop," ordering them here and there, wherever they were needed. Admiral Taylor's flotilla was directed to the beach at Malo, but there was nobody there. His ships then joined the general rescue effort centered on the mole. As Denny had predicted, it was impossible to draw up a detailed blueprint at Dover; Maund used his own judgment in guiding the flow of ships.

The mole itself got first call. As the destroyers and Channel steamers loomed out of the dusk, Maund gave them their berthing assignments. A strong tide was setting west, and the ships had an especially difficult time coming alongside. Admiral Wake-Walker, hovering nearby in the speedboat *MA/SB 10*, used her as a tug to nudge one of the destroyers against the pilings. At the base of the mole, Commander Renfrew Gotto and Brigadier Parminter, imperturbable as ever, regulated the flow of troops onto the walkway. The Green Howards, bayonets fixed, formed their cordon as planned, keeping the queues in order. There was plenty of light from the still-blazing city.

Shortly after 9:00 the last of the BEF started down the mole. Lieutenant-Colonel H. S. Thuillier, commanding the one remaining antiaircraft detachment, spiked his seven guns and guided his men aboard the destroyer *Shikari*. The 2nd Coldstream Guards filed onto the destroyer *Sabre*, still proudly carrying their Bren guns. With only a handful of men left, the Green Howards dissolved their cordon and joined the parade. The last unit to embark was probably the 1st King's Shropshire Light Infantry.

These last detachments ignored the order to leave behind their casualties. On the *Sabre* there were only fourteen stretcher cases, but over 50 wounded were carried aboard by their comrades. Commander Brian Dean, *Sabre*'s captain, never heard a complaint "and hardly ever a groan."

In the midst of the crowd streaming onto the mole walked two officers, carrying a suitcase between them. One was a staff officer, worn and rumpled like everyone else. The other looked fresh, immaculate in service dress. Calm as ever, General Alexander was leaving with the final remnants of his command. By prearrangement the *MA/SB 10* was waiting, and Admiral Wake-Walker welcomed the General aboard. They briefly checked the beaches to make sure all British units were off, then headed for the destroyer *Venomous*, still picking up troops at the mole.

Commander John McBeath of the *Venomous* was standing on his bridge when a voice from the dark hailed him, asking if he could handle "some senior officers and staffs." McBeath told them to come aboard, starboard side aft.

"We've got a couple of generals now—fellows called Alexander and Percival," Lieutenant Angus MacKenzie reported a few minutes later. He added that he had put them with a few aides in McBeath's cabin, "but I'm afraid one of the colonels has hopped into your bed with his spurs on."

Venomous pulled out about 10:00 p.m., packed with so many troops she almost rolled over. McBeath stopped, trimmed ship, then hurried on across the Channel. At 10:30 the destroyer *Winchelsea* began loading. As the troops swarmed aboard, Commander Maund noticed they were no longer British—just French. To Maund that meant the job was over, and he arranged with *Winchelsea*'s captain to take him along on the trip back to Dover.

Captain Tennant also felt the job was done. At 10:50 he loaded the last of his naval party onto the speedboat *MTB 102*; then he too jumped aboard and headed for England. Just before leaving, he radioed Ramsay a final signal: "Operation completed. Returning to Dover." Boiled down by some gifted paraphraser to just the words, "BEF evacuated," Tennant's message would subsequently be hailed as a masterpiece of dramatic succinctness.

Sub-Lieutenant Roger Wake was now the only British naval officer on the mole. With Tennant, Maund, and the other old hands gone—and with Clouston lost on the way over—Wake became pier master by inheritance, and it was not an enviable assignment. He was short-handed, and he was only a sub-lieutenant—not much rank to throw in a crisis.

At the moment it didn't make much difference. The mole was virtually empty. The British troops had left, and there were no French. "Plenty of ships, cannot get troops," Wake-Walker radioed Dover at 1:15 a.m. In two hours it would be daylight, June 3, and all loading would have to stop. Time was flying, but half a dozen vessels lay idle alongside the deserted walkway.

"Now, Sub, I want 700. Go and get them," Lieutenant E. L. Davies, captain of the paddle-sweeper *Oriole*, told Sub-Lieutenant Rutherford Crosby, as they stood together on the mole wondering where everybody was. Crosby headed toward shore, ducking and waiting from time to time, whenever a shell sounded close. At last, near the base of the mole, he came to a mass of poilus. There was no embarkation officer in sight; so he summoned up his schoolboy French. *"Venez ici, tout le monde!"* he called, gesturing them to follow him.

The way back led past another ship berthed at the mole, and her crew did their best to entice Crosby's group into their own vessel, like carnival barkers at a country fair. The rule was "first loaded, first away," and nobody wanted to hang around Dunkirk any longer than necessary. Crosby made sure none of his charges strayed—let the other crews find their own Frenchmen.

They were trying. Captain Nicholson, substitute skipper of the *Tynwald*, walked toward the shore, shouting that his ship could take thousands. The *Albury* too sent out ambassadors, hawking the advantages of the big minesweeper. She eventually rounded up about 200.

But other ships could find no one. The car ferry *Autocarrier* waited nearly an hour under heavy shelling . . . then was sent home, her cavernous interior still empty. It was the same with the destroyers *Express*, *Codrington*, and *Malcolm*. Wake-Walker kept them on hand as long as he dared; but as dawn approached, and still no French, they went back empty too.

Where were the French anyhow? To a limited extent it was the familiar story of the ships not being where the men were. As Walker made the rounds on *MA/SB 10*, he could see plenty of soldiers at the Quai Félix Faure and the other quays and piers to the west, but very few ships. He tried to direct a couple of big transports over there, but that was a strange corner of the harbor for Ramsay's fleet. When the steamer *Rouen* ran hard aground, the Admiral didn't dare risk any more.

There were still the little ships, and Wake-Walker deployed them to help. The trawler *Yorkshire Lass* penetrated deep into the inner harbor, as far as a vessel could go. Her skipper Sub-Lieutenant Chodzko had lost his ship the previous night, but that didn't make him any more cautious now. Smoke and flames were everywhere—buildings exploding, tracers streaking across the sky—as *Yorkshire Lass* ran alongside a pier crowded with Frenchmen. Chodzko called on the troops to come, and about 100 leapt aboard . . . then three Tommies, somehow left behind . . . then, as *Yorkshire Lass* threaded her way out again, a Royal Navy lieutenant-commander, apparently from one of the naval shore parties.

A little further out, Commander H. R. Troup nudged the War Department's fast motor boat *Haig* against another pier. Troup was one of Admiral Taylor's maintenance officers at Sheerness, but he too had wangled a ship for this big night. He picked up 40 poilus, ferried them to a transport waiting outside the harbor, then went back for another 39.

By now every kind of craft was slipping in and out, plucking troops from the various docks and quays. Collisions and near collisions were the normal thing. As *Haig* headed back out, a French tug rammed her. The hole was above the waterline; so Troup kept on. Two hundred yards, and *Haig* was rammed again by another tug. As Troup transferred his soldiers to the minesweeper *Westward Ho*, he was swamped when the minesweeper suddenly reversed engines to avoid still another collision. Troup now scrambled aboard *Westward Ho* himself, leaving *Haig* one more derelict in Dunkirk harbor.

Forty men here, 100 there, helped clear the piers, but most of the French weren't in Dunkirk at all. They were still on the perimeter, holding back General von Kuechler's "systematic attack." To the east the 12th Division fought all day to keep the Germans out of Bray-Dunes. Toward evening General Janssen was killed by a bomb, but his men fought on. Southeast, flooding held the enemy at Ghyvelde. In the center, Colonel Menon's 137th Infantry Regiment clung to Teteghem. Southwest at Spycker, two enterprising naval lieutenants commanded three 155 mm. guns, blocking the road for hours. All the way west, the 68th Division continued to hold General von Hubicki's panzers. A French observer in the church tower at Mardyck had an uncanny knack of catching the slightest German movement.

Corporal Hans Waitzbauer, radio operator of the 2nd Battery, 102nd Artillery Regiment, was exasperated. The battery had been promised Wiener schnitzel for lunch, but now here they were, pinned down by that sharp-eyed fellow in the church tower.

Waitzbauer, a good Viennese, wasn't about to give up his Wiener schnitzel that easily. With Lieutenant Gertung's permission, he darted back, leaping from ditch to ditch, to the company kitchen. Then, with his pot of veal in both hands, a bottle of red wine in his trouser pocket, and half a loaf of white bread in each of his jacket pockets, he scurried back again. Shells and machine-gun bullets nipped at his heels all the way, but he made it safely and distributed his treasures to the battery. Lieutenant Gertung's only comment was, "You were lucky."

With Kuechler's men pinned down in the east and west, the key to the advance was clearly Bergues, the old medieval town that anchored the center of the French line. If it could be taken, two good roads ran directly north to Dunkirk, just five miles to the north.

But how to take it? The town was circled by thick walls and a moat designed by the great military engineer Vauban. For a defense conceived in the seventeenth century, it was amazingly effective in the 20th. A garrison of 1,000 troops was well dig in, and they were supported by strong artillery plus naval guns at Dunkirk. The RAF Bomber Command gave help from the air.

Kuechler had been trying to take the place for two days, and it was still a stand-off. On the afternoon of June 2 it was decided to try a coordinated attack using Stukas and specially trained shock troops drawn from the 18th Regiment of Engineers.

At 3:00 p.m. the Stukas attacked, concentrating on a section of the wall that seemed weaker than the rest. Nearby the engineers crouched with flame-throwers and assault ladders. At 3:15 the bombers let up, and the men stormed the wall, led by their commander Lieutenant Voigt. Dazed by the Stukas, the garrison surrendered almost immediately.

Bergues taken, the Germans pressed on north toward Dunkirk, capturing Fort Vallières at dusk. They were now only three miles from the port, but at this point French General Fagalde scraped together every available man for a counterattack. It was a costly effort, but he managed to stop the German advance. Toward midnight the weary poilus began disengaging and working their way to the harbor, where they hoped the rescue fleet was still waiting.

Kuechler did not press them. In keeping with his orders for the "systematic attack," he took no unnecessary risks, and the Germans did not usually fight at night anyhow. Besides, there was a feeling in the air that the campaign was really over. Outside captured Bergues, one unit of the 18th Division sat in the garden of a cottage "singing old folk-songs, soldier-songs, songs of love and home." General Halder spent a good part of the day distributing Iron Crosses to deserving staff officers.

More than ever, all eyes were on the south. To the Luftwaffe, Dunkirk was now a finished story; it would be staging its first big raid on Paris tomorrow, June 3. Flying Officer B. J. Wicks, a Hurricane pilot shot down and working his way to the coast disguised as a Belgian peasant, noticed long columns of German troops—all heading south toward the Somme.

It was about 2:30 a.m. on the 3rd when the first of the French defenders, relieved from the counterattack, began filing onto the mole. Most of the ships had now gone back to Dover, but a few were still there. Sub-Lieutenant Wake struggled to keep order. He might lack rank, but he did have an unusual piece of equipment— a hunting horn.

It didn't do much good. The French seemed to know a thousand ways to slow down the embarkation. They tried to bring all their gear, their personal possessions, even their dogs. Many of them had inner tubes around their necks—improvised life preservers—and this bulky addition slowed them down even more. They invariably tried to crowd aboard the first boat they came to, rather than space themselves out over the full length of the mole. They insisted on keeping their units intact, never seemed to realize that they could be sorted out later in England. Right now the important thing was to get going before daylight.

Wake and his handful of seamen did their best, but his schoolboy French never rose to the occasion. What he really needed was someone like Clouston's assistant Michael Solomon, who was fluent in the language and could deal with the French officers. Lacking that, neither shouts of *"Allez vite"* nor blasts on the hunting horn could help. It was almost symbolic when some "damned Frenchman" (Wake's words) finally stepped on the horn and put it out of commission for good.

As it grew light, Admiral Wake-Walker—still patrolling in *MA/SB 10*—ordered all remaining ships to leave. The minesweeper *Speedwell* cast off; in an hour alongside the mole she had taken aboard only 300 French soldiers. Sub-Lieutenant Wake caught a small French fishing smack, and transferred to a large Channel steamer outside the harbor. The skoot *Hilda* lingered long enough for a final check of the beach at Malo— nobody there.

At 3:10, as the last ships pulled out, three new vessels slipped in. These were block ships, to be sunk at the harbor entrance under the direction of Captain E. Dangerfield. The hope was, of course, to deny the Germans future use of the port. But nothing seemed to go right this frustrating night. When the block ships were scuttled, the current caught one of them and turned it parallel to the Channel, leaving plenty of room to enter and leave.

"A most disheartening night," noted Admiral Wake-Walker on his return to Dover in the morning. He had hoped to lift over 37,000 men, actually got off only 24,000. At least 25,000 French—some said 40,000—were left behind. Wake-Walker tended to blame the French themselves for not providing their own berthing parties, but the British were the people used to running the mole. On May 31 Captain Tennant had, at Admiral Abrial's request, taken charge of both the British and French embarkation. It was asking a lot now to expect the French to take over on the spur of the moment.

To General Weygand sitting in Paris, it was a familiar story. Once again "perfidious Albion" was walking out, leaving the French to shift for themselves. Even before the night's misadventures, he fired off a telegram to the French military attaché in London, urging that the evacuation continue another night to embark the 25,000 French troops who were holding off the Germans. "Emphasize that the solidarity of the two armies demands that the French rearguard be not sacrificed."

Winston Churchill needed little convincing. He wired Weygand and Reynaud:

> We are coming back for your men tonight. Please ensure that all facilities are used promptly. For three hours last night many ships waited idly at great risk and danger.

In Dover at 10:09 on the morning of June 3, Admiral Ramsay signaled his command that their work was not over after all:

> I hoped and believed that last night would see us through, but the French who were covering the retirement of the British rearguard had to repel a strong German attack and so were unable to send their troops to the pier in time to be embarked. We

cannot leave our Allies in the lurch, and I call on all officers and men detailed for further evacuation to-night to let the world see that we never let down our Ally. . . .

On the destroyer *Malcolm* the morning had begun on a high note. She was just back from her seventh trip to Dunkirk, and was still in one piece. The last of the BEF had been evacuated, and everyone assumed that the operation was over. Breakfast in the ward room was a merry affair.

Lieutenant Mellis fell on his bunk hoping to catch up on his sleep. He was so tired he didn't even take his clothes off. Several hours later he was awakened by the sound of men's feet on the deck overhead. He learned that the crew was assembling for an important announcement by Captain Halsey, who had just returned from Ramsay's headquarters. Halsey came quickly to the point: "The last of the BEF was able to come off because the French took over the perimeter last night. Now the French have asked us to take them off. We can't do anything else, can we?"

No. But it was still a shock. For Mellis, it was the worst moment of the whole show. To enjoy that delicious feeling of relief and relaxation—and then to have it all snatched away—was almost more than he could stand. The ward room had planned a festive mess that evening, and decided to dress festively anyhow. When the *Malcolm* sailed on her eighth trip to Dunkirk at 9:08 p.m., June 3, her officers were wearing their bow ties and monkey jackets.

14

The Last Night

"If you've never seen any Germans, here they are." The announcement sounded strangely calm and detached to Edmond Perron, a minor Dunkirk official who had fled the blazing city with his family. The Perrons had found shelter on the farm of M. Wasel at Cappelle-la-Grande, a couple of miles to the south. As the fighting surged toward them, the Wasels and their guests retired to the stable for added protection. Now it was 3:00 p.m., June 3, and M. Wasel was peeking through the stable door and issuing bulletins on what he saw.

M. Perron peered out, too. Men in green uniforms covered the plain to the south—running . . . lying down . . . getting up . . . crouching . . . always advancing. But they did not come to the Wasel farm. Reaching its edge, they veered to the left to get around a water-filled ditch, then continued north toward Dunkirk.

General Lieutenant Christian Hansen's X Corps was closing in from the south. By 3:30 the 61st Division had passed the Wasel farm and occupied Cappelle itself. By evening the 18th Division, advancing from the southeast, had Fort Louis, an ancient landmark about a mile south of the port. Stukas helped reduce another little fort two miles to the east.

The French were also crumbling farther east. Colonel Menon's 37th Infantry were finally overwhelmed at Teteghem. By this time his 1st Battalion was down to 50 men. One machine gunner was working two guns, feeding them with scraps of ammunition picked up on the ground. Held up the better part of two days, the battered victors joined the other German units now converging on the port.

General Fagalde threw in everything he had left: the last of the 32nd Division . . . the coastal defense troops of the *Secteur Fortifié des Flandres* . . . the remains of the 21st Division Training Centre . . . his own *Gardes Mobiles*. Somehow he stopped them, although machine-gun bullets were now clipping the trees of suburban Rosendaël.

The end seemed very near to Sergeant Bill Knight of the Royal Engineers, who had somehow missed getting away with the last of the BEF. Now he was holed up in a cellar in Rosendaël with four other men from his unit. They had a truck, arms, plenty of food, but the German firing was so heavy that Knight felt they could never get to the harbor, even assuming the evacuation was still on.

The little party was pretty much resigned to surrender when two Belgian civilians, who had also taken cover in the cellar, began talking about slipping through the lines to their farms near the village of Spycker. Listening to them, an idea suddenly occurred to Knight: they might be cut off from the harbor, but why not go the other way? Why not slip through the encircling German Army and rejoin the Allies on the Somme?

A deal was quickly struck. Knight would give the Belgians transportation, if they would show him the little lanes and cow paths that might get them through the enemy lines unnoticed. Knight felt sure that the Germans were sticking to the main roads, and once through the cordon, it wouldn't be too hard to reach the Somme.

They set off at dusk, June 3, bouncing along the back streets that led southwest out of town. All night they continued driving, guided by the Belgians and by a road map picked up at a garage they passed.

Dawn on the 4th found them near Spycker. Here they dropped the two Belgians, and after a few final instructions continued heading southwest. They still used back roads, and when even these seemed dangerous, they lay low for a while in a field. Toward evening they had a lucky break. A German convoy appeared along the road, made up entirely of captured vehicles. They fell in behind, becoming the tail end of the convoy.

They made 20 to 25 miles this way, with only one narrow escape. A German motorcycle was escorting the convoy, and at one point it dropped back to make sure that none of the trucks were missing. Feeling that it would be just as jarring to find one truck too many, Knight slowed down, dropping far enough behind the convoy to appear to be no part of it. When the motorcycle returned to its regular position up front, Knight closed up again.

Wednesday, June 5, and the truck at last reached the Somme at Ailly. Here the British party had another break: a bridge still stood intact. It was not a highway bridge—just a cattle crossing—but it would do. Knight barreled across it into Allied lines.

No one else at Dunkirk was that enterprising. One and all believed that June 3 would be the last night, and at Bastion 32 the mood was heavy with gloom. There was no more fresh water; the medics had run out of bandages; communications were failing. "Enemy is reaching the outskirts," ran Abrial's last message, sent at 3:25 p.m. "I am having the codes burned, except for the M Code."

At 4:00 p.m. Admiral Ramsay's rescue fleet started out again. As before, the plan called for the big ships—the destroyers, the Channel steamers, the largest paddlers—to concentrate on the eastern mole. But this time the naval berthing party would be greatly strengthened. Commander Herbert James Buchanan would be in charge; four officers, fifty seamen, and several signalmen would be on hand. Four French officers were added to provide better communication. With luck, Ramsay hoped that 14,000 troops would be lifted off the mole between 10:30 p.m. and 2:30 a.m.

The minesweepers, skoots, and smaller paddle steamers would concentrate on the west pier, a shorter jetty just across from the mole, where crowds of French soldiers had waited in vain the previous night. This smaller flotilla should be able to take off another 5,000 men. The little ships—there were still scores of launches, motorboats, and small craft about—would again probe deep into the harbor where the larger vessels couldn't go. They would ferry the troops they found to the gunboat *Locust*, waiting just outside the port.

The ever-growing fleet of French trawlers and fishing smacks would take care of the Quai Félix Faure, cover the outer mole all the way west, and make a final check of Malo beach. These French boats were late arrivals, but now seemed to be everywhere.

All understood that this really would be the last night, and Ramsay tried to make sure of it with a strongly worded telegram to the Admiralty:

> After nine days of operations of a nature unprecedented in naval warfare, which followed on two weeks of intense strain, commanding officers, officers, and ships' companies are at the end of their tether. . . . If, therefore, evacuation has to be continued after tonight, I would emphasize in the strongest possible manner that fresh forces should be used for these operations, and any consequent delay in their execution should be accepted.

It was true, but hard to tell from the jaunty procession of vessels that once again streamed across the Channel. The destroyer *Whitshed* pulled out, her harmonica band playing on the foredeck. The cabin cruiser *Mermaiden* was manned by a sub-lieutenant, a stoker, an RAF gunner on leave, and a white-haired old gentleman who normally helped take care of Horatio Nelson's flagship *Victory* in Portsmouth. The motor launch *Marlborough* had lost her two solicitors—they only had the weekend off—but she boasted two equally dapper replacements: a retired colonel and an invalided army officer, said to be a crack shot with a Lewis gun.

The destroyer *Malcolm* looked especially dashing, with her officers dressed in their monkey jackets for the festive evening that never came off. The tug *Sun IV*, towing fourteen launches, was still skippered by Mr. Alexander, president of the tugboat company. The *MTB 102*, again carrying Admiral Wake-Walker, now sported a real admiral's flag—made from a red-striped dish cloth.

Wake-Walker arrived off the eastern mole at 10:00 p.m. and was relieved to find that tonight plenty of French troops were waiting. But once again the wind and the tide were against him, and he couldn't get alongside. When the *Whitshed* appeared at 10:20 with Commander Buchanan's berthing party, she had no better luck. The other ships too were unable to land, and a huge traffic jam built up at the entrance to the harbor.

Nearly an hour passed before Wake-Walker managed to get some lines ashore, and the berthing party was able to move into action. By 11:30 loading operations were under way, but a whole hour had been lost. What had been planned for four hours would have to be done in three.

Fortunately the Luftwaffe had turned its attention to Paris, and there was little shelling tonight. Many of the guns too had gone south, and Kuechler's advance was so close that his artillery were leery of hitting their own infantry. On the mole the British berthing party could hear machine-gun fire in the town itself. "*Vite, vite,*" a sailor shouted as the poilus tumbled aboard the *Malcolm*, "*Vite,* God damn it, *VITE!*"

Admiral Taylor's flotilla of small craft headed deeper into the harbor, to the Quai Félix Faure. The Admiral himself had gone ahead in the War Department's fast boat *Marlborough* to organize the loading. He understood there would be thousands of French waiting, but when he arrived, he found the quay deserted. Finally 300 to 400 French marines turned up and announced there was nobody else.

But they were enough, considering the size of Taylor's little ships. Most held fewer than 40 at a time. The *Mermaiden* was so crowded the helmsman couldn't see to steer. Directions had to be shouted over a babble of French voices.

As Taylor loaded the last of the marines, a German machine gun began chattering less than half a mile away. No more time to lose. Packing a final load into the *Marlborough*, he shoved off around 2:00 a.m. on the 4th. Dodging one of the many small craft darting about the harbor, *Marlborough* scraped over some fallen masonry and lost both her propellers and rudder. She was finally towed home by the large yacht *Gulzar*, piloted by a Dominican monk.

Mishaps multiplied. Nobody really knew the port, and the only light was from the flames consuming the waterfront. The Portsmouth Admiral's barge ran into a pile of rubble and was abandoned. . . .The trawler *Kingfisher* was rammed by a French fishing boat. . . .The minesweeper *Kellet* ran aground against the western breakwater. A tug towed her off, but she was too badly damaged to be of further use. Wake-Walker sent her home empty—one of only two ships not used this last hectic night.

The Admiral himself nipped about the harbor in *MTB 102*, busily juggling his fleet. The Quai Félix Faure was cleared . . . the eastern mole was under control . . . but the short jetty just west of the mole was a problem. The whole French 32nd Infantry Division seemed to be converging on it. At 1:45 a.m. Wake-Walker guided over a large transport, then the packet *Royal Sovereign* to help lift the crowd.

On the jetty, Commander Troup landed from the War Department's boat *Swallow*, took one look at the confusion, and appointed himself pier master. His chief problem was the usual one: the French troops refused to be separated from their units. Enlisting the help of a French staff officer, Captain le Comte de Chartier de Sadomy, Troup urged the poilus to forget their organization. In two hours they would all meet again in England. Take any boat. They seemed to understand: the big *Tynwald* came alongside, loaded 4,000 men in half an hour.

2:00 a.m., June 4, two small French torpedo boats, *VTB 25* and *VTB 26*, rumbled out of the harbor. Admiral Abrial and General Fagalde were leaving with their staffs. Behind them the massive steel doors of Bastion 32 now lay open and unguarded. Inside there was only a clutter of smashed coding machines and burnt-out candles.

2:25, gunboat *Locust*, stationed off the harbor mouth, received her last load of troops from Admiral Taylor's little ships. Her skipper, Lieutenant-Commander Costobadie, had done his duty, and it must have been a temptation to run for Dover. But he still had room; so he went instead to the eastern mole and topped off with another 100 men. Finally satisfied that *Locust* could hold no more, he headed for home.

2:30, the last French ships, a convoy of trawlers commanded by Ensign Bottex, emerged from the innermost part of the harbor. Packed with troops fresh from the fighting, he too turned toward Dover.

2:40, "heartened by bagpipes playing us out," the destroyer *Malcolm* slipped her lines at the eastern mole. Twenty minutes later the last destroyer of all, *Express*, left with a full load, including Commander Buchanan's berthing party.

3:00, French troops still crowded the short jetty just west of the mole. Commander Troup had been loading transports all night, but the jetty continued to fill up with new arrivals. Now the last big transport had gone, and Troup was waiting for a motorboat assigned to pick up himself, General Lucas of the French 32nd Division, and the general's staff at 3:00. The minutes ticked by, but no sign of the boat—not surprising on a night like this when a thousand things could go wrong.

Troup was beginning to worry, when at 3:05 the War Department's boat *Pigeon* happened by. She was miraculously empty, making a final swing through the harbor. Troup hailed her, and Sub-Lieutenant C. A. Gabbett-Mullhallen brought his craft alongside.

A thousand French soldiers stood at attention four deep, as General Lucas prepared to leave. Clearly they would be left behind—no longer a chance of escape—yet not a man broke ranks. They remained motionless, the light from the flames playing off their steel helmets.

Lucas and his staff walked to the edge of the pier, turned, clicked their heels, and gave the men a final salute. Then the officers turned again and made the long climb down the ladder to the waiting boat. Troup followed, and at 3:20 Sub-Lieutenant Gabbett-Mullhallen gunned his engines, quickly moving out of the harbor.

As these last ships left Dunkirk, they met a strange procession creeping in. Destroyer *Shikari* was in the lead. Following her were three ancient freighters, and flanking them were two speedboats, *MTB 107* and *MA/SB 10*. Captain Dangerfield was once again trying to bottle up the harbor by sinking block ships across the entrance. As the little flotilla moved into position, they were buffeted by the bow waves of the last ships racing out. Lieutenant John Cameron, skipper of the *MTB 107*, pondered the trick of fate that had brought him, "a settled barrister of 40," to be an actor in this awesome drama.

Suddenly an explosion. Enemy planes had apparently mined the channel—a parting present from the Luftwaffe. The first did no damage, but a second exploded under the leading block ship *Gourko*, sinking her almost instantly. As the two speedboats fished the survivors out of the water, the remaining block ships steamed on. But now there were only two of them, and the job would be that much harder.

While the block ships edged deeper into the harbor, *Shikari* paid a final visit to the eastern mole. It had been nearly empty when *Express* left, but now it was beginning to fill up again. Some 400 French troops tumbled aboard, including General Barthélémy, commanding the Dunkirk garrison. At 3:20 *Shikari* finally cast off—the last British warship to leave Dunkirk.

But not the last British vessel. Occasional motorboats were still slipping out, as Captain Dangerfield's two block ships reached the designated spot. With helms hard over, they attempted to line up at right angles to the Channel, but once again the tide and current were too strong. As on the previous night, the attempt was largely a failure. Hovering nearby, *MA/SB 10* picked up the crews.

Dawn was now breaking, and Lieutenant Cameron decided to take *MTB 107* in for one last look at the harbor. For nine days the port had been a bedlam of exploding bombs and shells, the thunder of artillery, the hammering of antiaircraft guns, the crash of falling masonry; now suddenly it was a grave-yard—the wrecks of sunken ships . . . abandoned guns . . . empty ruins . . . silent masses of French troops waiting hopelessly on the pierheads and the eastern mole. There was nothing a single, small motorboat could do; sadly, Cameron turned for home. "The whole scene," he later recalled, "was filled with a sense of finality and death; the curtain was ringing down on a great tragedy."

But there were still Englishmen in Dunkirk, some of them very much alive. Lieutenant Jimmy Langley, left behind because the wounded took up too much room in the boats, now lay on a stretcher at the 12th Casualty Clearing Station near the outskirts of town. The station—really a field hospital—occupied a huge Victorian house in the suburb of Rosendaël. Capped by an odd-looking cupola with a pointed red roof, the place was appropriately called the Chapeau Rouge.

The wounded had long ago filled up all the rooms in the house, then overflowed into the halls and even the grand staircase. Now they were being put into tents in the surrounding gardens. A French field hospital also lay on the grounds, adding to the crowd of casualties. The total number varied from day to day, but on June 3 there were about 265 British wounded at Chapeau Rouge.

Tending them were a number of medical officers and orderlies. They were there as the result of a curious but most fateful lottery. Even before the decision to leave behind the wounded, it had been clear that some would not be able to go. They were simply too badly hurt to be moved. To take care of them, orders had come down that one medical officer and 10 orderlies must be left behind for every 100 casualties. Since there were 200 to 300 wounded, this meant 3 officers and 30 orderlies would have to stay.

How to choose? Colonel Pank, the Station's commanding officer, decided that the fairest course was to draw lots, and at 2:00 p.m. on June 1 the staff gathered for what was bound to be a very tense occasion. Two separate lotteries were held—one among the 17 medical officers, the other among the 120 orderlies.

In each case all the names were put in a hat, and appropriately enough an English bowler was found in the cellar and used for this purpose. The rule was "first out, first to go"; the last names drawn would be those left behind. The Church of England chaplain drew for the enlisted men; the Catholic padre, Father Cockie O'Shea, drew for the officers.

Major Philip Newman, Chief of Surgery, listened to the drawing in agonized silence as the names were read out. Ten . . . twelve . . . thirteen, and still his name remained in the hat. As it turned out, he had good reason to fear: he was number seventeen of seventeen.

Later that afternoon a farewell service was held in the cupola. At the end Father O'Shea took Newman by the hand and gave him his crucifix. "This will see you home," the padre said.

One of those who stayed took no part at all in the lottery. Private W.B.A. Gaze was strictly a volunteer. An auctioneer and appraiser in peacetime, Gaze had been a machine gunner with a motor maintenance unit until the great retreat. Separated from his outfit, he had taken over an ambulance abandoned by its regular driver and was now a fixture at 12th CCS. The other men might know more about medicine, but he had skills of his own that came in handy at a time like this. He was a born scrounger, could fix anything, and had even located a new well, when Chapeau Rouge was running out of water. Major Newman regarded him as an "honorary member" of the unit, and Gaze reciprocated—of course he wasn't going to leave.

Most of the staff pulled out on the night of June 1. The 2nd was largely spent making futile trips to and from the docks, as false reports circulated that a hospital ship had arrived. That night a dispatch rider roared up with the news that walking wounded could be evacuated, if brought to the eastern mole. This last chance of escape was seized by many men who, under any normal definition, were stretcher cases. They rose from their cots and limped, hobbled, even crawled to the waiting trucks. One man used a pair of crutches made from a coal hammer and a garden rake.

June 3 was a day of waiting. The French troops were falling back, and Newman's main job was to keep them from occupying the house and using it for a last stand. A large red cross, made from strips of cloth, had been laid out on the lawn; the Luftwaffe had so far respected it; and Newman wanted to keep things that way. The French commandant seemed to understand. He didn't occupy the house, but he did continue digging on the grounds. Occasional shells began falling on the garden.

At dusk the French began pulling out, retiring still further into Dunkirk, and it was clear to everyone at Chapeau Rouge that the next visitors would be German. When, was anybody's guess, but the white German "victory rockets" were getting close.

While the wounded lay quietly on their cots and stretchers, the staff gathered in the basement of the house for a last dinner. They ate the best food they could find, topped off by some excellent red wine from the Chapeau Rouge cellar. Someone produced a concertina, but no one had the heart to sing.

Upstairs, Major Newman sought out a wounded German pilot named Helmut, who had been shot down and brought in several days earlier. It was clear to both that the roles of captor and captive were about to be reversed, but neither made much of it. What Newman did want was a crash course in German, to be used when the enemy arrived. Patiently Helmut taught him phrases like *Rotes Kreuz* and *Nichts Schiessen*—"Red Cross" ... "Don't shoot."

By midnight, June 3–4, the last French defenders had retired toward the docks, and there was nothing to do but keep waiting. As a sort of reception committee, Newman posted two enlisted men by the gate. An officer was stationed on the porch outside the front door. They had orders to call him as soon as the first Germans appeared. Then he laid out a clean uniform for the surrender and curled up on the stone floor of the kitchen for a few hours' sleep.

On the front steps Jimmy Langley lay on a stretcher just outside the front door. It was so hot and sticky—and the flies were so bad—he had asked to be moved into the open. He too was waiting, and even as he waited, he began thinking about what might happen next. He was a Coldstream Guards officer, and in the last war, the Coldstream were not known for taking prisoners. Had that reputation carried over? If so, there seemed a good chance that the Germans would pay him back in kind. He finally had a couple of orderlies carry his stretcher to a spot near the gate and set it down there. If he was going to be killed, he might as well get it over with.

15

Deliverance

"The Germans are here!" a voice was shouting, as an unknown hand shook Major Newman awake at 6 o'clock on the morning of June 4. Dead tired, Newman had been deeply asleep, even though lying on the stone floor of the kitchen at Chapeau Rouge. He gradually pulled himself together and began putting on the clean uniform he had laid out for the surrender.

Down near the gate Jimmy Langley lay on his stretcher watching a small party of German infantrymen enter the grounds. They might be about to kill him, but they looked as tired as the British. As they walked up the drive toward him, Langley decided his best chance lay in playing to the hilt the role of "wounded prisoner." Pointing to the Red Cross flag on the cupola, he gasped a request for water and a cigarette. The leader of the squad gave him both. Then Langley asked, a little tentatively, what would they like from him.

"*Marmelade,*" was the reply. For the first time Langley felt there was hope. No one about to kill him would be thinking primarily of marmalade.

Troops were pouring into the grounds now—some dirty and unkempt, but most freshly washed and cleanly shaven, the way Supermen should look. They fanned out over the yard, checking the tents and stretchers to make sure no armed Allied soldiers were still lurking about. "For you the war is over," a trooper curtly told Guardsman Arthur Knowles, lying wounded on his stretcher.

Satisfied that Chapeau Rouge met the standards of Geneva, the Germans relaxed and were soon mixing with their captives, swapping rations and sharing family pictures. Major Newman stood on the porch watching the scene, resplendent in his clean uniform but with no officer to take his surrender.

In two hours these Germans pushed on, replaced by administrative personnel who were far less friendly. The curious bond that sometimes exists between enemies at the front is rarely felt in the rear.

"*Wo das Meer?*" a departing infantryman asked Jimmy Langley, still lying on his stretcher. Langley had no idea where the sea was, but pointed confidently where he thought it might be. This couldn't be "helping the enemy"—they'd find it anyhow.

The French guns were completely silent now. As the Germans moved into town, white flags began sprouting everywhere. Sensing no opposition, Major Chrobek of the 18th Infantry Division piled his men into trucks and lurched through the debris-filled streets right to the waterfront. "Then our hearts leapt," exulted the division's normally staid Daily Intelligence Summary: "Here was the sea—the sea!"

At 8:00 a.m. a detachment of German marines took over Bastion 32. There was, of course, nobody there except a handful of headquarters clerks left behind by the departing generals and admirals.

Twenty minutes later a German colonel rolled up to Dunkirk's red brick *Hôtel de Ville* in the center of town. Here he was met by General Beaufrère, commanding the 68th Infantry and senior French officer left in the city. Beaufrère had taken off his steel helmet and now sported a gold-leaf kepi for the surrender ceremony. Sometime between 9:00 and 10:00 a.m. he met with General Lieutenant Friedrich-Carl Cranz, commanding the 18th Division, and formally handed over the city.

By 9:30 German units reached the foot of the eastern mole, but here they faced a problem. French troops were packed so tightly on the mole, it was impossible to round them up quickly.

As late as 10:00 o'clock, a French medical officer, Lieutenant Docteur Le Doze, escaped from the seaward end of the mole with 30 men in a ship's lifeboat.

It's hard to say exactly when Dunkirk officially fell. The Army Group B war diary put the time at 9:00 a.m. . . . X Corps said 9:40 . . . the 18th Army, 10:15. Perhaps the most appropriate time, symbolically anyhow, was the moment the swastika was hoisted on the eastern mole—10:20 a.m.

Now it was a case of mopping up. While Beaufrère dickered with Cranz, small parties of his 68th Division tried to escape to the west, but they were soon run down and captured. General Alaurent led a group from the 32nd Division in an attempt to break out via Gravelines, but they were rounded up at Le Clipon, just outside Dunkirk.

By 10:30 the last shots had been fired and the city was at peace. At Chapeau Rouge Major Newman could hear a golden oriole singing from the top of the oak tree close to the mansion. "This was his day."

A handful of dazed civilians began emerging from the city's cellars. Staring at the blackened walls and piles of rubble, a gendarme—covered with ribbons from the First World War—cried like a child. On the rue Clemenceau a small fox terrier sat guarding the body of a French soldier. Somewhere in the ruins a portable radio, miraculously intact, was playing "The Merry Widow Waltz."

Father Henri Lecointe, assistant curate of Saint Martin's parish, picked his way through the rubble to his church. The door was blown in, the windows gone, but it still stood. Entering, he was surprised to hear the organ playing a Bach chorale. Two German soldiers were trying it out—one at the console, the other in the loft, pumping the bellows.

Foreign correspondents—never far behind when the Wehrmacht was victorious—poked among the ruins, interviewing survivors. The Assistant Chief of Police, André Noël, remarked that he was an Alsatian from Metz and had served in the German Army during the First War.

"Now you can go back to your old regiment," dryly observed a lieutenant-colonel standing by.

As Georg Schmidt, one of Joseph Goebbels's propaganda men,

photographed the scene, his section chief drove up and reminded him that Goebbels expected pictures of British POW's—did
Schmidt have any?

Schmidt replied that the British were all gone.

"Well," said his chief, "you're an official photographer. If
you don't get any pictures of British POW's, then you *were* an
official photographer!"

Schmidt needed no further encouragement. He hurried over
to the POW compound, where he found 30,000 to 40,000
French, but still no British. He looked harder and was finally rewarded. Scattered here and there were two or three dozen
Tommies. Schmidt put them up front and began taking his pictures. The day was saved.

Most of the British were indeed gone, but they took an aston-
ishingly large number of French troops with them. Over 26,000
jammed the decks of the last ships to leave Dunkirk. As the *Medway Queen* groped through an early-morning fog toward Dover,
an officer strummed a mandolin on the after deck, trying to
cheer up the already homesick poilus. On the destroyer *Sabre*
Commander Brian Dean drew cheers by addressing his passengers in French. There was much banter comparing the accom-
modations on the crowded *Sabre* with those on the luxury liner
Normandie.

Generally speaking, the passage back was uneventful—but
not always. As the Belgian trawler *Maréchal Foch* neared the
English coast, the minesweeper *Leda* loomed out of the fog and
rammed her. The "*Foch*" sank instantly, pitching 300 soldiers
into the water.

The French motorboat *VTB 25*, carrying Admiral Abrial and
other high-ranking officers, heard cries and rushed to the scene.
But the fog knew no favorites: *VTB 25* ran into a piece of wreckage and lost her propeller. Now she wallowed helplessly in the
sea.

Eventually the destroyer *Malcolm* came up. Captain Halsey's
smooth-working crew picked up 150 survivors and threw a
line to *VTB 25*. Somewhat ignominiously, Admiral Abrial was finally towed into Dover around 6:00 a.m.

About this time the fog lifted, but that didn't help a young
French ensign named Tellier, commanding the auxiliary dredge

Emile Deschamps. He was thoroughly lost, and when he asked directions from a passing ship, he couldn't understand the answer. He tried to follow the crowd, and was just off Margate when the *Emile Deschamps* struck a magnetic mine and blew up. She sank in less than half a minute with most of the 500 men aboard.

Lieutenant Hervé Cras managed to swim clear of the wreck. He was getting accustomed to this sort of thing, having also gone down on the destroyer *Jaguar* the previous week. Now, as he tread water gasping for breath, he was hailed by a shipmate, Lieutenant Jacquelin de la Porte de Vaux: "Hello, Hello! Let's sing."

With that, de la Port de Vaux burst into *"Le Chant du Départ"*—"The Song of Departure"—a well-known French march. Cras was in no mood to join in, and gradually drifted away. Later, after both men were rescued, de la Porte de Vaux chided him for not singing in the water, "as all sailors with their hearts in the right place must do in such circumstances."

Perhaps he was right. Certainly the men who manned the evacuation fleet needed every conceivable device to keep up their spirits. The *Emile Deschamps* was the 243rd vessel lost, and many of the crews had now reached the breaking point. During the morning of the 4th, Admiral Abrial met with Ramsay in Dover Castle, and they agreed that the time had come to end "Dynamo." Abrial observed that the Germans were closing in; the French had now used up all their ammunition; and the 30,000 to 40,000 men left behind weren't combat units. He was wrong only on the last point: the troops standing forlornly on the pierheads of Dunkirk included some of France's best.

Paris gave its formal approval at 11:00, and at 2:23 p.m. the British Admiralty officially announced the end of Operation Dynamo. Released at last from the strain and tension, Ramsay drove up to Sandwich and celebrated with a round of golf. He shot a 78—by far the best score in his life.

The past several days had been so all-consuming that he never had time even to write "darling Mag," but she had kept the asparagus and gingerbread coming, and now on June 5 he once again took up his pen: "The relief is stupendous, and the results beyond belief." He tried to describe what had been achieved, but it sounded awkward and full of self-praise. He was really a man of action, not a man of letters. He quickly wrapped his effort up: "Tons of love, darling Mag, you are such a comfort to me."

Along with relief went a deep feeling of vindication. Ramsay had never gotten over his years in eclipse; his break with Admiral Backhouse hurt too deeply. Now Dunkirk made up for everything, and the grateful letters that poured in seemed doubly sweet.

He cherished them all, including one from his barber. But the most touching was a letter signed simply "Mrs. S. Woodcock," a British soldier's mother he had never met:

> As a reader of the Daily Express and after reading in today's paper of your wonderful feat re Dunkirk, I feel I must send you a personal message to thank you. My son was one of the lucky ones to escape from there. I have not seen him, but he is somewhere in England, and that's good enough. My youngest boy John Woodcock died of wounds received in Norway on April 26; so you can guess how thankful I feel and grateful to you. . . .

It was a nation already overflowing with gratitude and relief when Winston Churchill went to the House of Commons on the evening of June 4 to report on the evacuation. The benches were filled; the Public Gallery, the Peers Gallery, and the Distinguished Strangers Gallery all packed. The crowd welcomed him with a rousing cheer, then sat enthralled by that rarity—a speech devoted mainly to bad news but which, nevertheless, inspires men with hope and courage.

He thrilled the House with his ringing peroration—"We shall fight on the beaches, we shall fight on the landing grounds, we shall fight in the fields and in the streets"—but what impressed astute observers the most was his frankness in facing unpleasant facts. The *News Chronicle* praised the speech for its "uncompromising candour." Edward R. Murrow called it "a report remarkable for its honesty, inspiration, and gravity."

This was as Churchill wanted it. The rescue of the Army must not lull the nation into a paralyzing euphoria. "We must be very careful," he warned, "not to assign to this deliverance the attributes of a victory. Wars are not won by evacuations."

For the moment his warnings did little good. The returning troops were greeted—often to their own amazement—like conquering heroes. Captain John Dodd of the 58th Field Regiment, Royal Artillery, had expected sullen and angry faces, possibly hostile crowds, and a stigma that would stick for all time. Instead, he found nothing but joy and thankfulness, as if the BEF had been the victors, not the vanquished.

When the troops tumbled ashore at Ramsgate, the women of the town swamped them with cups of cocoa, buried them in sandwiches. The manager of the Pavilion Theatre gave away all his cigarettes and chocolate. A director of the Olympia Ballroom bought up all the socks and underwear in town, and handed them out as needed. A grocery store at Broadstairs gave away its entire stock of tea, soup, biscuits, butter, and margarine. A wealthy Scotsman at St. Augustines bought every blanket in town, sending them all to Ramsgate and Margate.

As fast as possible the returning troops were loaded into special trains and taken to assembly points scattered over England and Wales. Here the various units would be rested and reorganized. As the trains moved through the countryside, crowds gathered at the station platforms along the way, showering them with still more cigarettes and chocolate. Bedsheet banners hung from the windows of London's suburbs with messages like "HARD LUCK, BOYS" and "WELL DONE, BEF." Children stood at road crossings waving Union Jacks.

Lady Ismay, wife of Churchill's military adviser, was changing trains at Oxford when one of these "Dunkirk Specials" pulled in. The people on the platform, until now bored and apathetic, saw the weary faces, the bandages, the torn uniforms, and suddenly realized who these new arrivals were. In a body the crowd rushed the station refreshment stand and showered the exhausted soldiers with food and drink. That night when General Ismay told her how well the evacuation was going, she replied, "Yes, I have seen the miracle with my own eyes."

"Miracle"—that was the word. There seemed no other way to describe such an unexpected, inexplicable change in fortune. In his address to Parliament Winston Churchill called it a "miracle of deliverance." Writing a naval colleague, Admiral Sir William James of Portsmouth could only "thank God for that miracle at Dunkirk." Gort's Chief of Staff, General Pownall, noted in his diary, "The evacuation from Dunkirk was surely a miracle."

Actually, there were several miracles. First, the weather. The English Channel is usually rough, rarely behaves for very long. Yet a calm sea was essential to the evacuation, and during the nine days of Dunkirk the Channel was a millpond. Old-timers still say they have never seen it so smooth.

At one point a storm seemed to be heading for the coast, but veered up the Irish Channel. Northerly winds would have kicked up a disastrous surf, but the breeze was first from the southwest, later shifting to the east. On only one morning, May 31, did an on-shore breeze cause serious trouble. On June 5— the day after the evacuation was over—the wind moved to the north, and great breakers came rolling onto the empty beaches.

Overhead, clouds, mist, and rain always seemed to come at the right moment. The Luftwaffe mounted three all-out assaults on Dunkirk—May 27, 29, and June 1. Each time the following day saw low ceilings that prevented any effective follow-up. It took the Germans three days to discover the part played by the eastern mole, mainly because the southwesterly breezes screened it with smoke.

Another miracle was Adolf Hitler's order of May 24, halting his tanks just as they were closing in for the kill. That day Guderian's panzers had reached Bourbourg, only ten miles southwest of Dunkirk. Nothing stood between them and the port. The bulk of the BEF still lay near Lille, 43 miles to the south. By the time the tanks began rolling again in the predawn hours of May 27, the escape corridor had been established, the BEF was pouring into Dunkirk and Ramsay's rescue fleet was hard at work.

Hitler's "halt order" seems so mysterious that it has even been suggested that he was deliberately trying to let the BEF escape. With her army still intact, the theory runs, Britain might feel she could more honorably sit down at the peace table.

Anyone who was at Dunkirk will have a hard time believing that. If Hitler was secretly trying to let the British go home, he was slicing it awfully thin. He almost failed and caught them all.

Nor did he confide this secret to the Luftwaffe, the artillery, or the S-Boats. All were doing their best to disrupt the evacuation; none were told to go easy. Finally, there were the ideas tossed off by Hitler himself, suggesting better ways to raise havoc on the beaches.

The most convincing evidence indicates that Hitler was indeed trying to block the evacuation, but wasn't willing to risk his armor to do it. The British looked finished anyhow; Flanders was poor tank country; his lines were already stretched thin; the brief counterattack at Arras disturbed him; 50% of his tanks were said to be out of action; he needed that armor for the next phase of the campaign, the drive across the Somme and into the heart of France.

It was understandable, especially for any German who had been through the First War. France was crucial, and Paris was the key. It had eluded them then; there must be no mistake this time. Far better to risk a miracle at Dunkirk than risk a second "Miracle of the Marne."

The decision was all the easier when Hermann Göring announced that his Luftwaffe could handle Dunkirk alone. Hitler didn't buy this for very long—he lifted the "halt order" several days before it became clear that Göring couldn't deliver—but the General Field Marshal's boast certainly played a part.

By May 27, when the tanks got going again, the great German drive had lost its momentum, and the panzer generals themselves were thinking of the south. Guderian, once an impassioned advocate for using his armor at Dunkirk, now only had eyes for the Somme.

Still another miracle was provided by the Luftwaffe itself. Perhaps Göring could never have stopped the evacuation, but he could have caused far more mischief. The German planes rarely strafed the crowded beaches; they never used fragmentation bombs; they never attacked tempting targets like Dover or Ramsgate. None of this was through lack of desire; it was through lack of doctrine. The Stuka pilots had been trained for ground support, not for interdiction. The fighters were expected to stay upstairs, covering the bombers, not to come down and mix it up. Whatever the reasons, these lapses allowed additional thousands of men to come home.

"Had the BEF not returned to this country," General Brooke

later wrote, "it is hard to see how the Army could have recovered from the blow." That was the practical significance of Dunkirk. Britain could replace the 2,472 lost guns, the 63,879 abandoned vehicles; but the 224,686 rescued troops were irreplaceable. In the summer of 1940 they were the only trained troops Britain had left. Later, they would be the nucleus of the great Allied armies that won back the Continent. The leaders—Brooke, Alexander, and Montgomery, to name only three—all cut their teeth at Dunkirk.

But the significance of Dunkirk went far beyond such practical considerations. The rescue electrified the people of Britain, welded them together, gave them a sense of purpose that the war had previously lacked. Treaty obligations are all very well, but they don't inspire men to great deeds. "Home" does, and this is what Britain was fighting for now.

The very sense of being alone was exhilarating. The story was told of the foreigner who asked whether his English friend was discouraged by the successive collapse of Poland, Denmark, Norway, the Lowlands, and now France. "Of course not," came the stout-hearted reply. "We're in the finals and we're playing at home."

Some would later say that it was all clever propaganda that cranked up the country to this emotional peak. But it happened too quickly—too spontaneously—for that. This was a case where the people actually led the propagandists. The government's fears were the opposite—that Dunkirk might lead to overconfidence. It was Winston Churchill himself who stressed that the campaign had been "a colossal military disaster," and who warned that "wars are not won by evacuations."

Ironically, Churchill was a prime mover in creating the very mood he sought to dispel. His eloquence, his defiance, his fighting stance were almost bewitching in their appeal. Like Abraham Lincoln in the American Civil War, he was perfectly cast.

Another ingredient was the sense of national participation that Dunkirk aroused. Modern war is so impersonal, it's a rare moment when the ordinary citizen feels that he's making a direct contribution. At Dunkirk ordinary Englishmen really did go over in little boats and rescue soldiers. Ordinary housewives really did succor the exhausted troops reeling back. History is

full of occasions when armies have rushed to the aid of an embattled people; here was a case where the people rushed to the
aid of an embattled army.

Above all, they pulled it off. When the evacuation began,
Churchill thought 30,000 might be saved; Ramsay guessed
45,000. In the end, over 338,000 were landed in England, with
another 4,000 lifted to Cherbourg and other French ports still
in Allied hands. "Wars are not won by evacuations," but, for
the first time, at least Adolf Hitler didn't have everything his
own way. That in itself was cause for celebration.

Curiously, the Germans felt like celebrating too. Years later,
they would see it differently. Many would even regard Dunkirk
as the turning point of the whole war: If the BEF had been captured, Britain would have been defeated. . . . If that had happened, Germany could have concentrated all her strength on
Russia. . . . If that had happened, there would have been no Sta-
lingrad. . . . and so on. But on June 4, 1940, none of these "ifs"
were evident. Except, perhaps, for a few disgruntled tank commanders, the victory seemed complete. As the magazine *Der Adler* put it:

> For us Germans the word "Dunkirchen" will stand
> for all time for victory in the greatest battle of annihi-
> lation in history. But for the British and French who
> were there, it will remind them for the rest of their
> lives of a defeat that was heavier than any army had
> ever suffered before.

As for the escape of "a few men" back to England, *Der Adler* reassured its readers that this was no cause for alarm: "Every
single one of these completely demoralized soldiers is a bacillus
of disintegration. . . ." The *Völkischer Beobachter* told how wom-
en and children burst into hysterical tears as the battered troops
staggered home.

And they would never be back. Landing craft, "mulberries,"
fighter-bombers, sophisticated radar, the whole paraphernalia
of the 1944 counterstroke hadn't even been invented. Viewed
with 1940 eyes, it wasn't all that important to annihilate the
BEF. It had been thrown into the sea, and that was enough.

Only the French were bitter. Whether it was Weygand sniping at General Spears in Paris or the lowliest poilu giving up the eastern mole, the overwhelming majority felt abandoned by the British. It did no good to point out that 123,095 French *were* rescued by Ramsay's fleet, 102,570 in British ships.

Goebbels joyfully fanned the flames. The crudest propaganda poured out of Berlin. In a little book called *Blende auf-Tiefangriff,* correspondent Hans Henkel told how the fleeing British in one rowboat forced several Frenchmen at pistol-point to jump into the sea. The survivors now stood before Henkel, cursing the *"sales anglais."*

> Then I asked, "But why do you have an alliance with these '*sales anglais,*' these dirty Englishmen?"
>
> "But we didn't do this! It was done by our wretched government, which then had the nerve to save them!"
>
> "You didn't have to keep that government!"
>
> "What could we do? We weren't asked at all." And one added, "It's the Jews who are to blame."
>
> "Well, fellows, what if we now fought the English together?"
>
> They laughed and said with great enthusiasm, "Yes, we'd join up immediately."

In London the French naval attaché Admiral Odend'hal did his best to put the matter in perspective. He was a good Frenchman, but at the same time tried to give Paris the British point of view. For his pains, Admiral Darlan wrote back asking whether Odend'hal had "gone into the British camp."

"I have not gone into the British camp," Odend'hal replied, "and I would be distressed if you believed it." To prove his loyalty he then reeled off some of his own run-ins with the British, adding:

> But it is not with the English but with the Boches that we are at war. Whatever may have been the British faults, the events of Dunkirk must not leave us with bitterness. . . .

His advice was ignored.

Such matters of state made little difference to the men of the BEF these early days of June. They only knew that they were home, and even that was hard to believe. As the train carrying Captain John Dodd of the Royal Artillery steamed slowly through the Kentish countryside, he looked out the window at the passing woods and orchards. "Good gun position . . . good hideout for vehicles . . . good billets in that farm," he thought—then suddenly realized he was at last free from such worries.

Signalman Percy Charles, wounded at Cassel, boarded a hospital train from Northfield. It traveled all night and at 7:00 the following morning Charles was awakened by brilliant greenish lights streaming through the window. He glanced around and noticed that the other men in the compartment were crying. Then he looked out the window, and the sight he saw was "what the poets have been writing about for so many centuries." It was the green English countryside. After the dirt, the blackened rubble, the charred ruins of northern France, the impact of all this fresh greenness was too much. The men simply broke down.

General Brooke, too, felt the contrast. After landing at Dover, he checked in with Ramsay, then drove up to London in a staff car. It was a lovely sunny morning, and he thought of the horror he had just left: burning towns, dead cows, broken trees, the hammer of guns and bombs. "To have moved straight from that inferno into such a paradise within the spell of a few anguished hours made the contrast all the more wonderful."

In London he conferred briefly with General Dill, then caught the train to Hartley Wintney and home. He was overwhelmingly sleepy now, and walked up and down the compartment in a desperate effort to stay awake. If he so much as closed his eyes, he was afraid he'd fall asleep and miss the station.

His wife and children were waiting on the platform. They whisked him home for a nursery tea, and then to bed at last. He slept for 36 hours.

How tired they all were. Major Richardson of the 4th Division staff had managed only sixteen hours of sleep in two weeks. During one stretch of the retreat he went for 62 hours straight without even a nap. Finally reaching the Division assembly point at Aldershot, he threw himself on a bed and slept for 30 hours. Captain Tufton Beamish, whose 9th Royal Northumberland Fusiliers saved the day at Steenbecque, topped them all with 39 hours.

The rescuers were just as weary. Lieutenant Robin Bill, whose minesweepers were in constant demand, had five nights in bed in two weeks. Lieutenant Greville Worthington, in charge of unloading at Dover, stumbled groggily into the mess one morning. When bacon and eggs were put before him, he fell asleep with his beard in the plate. Commander Pelly, skipper of the destroyer *Windsor*, discovered that his only chance for a rest was during turn-around time at Dover. Even then he never took a nap, fearing that he wouldn't have a clear head when he woke up. Instead, he simply sat on the bridge, nursing a whisky and soda. It must have worked, for he never went to sleep for ten days.

No one was more tired than civilian volunteer Bob Hilton. He and his partner, cinema manager Ted Shaw, had spent seventeen hours straight rowing troops out to the skoots and small paddlers from the beach near the mole. Not even Hilton's training as a physical education instructor prepared him for a test like that, but somehow he managed it. Now the job was done, and they were back at Ramsgate.

They could have used some rest, but they were ordered to help take the little ships back up the Thames to London. To make matters worse, they were assigned the *Ryegate II*, the balky motor yacht they had sailed to Dunkirk and abandoned when her screws fouled. Wearily they set off, around the North Foreland . . . into the Thames estuary . . . and on up the river itself.

The cheering really began after Blackfriars Bridge. Docklands and the City had been too busy to watch the passing of this grimy, oil-stained fleet. But as *Ryegate II* passed the training ship *Discovery*, moored alongside the Embankment, her Sea Scouts set up a mighty cheer. It grew ever louder as the yacht continued upstream. Chelsea . . . Hammersmith . . . Twickenham . . . every bridge was lined with shouting people.

Hilton and Shaw ultimately delivered *Ryegate II* to her boatyard and walked to the tube, where they parted company. After rowing together, side by side, for seventeen hours, it would be reasonable to suppose they remained lifelong friends. As a matter of fact, they never met again.

Hilton took the tube home. As he entered the train, any idea he may have had that he would be greeted as a hero quickly vanished. He had a three-day growth of beard; his clothes were covered with oil; he reeked to high heaven. His fellow passengers quickly moved to the far end of the car.

He reached the front door and discovered he had forgotten his keys. He rang the bell, the door opened, and his wife Pamela was standing there. She took one look at "this tramp" and threw her arms around him. He was a hero to someone, after all.

Written Source Materials

"I am sorry I am unable to get the details and events to dates," writes Sapper Joe Coles of the 223rd Field Park Company, Royal Engineers. "That was an impossibility even a few days after Dunkirk. This I can only put down to continual fatigue and the atmosphere of continual emergency, 24 hours a day."

He isn't the only one with this problem. The days had a way of merging into one another for most of the participants, and the passage of more than 40 years doesn't make memories any sharper. Personal recollections are indispensable in recapturing the atmosphere and preserving many of the incidents that occurred, but overreliance on human memory can be dangerous too. For that reason, I spent even more time examining the written source materials on Dunkirk than in interviewing and corresponding with those who were there.

The Public Record Office in London was the starting point. The basic Admiralty files dealing with the evacuation are ADM 199/786-796. These have been well mined, but fascinating nuggets still await the diligent digger. For instance, ADM 199/792 contains not only Admiral Wake-Walker's familiar 15-page account, but an earlier, far more detailed 41-page account that has lain practically untouched through the years—apparently because it is so faint and hard to read. A powerful magnifying glass pays handsome dividends.

ADM 199/788-B and ADM 199/796-B, dealing with ships reluctant to sail, are still "off-limits" to researchers, but it is possible to work around this restriction and piece together the story from other documents.

Additional Dunkirk material pops up elsewhere in the Admiralty files. ADM 199/360 contains day-by-day information on the weather. ADM 199/2205-2206 includes much of the radio traffic between Dover and Dunkirk, and between ships and the shore. ADM 116/4504 has the story of the bizarre "lethal kite barrage."

The RAF role at Dunkirk can be traced through the Operational Record Books at the PRO, but most of these are too detailed for all but the most exacting scholars. AIR 20/523 does include a useful overview of the Fighter Command's contribution. The War Office records tend to mire the reader in the campaign, although occasionally some documents bear specifically on the evacuation. WO 197/119 has an excellent account of Brigadier Clifton's improvised defense at Nieuport; also a report by Colonel G.H.P. Whitfield, area commandant, depicting the chaos in Dunkirk itself until Captain Tennant arrived.

In some ways the most valuable materials at the PRO are the War Cabinet Historical Section series, CAB 44/60-61 and CAB 44/67-69, not released until 1977. The telephone played an enormous role in the decisions involving Dunkirk, and these CAB files contain detailed accounts of many of the calls, along with the texts of pertinent letters and telegrams.

The PRO is not the answer to everything. Probably the most useful single source of information on the evacuation is the three-volume annotated index of participating ships at the Ministry of Defense's Naval Historical Branch. Labeled "Alphabetical List of Vessels Taking Part, with Their Services," these volumes are occasionally updated as new information trickles in. They include valuable data on the French ships contributed by the French naval historian Hervé Cras.

Another extremely useful source is an account of RAF operations prepared by historian Denis Richards for the Air Historical Branch. Entitled *RAF Narrative: The Campaign in France and the Low Countries, September 1939–June 1940,* this volume gives day-by-day coverage of the evacuation.

Then there are the records so lovingly kept by most of the famous British regiments. These usually include battalion war diaries and often individual accounts. I paid most rewarding visits to the regimental headquarters of the Coldstream Guards, the Grenadier Guards, the Queen Victoria's Rifles, the Gloucestershires, and the Durham Light Infantry.

The formal dispatches of Lord Gort and of Admiral Ramsay complete the official side of the Dunkirk story. Gort's dispatch appeared as a Supplement to the *London Gazette,* October 17, 1941; Ramsay's account as a Supplement to the *Gazette* of July 17, 1947. They are helpful in fixing dates and places, but neither could be called a distinguished piece of battle literature.

There's no end to the unofficial material on Dunkirk. The Imperial War Museum is a cornucopia of unpublished diaries, journals, letters, memoirs, and tapes. I found the following especially valuable: Corporal P. G. Ackrell's account of early turmoil on the Dunkirk waterfront; W.B.A. Gaze's recollections of the 12th Casualty Clearing Station; Commander Thomas Kerr's letters to his wife on conditions at Malo and Bray-Dunes; Admiral Sir L. V. Morgan's reflections as Ramsay's Chief of Staff; Chaplain R. T. Newcomb's impressions as a padre caught up in the great retreat; Signalman L. W. Wright's manuscript, "Personal Experience in the Defence of Calais."

Few of the shipping companies that provided vessels have saved their records (many were destroyed in the blitz), but the Tilbury Contracting Group has preserved accounts by three of its skippers. Tough's Boatyard has a useful file of papers and clippings describing its contribution.

Numerous unpublished accounts have been made available to me by participants and their families. These include no fewer than fourteen diaries. Contemporary letters have been another important source, especially an almost-running commentary from Admiral Ramsay to his wife.

The voluminous published material on Dunkirk began to appear even before the evacuation was over. The *Times* and the other London papers are curiously bland, but not so the local press of the south and southeast coast. Their accounts make fresh, vivid reading even today. The cream of the crop: *The Evening Argus* (Brighton), June 5; *Bournemouth Times and Directory*, June 14; *The East Kent Times* (Ramsgate), June 5; *The Kentish Gazette and Canterbury Press*, June 8; *Folkestone, Hythe and District Herald*, June 8; *Isle of Thanet Gazette* (Margate), June 7; *Sheerness Times and Guardian*, June 7. The Dover *Express* is, of course, a "must" for the whole period.

A number of eyewitness accounts also appeared in various periodicals at the time. Some good examples: *The Architectural Association Journal*, September-November, 1940, "And So—We Went to Dunkirk" (Anonymous); *Blackwood's*, August 1940, "Prelude to Dunkirk" by Ian Scott, and in November 1940, "Small Change from Dunkirk" by M.C.A. Henniker; *Fortnightly Review*, July 1940, "Dunkirk" by E. H. Phillips; *King's Royal Rifle Corps Chronicle*, 1940, an important letter by Sub-Lieutenant Roger Wake, RN, who served as acting pier master on the eastern mole, night of June 2-3.

The magazine *Belgium*—published in London during the war and frankly Allied propaganda—occasionally carried articles on Belgian participants at Dunkirk. Georges Truffant's piece in the issue of July 31, 1941, deserves special mention.

Through the years newspapers have often marked the anniversary of Dunkirk with fresh material. The Scarborough *Evening News*, for instance, commemorated the tenth anniversary with a splendid series by "A Green Howard," appearing April 24, 26, and May 1, 1950. Just about every paper in England must have marked the 40th anniversary. Especially striking was the series in the Manchester *Evening News*, March 10, 11, 12, 13, 14, 1980.

Magazines and service journals are another continuing source of information. Hitler's role is analyzed in the *Army Quarterly*, January 1955, "The Dunkirk Halt Order—a Further Reassessment" by Captain B. H. Liddell Hart; and again in the *Quarterly*, April 1958, "Hitler and Dunkirk" by Captain Robert B. Asprey. The Belgian surrender is examined in *History Today*, February 1980, "The Tragedy of Leopold III" by James Marshall-Cornwall. Alexander's takeover and the last days are recalled in the *Army Quarterly*, April 1972, "With Alexander to Dunkirk" by General Sir William Morgan. But beware of General Morgan's contention that Admiral Abrial still didn't plan to evacuate as late as May 31. Alexander himself refutes this in his report.

Particular ships get their due in a host of articles through the years: *Malcolm,* in "Mostly from the Bridge" by Captain David B. N. Mellis, *Naval Review,* October 1976; *Harvester,* in "Dunkirk: The Baptism of a Destroyer" by Hugh Hodgkinson, *Blackwood's,* June 1980; *Massey Shaw,* in "New Bid to Save London Fireboat," *Lloyd's Log,* October 1981; the sprit-sailing barges, in "The Little Ships of Ipswich" by J. O. Whitmore, *East Anglian Magazine,* July 1950. The medical effects of continuing fear and exhaustion are intelligently discussed by James Dow in *Journal of the Royal Naval Medical Service,* Spring 1978.

No discussion of periodicals would be complete without some mention of the *Dunkirk Veterans Association Journal.* This little quarterly not only keeps the DVA members in touch, but serves as a clearinghouse for all sorts of questions and answers concerning the evacuation. It was through its columns, for instance, that the indefatigable Sam Love tracked down the story of the *Hird,* the ship that returned to France before unloading at Dover.

The books on Dunkirk could fill a warehouse. At least fifteen different titles are devoted entirely to the evacuation or the events leading up to it. From John Masefield's *Nine Days Wonder,* 1941, to Nicholas Harman's *Dunkirk: The Necessary Myth,* 1980, I have learned from them all. Two stand out especially: A. D. Divine's *Dunkirk,* 1944, and Gregory Blaxland's *Destination Dunkirk,* 1973. Mr. Divine was there himself with the little ships, while Mr. Blaxland has written the very model of a campaign history—clear, candid, and complete.

Not limited to Dunkirk, but covering the campaign in detail, are two official histories: Captain S. W. Roskill, *The Navy at War, 1939–45,* 1960; and Major L. F. Ellis, *The War in France and Flanders, 1939–1940,* 1953. Ellis's maps should be the envy of every military historian.

Published memoirs and diaries abound, written by both the known and the unknown. The leaders include: Clement R. Attlee, *As It Happened,* 1954; Duff Cooper, *Old Men Forget,* 1953; Hugh Dalton, *The Fateful Years,* 1957; Anthony Eden, *The Reckoning,* 1965; General Lord Ismay, *Memoirs,* 1960; R. MacLeod, (ed.), *The Ironside Diaries*, 1962; Field-Marshal the Viscount Montgomery, *Memoirs*, 1958; Lieutenant-General Sir Henry Pownall, *Diaries*, 1972; Major-General Sir Edward Spears, *Assignment to Catastrophe*, 1954; Sir Arthur Bryant, *The Turn of the Tide*, 1957, based on the diaries of Field Marshal Lord Alanbrooke. In a class by himself: Winston S. Churchill, *Their Finest Hour*, 1949.

Others are less famous but sometimes more revealing: Sir Basil Bartlett, *My First War*, 1940; Eric Bush, *Bless Our Ship*, 1958; Sir H. E. Franklyn, *The Story of One Green Howard in the Dunkirk Campaign*, 1966; Gun Buster (pseud.), *Return via Dunkirk*, 1940; Sir Leslie Hollis, *One Marine's Tale*, 1956; J. M. Langley, *Fight Another Day*, 1974; A.R.E. Rhodes, *Sword of Bone*, 1942; General Sir John G. Smyth, *Before the Dawn*, 1957; Colonel L.H.M. Westropp, *Memoirs*, 1970.

Useful biographies cover some of the leading figures. For Admiral Ramsay, see David Woodward, *Ramsay at War*, 1957; and W. S. Chalmers, *Full Cycle*, 1958. Lord Gort is gently handled by Sir John Colville in *Man of Valour*, 1972. Lord Alanbrooke is examined by General Sir David Fraser in *Alanbrooke*, 1982. Field Marshal Montgomery gets full-dress treatment from Nigel Hamilton in *Monty: The Making of a General*, 1981. *John Rutherford Crosby* by George Blake, 1946, is a touching, privately published tribute to a young, little-known sub-lieutenant (later a casualty) that somehow captures the glow of Dunkirk better than many more ambitious books.

Then there are the unit and regimental histories. I have made use of 54 of these volumes, and have come to appreciate the loving care with which all have been prepared. I have relied especially on D. S. Daniell, *Cap of Honour* (Gloucestershire Regiment), 1951; Patrick Forbes and Nigel Nicolson, *The Grenadier Guards in the War of 1939–1945*, 1949; Jeremy L. Taylor, *Record of a Reconnaissance Regiment*, section headed "The Fifth Glosters," by Anothony Scott, 1950. David Quilter, *No Dishonourable Name* (2nd Coldstream Guards), 1947; David Russik, *The DLI at War*, 1952; W. Whyte, *Roll of the Drum* (King's Royal Rifle Corps), 1941; and Robin McNish, *Iron Division: The History of the 3rd Division*, 1978.

Other books are important for specific aspects of the story.

The defense of Calais: Airey Neave, *The Flames of Calais*, 1972. The role of the railways: Norman Crump, *By Rail to Victory*, 1947, and B. Darwin, *War on the Line*, 1946. Reaction along the southeast coast: Reginald Foster, *Dover Front*, 1941. The air battles: Douglas Bader, *Fight for the Sky*, 1973, Larry Forrester, *Fly for Your Life*, 1956; B. J. Ellan (pseud.), *Spitfire!* 1942, and Denis Richards, *The Royal Air Force, 1939–1945*, 1953.

Many of these titles concern the rescue fleet. The little ships: Nicholas Drew (pseud.), *The Amateur Sailor*, 1946; and A. A. Hoehling, *Epics of the Sea*, 1977. Role of the Royal National Lifeboat Institution: Charles Vince, *Storm on the Waters*, 1946. The MTB's and MA/SB's: Peter Scott, *The Battle of the Narrow Seas*, 1945. The *Massey Shaw*: H. S. Ingham, *Fire and Water*, 1942. The *Medway Queen*: The Paddle Steamer Preservation Society, *The Story of the Medway Queen*, 1975. The *Clan MacAlister*: G. Holman, *In Danger's Hour*, 1948.

For the French side of Dunkirk I found especially useful the official French Navy study, *Les Forces Maritime du Nord, 1939–1940*, prepared by Dr. Hervé Cras. It is not generally available to the public, but I was given access to a set, and also to several important letters written by Admiral J. Odend'hal, head of the French Naval Mission in London, to his superiors in Paris.

Published memoirs of the French leaders are not very satisfactory. Premier Reynaud's *In the Thick of the Fight*, 1955, is heavy and self-serving. (He even calls it his "Testimony.") General Weygand's *Recalled to Service*, 1952, comes from an obviously bitter man. Jacques Mordal's *Dunkerque*, 1968, tries to combine a memoir with straight history. "Jacques Mordal," incidentally, is a pseudonym used by the historian Hervé Cras. Edmond Perron's *Journal d'un Dunkerquois*, 1977, depicts what it was like to be an ordinary citizen of Dunkirk trapped in the battle.

Good general histories include Rear-Admiral Paul Auphan (with Jacques Mordal), *The French Navy in World War II*, 1957; General André Beaufre, *1940: The Fall of France*, 1967; Guy Chapman, *Why France Collapsed*, 1968; and William L. Shirer, *The Collapse of the Third Republic*, 1969.

The German archival sources are amazingly complete. It's

difficult to understand how, in the final *Götterdämmerung* of the Third Reich, so much could have survived, but the very swiftness of the collapse enabled the Allied armies to seize vast quantities of records intact, to be examined and later returned to the owners.

It's all now in the lovely city of Freiburg, meticulously filed in the Bundesarchiv/Militärarchiv, and the Dunkirk material can be easily located. I found most useful the war diaries and situation reports of Army Groups A and B; the Sixth and Eighteenth Armies; IX, X, XIV, and XIX Corps; 18th Infantry Division; 1st, 2nd, and 10th Panzer Divisions; Luftwaffe Air Fleet 2; Fliegerkorps VIII; First Naval War Command; the motor torpedo boat *S 30*; and the submarine *U 62*.

The Bundesarchiv also contains a number of unpublished firsthand accounts covering the Dunkirk campaign. File Z A_3/50 includes recollections of Field-Marshal Kesselring and Luftwaffe Generals Hans Seidemann and Josef Schmidt. File RH37/6335 contains a vivid account by an unidentified soldier in XIX Corps, covering the whole period from the dash to the sea on May 20 to the fall of Bergues, June 2. File Z 305 is the published diary of Hans Waitzbauer, an observant young radio operator serving in the 102nd Artillery Regiment.

The most important diary of all was that kept by General Franz Halder, Chief of the Army General Staff at the time of Dunkirk. It provides not only an hour-by-hour record of events but candid comments on the various personalities at OKH and OKW. The copy I used is an English translation on file at the Bibliothek für Zeitgeschichte in Stuttgart.

The contemporary published material faithfully follows the Nazi line, but the press does convey the feeling of euphoria that swept Germany that intoxicating May and June of 1940. Three good examples: *Der Adler*, June 11 and 25; *Die Wehrmacht*, June 19; and *Völkischer Beobachter*, almost any day.

The German books of the period are just as slanted, but occasionally something useful turns up. Fritz Otto Busch, *Unsere Schnellboote im Kanal* (no date) gives a good picture of S Boat operations. Herbert W. Borchert, *Panzerkampf im Westen* (1940) has interesting anecdotes on the thrust of the panzers. Heinz Guderian, *Mit den Panzern in Ost und West* (1942) is really a compilation of eyewitness stories brought out under Guderian's name, but it does include a good piece on Calais by a Colonel Fischer, who was there. Hans Henkel, *Blende auf-Tiefangriff* (1941) has a chapter on Dunkirk that gives a vivid picture of the utter desolation that greeted the entering German troops.

The years since the war have seen an enormous output of German articles and books touching on Dunkirk. The propaganda is gone, often replaced by wishful thinking, second-guessing, and buck-passing. Some of these sources have English translations: Guenther Blumentritt, *Von Runstedt: The Soldier and the Man*, 1952; Adolf Galland, *The First and the Last*, 1954; Heinz Guderian, *Panzer Leader*, 1952; Hans-Adolf Jacobsen, *Decisive Battles of World War II*, 1965; Albert Kesselring, *Memoirs*, 1953; Werner Kreipe, *The Fatal Decisions*, 1956; Walter Warlimont, *Inside Hitler's Headquarters*, 1964. Pertinent interviews can be found in B. H. Liddell Hart, *The German Generals Talk*, 1948.

Hitler's "halt order" is picked apart by all these authorities, as it is by other, less familiar writers who have not yet been translated into English: Wolf von Aaken, *Inferno im Westen*, 1964; Peter Bor, *Gespräche mit Halder*, 1950; Gert Buchheit, *Hitler der Feldherr; die Zerstörung einst Legende*, 1958; Gerhard Engel, *Heeres-Adjutant bei Hitler, 1938–1943*, 1974; Ulrich Liss, *Westfront 1939–1940*, 1959.

For general background I often turned to Len Deighton's *Blitzkrieg: From the Rise of Hitler to the Fall of Dunkirk*, 1980; William L. Shirer's classic *The Rise and Fall of the Third Reich*; Telford Taylor's *The March of Conquest*, 1958; and John Toland's immensely readable *Adolf Hitler*, 1978. All helped fill me in, and Taylor's appendices proved indispensable.

Acknowledgments

"My own feelings are rather of disgust," writes a member of the 67th Field Regiment, Royal Artillery. "I saw officers throw their revolvers away ... I saw soldiers shooting cowards as they fought to be first in a boat."

"Their courage made our job easy," recalls a signalman with the Naval Shore Party, describing the same men on the same beaches, "and I was proud to have known them and to have been born of their generation."

To a clerk in 11th Brigade Headquarters, the evacuation was "absolute chaos." To a man in III Corps Headquarters, it was a "debacle" ... a "disgrace." But to a dispatch rider with the 4th Division, it was thrilling evidence "that the British were an invincible people."

Could they all be talking about the same battle? As I pieced the story together, sometimes it seemed that the only thing the men of Dunkirk agreed upon was their desire to be helpful. Over 500 answered my "call to arms," and there seemed no limit to the time and trouble they were willing to take.

Lieutenant-Colonel James M. Langley spent three days showing me around the perimeter, with special attention to the segment of the line held by the 2nd Coldstream Guards. Harold

Robinson, Hon. General Secretary of the Dunkirk Veterans Association, arranged for me to join the DVA's annual pilgrimage in 1978. It was a splendid opportunity to get to know some of these men personally, listen to their recollections, and feel the ties that bind them together. I'm especially grateful for the time given me by the Reverend Leslie Aitken, Fred Batson, and Arthur Elkin.

The DVA Headquarters in Leeds generously put me in touch with the organization's branches all over the world, and as a result I've received valuable assistance from such varied places as Cyprus, Zimbabwe, Malta, Libya, Italy, Canada, Australia, and New Zealand. The London Branch was particularly helpful, which calls for an extra word of thanks to Stan Allen, Ted Rabbets, and Bob Stephens. For making my cause so widely known, I'm indebted to Captain L. A. Jackson ("Jacko"), editor of the DVA's lively *Journal*.

Everyone was helpful, but as the work progressed, I found myself leaning more and more on certain individuals, whom I came to regard as "my" experts in certain areas. These included the Viscount Bridgeman on events at GHQ; Captain Eric Bush on the Royal Navy; Air Vice-Marshal Michael Lyne on the RAF; Captain Stephen Roskill on the Dynamo Room; John Bridges on the Grenadier Guards; Sam Love on the *Hird*; W. Stanley Berry on the Small Vessels Pool; and Basil Bellamy on the Ministry of Shipping. General Sir Peter Hunt gave me a crash course on British Regiments, and it's a lucky American indeed whose tutor on such an intricate matter is a former Chief of the Imperial General Staff.

The participants not only poured out their recollections; they cheerfully rummaged through trunks and attics for long-forgotten papers that might throw further light on their experiences. Old diaries were dusted off by A. Baldwin, J. S. Dodd, F. R. Farley, A. R. Jabez-Smith, W. P. Knight, J. M. Langley, R. W. Lee, I.F.R. Ramsay, and N. Watkin. Others sent in detailed accounts originally written when memories were green— for instance, G. W. Jones, E. C. Webb, and R. M. Zakovitch. Fred Walter contributed a remarkable 31-page handwritten account of Calais, which gave a better picture of that controversial episode than anything else I've seen.

Families gallantly pitched in where the participants themselves had passed on. Mrs. E. Barker sent in the diary of her father, Major J. W. Gibson; Roy L. Fletcher contributed a fascinating account by his father, Seaman C. L. Fletcher. Mrs. D. Forward extracted an interesting letter from her brother Syd Metcalf. Helpful widows included Mrs. Nancy Cotton and Mrs. C. Smales.

Two cases deserve special mention. First, David F. Ramsay made available some personal correspondence of his distinguished father, Admiral Sir Bertram Ramsay, including a file of letters to Mrs. Ramsay that vividly depicts the blend of desperation and determination that permeated the Dynamo Room. Second, through the good offices of my friend Sharon Rutman, Mrs. Sylvia Sue Steell contributed a letter from her gallant uncle, Commander Charles Herbert Lightoller. It mirrors the spirit of the men who sailed the little ships, and shows that Commander Lightoller had lost none of the zeal that served him so well as Second Officer on the *Titanic*.

Other firsthand accounts were collected and forwarded to me by various branches of the DVA, and for this good work I'm particularly grateful to E. C. Webb of the Glasgow Branch and A. Hordell of the Stoke-on-Trent Branch. A special word of thanks, too, for my friend Edward de Groot, who called my attention to Lieutenant Lodo van Hamel, the only skipper in Admiral Ramsay's rescue fleet to fly the Dutch flag. Further details on van Hamel's service were generously provided by Commander F. C. van Oosten, Royal Dutch Navy, Ret., Director of Naval History.

In France I was lucky to have the all-out assistance of Hervé Cras, Assistant Director of the Musée de la Marine, who survived the destroyer *Jaguar* and the minesweeper *Emile Deschamps*, both lost at Dunkirk. Besides being a participant, Dr. Cras lent me important French records and arranged for two key interviews: one with Rear-Admiral Paul Auphan, who explained the thinking at Darlan's headquarters; and the other with Vice-Admiral Gui de Toulouse-Lautrec, who described the loss of his destroyer, *Siroco*. I only wish Hervé Cras were still alive to read these words of heartfelt gratitude.

At a different level F. Summers (then Fernand Schneider)

provided a fascinating glimpse of life on a French minesweeping trawler. Mr. Summers came from Dunkirk, and he enjoyed the unusual distinction of starting the war in the French Navy and ending it in the Royal Navy—all in all, a unique point of view.

In Germany I concentrated on old aviators, since so much of Dunkirk revolved around the successes and failures of the Luftwaffe. I felt my questions were answered with candor, and I'm deeply grateful to Wolfgang Falck, Adolf Galland, and Hans Mahnert. Colonel Rudi Erlemann was only a small boy in 1940, but by the time I cornered him he was Air Attaché at the German Embassy in Washington, and full of insight on the Luftwaffe's performance.

For other glimpses of the German side, I'm indebted to Willy Felgner, a signalman with the 56th Infantry Division; Vice-Admiral Friedrich Ruge, a wise old sailor full of thoughtful comment on the German Navy's performance; Georg Smidt Scheeder, photographer with Goebbels's propaganda company; and Albert Speer, who had at least one conversation with Hitler touching on Dunkirk. Speer felt, incidentally, that anyone who believed that Hitler wanted to "let the English escape" didn't understand the Fuehrer very well.

The written material on Dunkirk is voluminous; fortunately an army of dedicated archivists and librarians stands ready to aid the probing scholar. At the Imperial War Museum in London, Dr. Noble Frankland's helpful staff made me feel like one of the family. Rose Coombs, Keeper of Special Collections, is a heroine to countless American researchers, and I'm no exception.

David Brown, head of the Naval Historical Branch, gave me a warm welcome, and his assistant, Miss M. Thirkettle, made available her encyclopedic knowledge of what ships were and what were not at Dunkirk. Andrew Naylor, Librarian of the Royal United States Institute, and Richard Brech of the Royal Air Force Museum both had many useful suggestions.

The Secretaries of the various Regimental Headquarters scattered throughout Britain were invariably helpful. I'm especially grateful to Lieutenant-Colonel F.A.D. Betts of the Coldstream Guards; Major Oliver Lindsay of the Grenadier Guards;

Lieutenant-Colonel R. E. Humphreys of the Durham Light Infantry; Lieutenant-Colonel H.L.T. Radice of the Gloucestershire Regiment; and Lieutenant-Colonel W.R.H. Charley of the Royal Irish Rangers. Miss E. M. Keen of the Queen Victoria's Rifles Association not only produced records but organized a session where I could meet and talk with several of the veterans of Calais.

On the nautical side, the Association of Dunkirk Little Ships was always helpful in identifying various vessels. This organization must be the most unusual yacht club in the world: the boat, rather than the owner, is elected to membership. Through the Association's efforts, 126 of the Dunkirk little ships have now been carefully preserved. The group's Archivist, John Knight, knows them all and generously shares his knowledge. A special word of thanks to Harry Moss, owner of *Braymar*, who hosted me at the 1978 Fitting-Out Dinner.

A visit to Tough's Boatyard paid great dividends in learning how these little ships were collected and manned. Mr. Robert O. Tough, present head of the family enterprise, took time off from a busy day to dig out the yard's files on the evacuation. I was unable to get to Tilbury, but that didn't deter Mr. C. E. Sedgwick, Group Secretary of the Tilbury Contracting Group. He generously struck off for me photocopies of the actual reports submitted by the masters of three of the company's dredges at Dunkirk.

The German archivists matched their British counterparts in patience and helpfulness. Nothing seemed too much trouble, as they tirelessly pulled books and records for my perusal. Heartfelt thanks to the splendid staffs at the Bundesarchiv/Militärarchiv in Freiburg, at the Bibliothek für Zeitgeschichte in Stuttgart, and at the Institut für Zeitgeschichte in Munich. The Bundesarchiv in Koblenz is a treasure house of photographs, and I appreciate the effort here, too, in providing everything I needed.

A writer can always use helpful leads, and fortunately there were any number of knowledgeable people on both sides of the Atlantic willing to point me in the right direction. In England this loyal band included Leo Cooper, David Curling, David Divine, Dick Hough, Peter Kemp, Ronald Lewin, Roger Machell,

Martin Middlebrook, Denis Richards, Stephen Roskill, and Dan Solon. In America there were Dolph Hoehling, Tom Mahoney, Sam Meek, Drew Middleton, Roger Pineau, Ed Schaefer, Jack Seabrook, Bill Stump, and John Toland. Some, like Ronald Lewin and John Toland, took time out from their own books to help me—a sacrifice that perhaps only another writer can truly appreciate.

One bit of unusual generosity deserves separate mention. In 1970 the late Robert Carse wrote *Dunkirk—1940*, an interesting book that made use of many firsthand accounts. Ten years later—to my grateful surprise—Mr. Carse's daughter Jean Mitchell and a family friend, Vice-Admiral Gordon McLintock, USN (Ret.), turned over to me Mr. Carse's notes and correspondence with various Dunkirk participants. Although in the end I did not include any of this material in my book, it served as valuable background and a useful cross-check on my own sources. I deeply appreciate the thoughtfulness of both Mrs. Mitchell and Admiral McLintock.

There remain those who worked directly on the project over the long haul. Marielle Hoffman performed all sorts of heroics as my interpreter/translator in France. Karola Gillich did the same in Germany. I'm also indebted to my friend Roland Hauser, who scanned for me the German press coverage of Dunkirk in 1940 and took on several special research assignments.

In England Caroline Larken excelled in lining up interviews, checking various points, and helping me screen the press. Alexander Peters did useful reconnaissance at the PRO. Susan Chadwick efficiently handled the traffic at Penguin as the accounts poured in. My editor there, Eleo Gordon, constantly performed services above and beyond the call of duty.

In New York Scott Supplee came to town intending to write short-story fiction—and stayed to become the city's greatest authority on British regimental histories. Preston Brooks, whose father did research for me in 1960, carried on the family tradition. His fluent knowledge of French also came in handy at a critical time. Patricia Heestand not only carried out her share of research, but did yeoman work in compiling the List of Contributors and the Index. Colin Dawkins lent his shrewd eye to the selection and arrangement of illustrations. At Viking my editor, Alan Williams, was as patient and perceptive as ever.

Finally, there are those who lived with the book on an almost daily basis. Dorothy Hefferline handled the voluminous correspondence and helped out on all sorts of dire emergencies. The long-suffering Florence Gallagher deserves a medal for completing her 34th year of deciphering my foolscap.

But all these people—helpful as they were—would not have been enough without the cooperation of the participants listed on the following pages. They get no blame for my mistakes, but a full share of the credit for whatever new light is thrown on the events that unfolded at Dunkirk in the memorable spring of 1940.

List of Contributors

The miracle of Dunkirk was largely the achievement of British soldiers, sailors, fliers, and civilians—all working together—so it is fitting that the same combination has made possible this book. All contributors are listed alphabetically, regardless of rank or title. Where supplied, retired rank and honors are indicated.

Each name is followed by the participant's unit or service, to give some idea of vantage point; where appropriate, ship names are also included. In a few cases the participant is no longer living, and his account has been made available by some member of the family. These names are marked by an asterisk.

Lt.-Col. G. S. Abbott, TD, JP—BEF, Royal Artillery, 57th Anti-Tank Regiment
Douglas Ackerley—BEF, The King's Own Scottish Borderers
E. Acklam—BEF, Royal Artillery, 63rd Medium Regiment
L. J. Affleck—BEF, 2nd Division, Signals
Lt.-Cdr. J. L. Aldridge, MBE—HMS *Express*
Andrew Alexander—BEF, GHQ Signals; HMS *Calcutta*
P. D. Allan—BEF, Royal Artillery; HMS *Vimy*

George Allen—BEF
Stanley V. Allen—RN, HMS *Windsor*
H. G. Amphlett—BEF, 14th City of London Royal Fusiliers
Michael Anthony—RNVR, *Aura, Yorkshire Lass*
G. W. Arnold—BEF, Royal Engineers, 573rd Field Squadron
E. W. Arthur—RN, HMS *Calcutta*
Jean Gardiner Ashenhurst—nurse, Royal Victoria Hospital, Folkestone
C. J. Atkinson—RN, HMS *Basilisk*
Thomas Atkinson—BEF, RASC, 159th Welsh Field Ambulance
Mrs. M. Austin—Red Cross nurse, southern England

William H. Bacchus—BEF, RAMC, 13th Field Ambulance
Lt.-Col. L.J.W. Bailey—BEF, Royal Artillery, 1st Heavy Anti-Aircraft Regiment
Alfred Baldwin—BEF, Royal Artillery; *Maid of Orleans*
Brigadier D. W. Bannister—BEF, Royal Artillery, 56th Medium Regiment
R. H. Barlow—BEF, RAOC, 11th Infantry Brigade; HMS *Sandown*
Oliver D. Barnard—BEF, 131st Brigade, Signals; *Dorrien Rose*
A. F. Barnes, MSM—BEF
Douglas Barnes—BEF, Royal Artillery, 1st Heavy Anti-Aircraft Regiment; HMS *Javelin*
S. Barnes—RN, HMS *Widgeon*
A. F. Barnett—BEF
R. Bartlett—personnel ships, detached duty from Royal Artillery, 64th Regiment, *Queen of the Channel*
D. F. Batson—BEF, RASC
R. Batten—BEF, 48th Division, Royal Engineers
F. A. Baxter—BEF, RAOC, No. 2 Ordnance Field Park; *Bullfinch*
H. J. Baxter, BEM—RN, HMS *Sandhurst*
Ernest E. Bayley—BEF, 3rd Division, Signals; HMS *Mosquito*
J. Bayliff—BEF, 2nd Division, RASC; HMS *Mosquito*
C. E. Beard—BEF, RASC; *Bullfinch*
J. Beardsley—BEF, Royal Engineers
L. C. Beech—BEF, 3rd Division, Signals
Basil E. Bellamy, CB—civilian, Ministry of Shipping
R. Bellamy—BEF, Middlesex Regiment

C. N. Bennett—BEF, 5th Northamptonshire Regiment; HMS *Ivanhoe*

Lt.-Col. John S. W. Bennett—Royal Engineers, 250th Field Company

Lt.-Cdr. the Rev. Peter H. E. Bennett—RN, *New Prince of Wales, Triton*, HMS *Mosquito*

Myrette Bennington—WRNS, Naval HQ, Dover

W. S. Berry—civilian, Admiralty, Small Vessels Pool

Herbert V. Betts—Constable, Police War Reserve, Ramsgate

Cdr. Robert Bill, DSO, FRICS, FRGS—RN, Naval HQ, Dover; HMS *Fyldea*

Tom Billson—BEF, RASC; *Royal Daffodil*

R. H. Blackburn—BEF, CMP; *Hird*

L. Blackman—BEF, Royal Artillery, 1st Light Anti-Aircraft Battery

Robert Blamire—BEF, Infantry

R. J. Blencowe—BEF, Royal Artillery

G. Bollington—BEF, RASC, 3rd Division

Capt. L.A.A. Border—BEF, RASC, 44th Division; *Prudential*

George Boston—BEF, 143rd Infantry Brigade

Frank H. Bound—BEF, 2nd Cameronians

D. Bourne—BEF, RASC; HMS *Beatrice*

Eric Bowman—BEF, 7th Green Howards

Cdr. V.A.L. Bradyll-Johnson—RN, Eastern Arm, Dover breakwater

E. P. Brett—BEF, Signals; HMS *Calcutta*

Maj. Anthony V. N. Bridge—BEF, 2nd Dorset Regiment

Viscount Robert Clive Bridgeman, KBE, CB, DSO, MD, JP— GHQ, acting Operations Officer; HMS *Keith, Vivian*

John Bridges—BEF, 1st Grenadier Guards; HMS *Ivanhoe*, HMS *Speedwell*

Maj.-Gen. P.H.W. Brind—BEF, 2nd Dorset Regiment; HMS *Javelin*

W. Brown—RN, HMS *Grenade, Fenella*, HMS *Crested Eagle*

D. A. Buckland—BEF, Royal Artillery, 54th Light Anti-Aircraft Regiment

K. S. Burford—BEF, 1/7th Middlesex Regiment

Frederick J. Burgin—BEF, Royal Engineers

Lord Burnham, JP, DL—BEF, 2nd Division, Royal Artillery; HMS *Worcester*

G. H. Burt—BEF, 2nd Dorset Regiment

Capt. Eric Bush—RN, Adm. Ramsay's staff, Dunkirk beaches; HMS *Hebe*

Charles K. Bushe, SJAB—BEF, Royal Artillery, 52nd Field Regiment

R. G. Butcher—BEF, 1st Division

George H. Butler—BEF, Royal Artillery, 2nd Field Regiment; HMS *Worcester*

Olive M. Butler—civilian, Basingstoke, return of troops

Charles V. Butt—BEF, RASC

Capt. J.S.S. Buxey—BEF, Royal Artillery, 139th Field Regiment; *Lady of Mann*

Maj. Donald F. Callander, MC—BEF, 1st Queen's Own Cameron Highlanders

Lord Cameron, Kt, DSC, LLD, FRSE, HRSA, FRSGS, DI—RNVR, *MTB 107*

Lt.-Col. T.S.A. Campbell—BEF, 3rd Division, Signals

Moran Caplat—RNVR, *Freshwater*

David H. Caple—BEF, RASC, 3rd Division, 23rd Ammunition Company

Maj. B. G. Carew Hunt, MBE, TD—BEF, 1/5th Queen's Royal Regiment

D. C. Carter—BEF, 2nd Division, 208th Field Company; *Fisher Boy*

Robert Carter—BEF, 48th Division, Signals

P. Cavanagh—RN, HMS *Grenade*

P. C. Chambers—BEF, Royal Engineers

Mowbray Chandler—BEF, Royal Artillery, 57th Field Regiment; *Fenella*, HMS *Crested Eagle*

R. Chapman—BEF

Percy H. Charles—BEF, 44th Division, Signals; *Canterbury*

J. Cheek—BEF, RASC, 44th Division; HMS *Sabre*

Lord Chelwood, MC, DL—BEF, 9th Royal Northumberland Fusiliers; HMS *Malcolm*

Col. J.M.T.F. Churchill, DSO, MC—BEF, 2nd Manchester Regiment; HMS *Leda*

J. B. Claridge—BEF, 4th Division, 12th Field Ambulance; HMS *Ivanhoe*

Charles Clark—BEF, 4th Royal Sussex Regiment

E. Clements—RN, HMS *Gossamer*

D. J. Coles—BEF, Royal Engineers, 223rd Field Park Company

Col. J. J. Collins, MC, TD—BEF, GHQ, Signals

Sir John Colville, CB, CVO—Assistant Private Secretary to Winston Churchill

A. Cordery—BEF, RASC; HMS *Icarus*

W. F. Cordrey—BEF, 2nd Royal Warwick Regiment

Henry J. Cornwell—BEF, Royal Engineers, 250th Field Company

*Walter Eric Cotton—BEF, Signals

L.H.T. Court—BEF, 2nd Coldstream Guards

David F. Cowie—BEF, 1st Fife and Forfar Yeomanry

Lt.-Cdr. I.N.D. Cox, DSC—RN, HMS *Malcolm*

F. J. Crampton, RSM—BEF, II Corps, Signals, attached to 51st Heavy Regiment, RA

George Crane—BEF, 12th Royal Lancers

Joyce Crawford-Stuart—VAD Guildford, Surrey

Maj. H. M. Croome—BEF, 5th Division, Field Security

Thomas Henry Cullen—BEF, RAOC, 19th HQ Field Workshops, attached to 1st Division

Frank Curry—BEF, 1st East Lancashire Regiment

R. G. Cutting—BEF, 44th Division, Signals

Maj. F. H. Danielli—BEF, RASC, 3rd GHQ Company

George David Davies—RNR, *Jacinta*, *Thetis*

F. Davis—BEF, Royal Artillery, 4th Heavy Anti-Aircraft

John Dawes—RN, Naval Shore Party; HMS *Wolfhound*

H. Delve—BEF, RASC, II Corps; *Westwood*

Raphael de Sola—civilian, ship's lifeboat

Charles James Dewey—BEF, 4th Royal Sussex Regiment

C.C.H. Diaper—RN, HMS *Sandown*

Harold J. Dibbens—BEF, I Corps, 102nd Provost Company; HMS *Windsor*

Robert Francis Dickman—BEF, 4th Division, Signals; *Ben-My-Chree*

G. W. Dimond—BEF, Royal Artillery, Brigade Anti-Tank Company

A. D. Divine—civilian, *Little Ann*, *White Wing*

K. Dobson—Infantry, Suffolk coast defense

John S. Dodd, TD—BEF, Royal Artillery, 58th Field Regiment; HMS *Sabre*

A. H. Dodge—BEF, Royal Artillery, 13th Anti-Tank Regiment

Harry Donohoe—BEF, 1st Division, Signals

Maj.-Gen. Arthur J. H. Dove—GHQ; HMS *Wolfhound*

James Dow—Royal Naval Medical Service; HMS *Gossamer*, HMS *Mosquito*

James F. Duffy—BEF, Royal Artillery, 52nd Heavy Regiment

F. G. Dukes—BEF, Signals, Division HQ; HMS *Shikari*

Reginald E. Dunstan—BEF, RAMC, 186th Field Ambulance

Col. L. C. East, DSO, OBE—BEF, 1/5th Queen's Royal Regiment

R. G. Eastwell—BEF, 5th Northamptonshire Regiment; HMS *Niger*

G. Edkins—civilian, Surrey, return of troops

R. Edwards—BEF, RASC, ambulance driver

R. Eggerton—BEF; HMS *Esk*

A. L. Eldridge, RMPA, RMH—BEF, 3rd Grenadier Guards

Arthur Elkin, MM—BEF, 3rd Division, Military Police, General Montgomery's bodyguard

A. W. Elliott—civilian, *Warrior*

C. W. Elmer—BEF, 2nd Coldstream Guards

Charles J. Emblin—RN, HMS *Basilisk*

Lt.-Col. H. M. Ervine-Andrews, VC—BEF, 1st East Lancashire Regiment

Alwyne Evans—BEF, 5th Gloucestershire Regiment; hospital carrier *Paris*

Col. H. V. Ewbank—BEF, 50th Division, Signals; HMS *Sutton*

Cdr. R. G. Eyre.—RN *MA/SB 10*

Julian Fane—BEF, 2nd Gloucestershire Regiment

F. R. Farley—BEF, RAOC, 1/7th Middlesex Regiment; HMS *Halcyon*

F. A. Faulkner—BEF, 1st Division, Signals

H. W. Fawkes—BEF, RAOC, electrician

Rosemary Keyes Fellowes—WRNS, Naval HQ, Dover

F. Felstead—BEF, Signals; HMS *Royal Eagle*

John Fernald—civilian, ship's lifeboat
Col. John H. Fielden—BEF, 5th Lancashire Fusiliers
Maj. Geoffrey H. Fisher—BEF, RASC
Rear-Adm. R. L. Fisher, CB, DSO, OBE, DSC—HMS *Wakeful, Comfort, Hird*
*Carl Leonard Fletcher, DSM—RN, HMS *Wolfhound*, HMS *Crested Eagle, Fenella*, HMS *Whitehall*
B.G.W. Flight—BEF, RASC, No. 1 Troop Carrying Company
E. H. Foard, MM—BEF, Royal Engineers, No. 2 Bridge Company, RASC
Capt. R. D. Franks, CBE, DSO, DSC—RN, HMS *Scimitar*
K. G. Fraser—Merchant Navy, *Northern Prince*, London docks
Brig. A. F. Freeman, MC—BEF, Signals, HQ II Corps
W. C. Frost—BEF, RAMC, 1th Casualty Clearing Station
Mrs. D. M. Fugeman—civilian, Wales, return of troops
Ronald Wilfred Furneaux—BEF, 1/5th Queen's Royal Regiment

H. E. Gentry—BEF, Royal Artillery, 32nd Field Regiment; HMS *Malcolm*
Lottie Germain—refugee; *Sutton*
*Maj. J. W. Gibson, MBE—BEF, 2nd East Yorkshire Regiment; HMS *Lord Howe*
Alfred P. Gill—BEF, RASC, 44th Division, 132nd Field Ambulance; *Hird*
Air Marshal Sir Victor Goddard, KCB, CBE, MA—RAF, Air Adviser to Lord Gort
Eric V. Goodbody—RN, Yeoman of Signals, GHQ; HMS *Westward Ho*
Mark Goodfellow—BEF, RASC, 55th West Lancashire Division
Thomas A. Gore Browne—BEF, 1st Grenadier Guards
Bessie Gornall—civilian, London, return of troops
S. E. Gouge—BEF, RASC; HMS *Intrepid*
William Douglas Gough—BEF, Royal Artillery, 1st Medium Regiment
Captain J. R. Gower, DSC—RN, HMS *Albury*
Air Vice-Marshal S. B. Grant, CB, DFC—RAF, 65 Squadron, Hornchurch
Col. J.S.S. Gratton, OBE, DL—BEF, 2nd Hampshire Regiment

D.K.G. Gray—BEF, RAMC, 12th Casualty Clearing Station

A. H. Greenfield—BEF, Royal Artillery, Anti-Tank Regiment

G. A. Griffin—BEF, RASC, driver

E. N. Grimmer—BEF, Royal Engineers, 216th Field Company; HMS *Malcolm*

Bob Hadnett, MM—BEF, 48th Division, Signals, Dispatch Rider

E. A. Haines—BEF, 1st Grenadier Guards; HMS *Speedwell*

David Halton—BEF, 1st Division, Signals

V. Hambly—civilian, Ashford, Kent, return of troops

M. M. Hammond—BEF, RAMC, 1st Field Ambulance

Lt.-Col. C. L. Hanbury, MBE, TD, DL—BEF, Royal Artillery, 99th Field Regiment

E. S. Hannant—BEF, Infantry, Machine-Gunner

W. Harbord—BEF, RASC

George Hare—BEF, I Corps, 102nd Provost Company; HMS *Windsor*

S. Harland—BEF, 2nd Welsh Guards

R. A. Harper—BEF, RAF, Lysander spotter plane, attached to 56th Highland Medium Artillery; HMS *Grafton*

K.E.C. Harrington—BEF, 48th Division, RAMC, 143rd Field Ambulance

E. Harris—BEF, Royal Engineers, 135th Excavator Company; HMS *Calcutta*

F. H. Harris—BEF, 4/7th Royal Dragoons

Leslie F. Harris—BEF, RAMC, 7th Field Ambulance

Tom Harris—BEF, Royal Engineers, I Corps, 13th Field Survey Company; hospital carrier *Paris*

Thomas Collingwood Harris—BEF, RAOC, No. 1 Recovery Section

Ted Harvey—civilian, *Moss Rose*, Cockle Boats, *Letitia*

Jeffrey Haward, MM—BEF, 3rd Division, Machine Gun Battalion

Maj. S. S. Hawes—BEF, RASC, 1st Division; HMS *Grafton*, HMS *Wakeful*

E. A. Hearl—BEF, RAMC, 132nd Field Ambulance

Ernest A. Heming—BEF, RAOC, Field Rank Unit

Oliver Henry—BEF, Infantry, Machine Gun Battalion

Col. J. Henton Wright, OBE, TD, DL—BEF, Royal Artillery, 60th Field Regiment; *Royal Sovereign*

Sam H. Henwood—BEF, 3rd Division, Signals; HMS *Sandown*

Maj. John Heron, MC, TD—BEF, 2nd Dorset Regiment

Thomas Hewson—BEF, RAOC, attached to Field Artillery Unit

Col. Peter R. Hill, OBE, TD—BEF, RAOC, II Corps, 2nd Ordnance Field Park

C.F.R. Hilton, DSC—civilian, *Ryegate II*

Michael Joseph Hodgkinson—BEF, RAOC, 14th Army Field Workshop

William Holden—BEF, 3rd Division, Signals; HMS *Sandown*

Robert Walker Holding—BEF, Royal Sussex Regiment; HMS *Codrington*

F. Hollis—BEF, 7th Green Howards

Brig. A. Eric Holt—BEF, 2nd Manchester Regiment

C. G. Hook—BEF, RASC; *Tynwald*

Alan Hope—BEF, Royal Artillery, 58th Field Regiment

R. Hope—BEF, 2nd Manchester Regiment

Ronald Jeffrey Hopper—BEF, RASC, 50th Division

Richard Hoskins—BEF, RASC, driver

Brig. D.J.B. Houchin, DSO, MC—BEF, 5th Division

H. Howard—BEF, RASC, 4th Division

Jeffrey Howard, MM—BEF, 1/7th Middlesex Regiment

Dennis S. Hudson—RN, signalman, HMS *Scimitar*

Mrs. Pat Hunt—civilian, Portland and Weymouth, return of troops

Gen. Sir Peter Hunt, GCB, DSO, OBE—BEF, 1st Cameron Highlanders

Major Frank V. Hurrell—BEF, RASC

Freddie Hutch—RAF, 4th Army Cooperation Squadron; *Maid of Orleans*

L. S. Hutchinson—BEF, Royal Artillery, Medium Regiment

W. J. Ingham—BEF, Field Security Police; HMS *Sabre*

A. R. Isitt—BEF, 2nd Coldstream Guards; HMS *Vimy*

Byron E. J. Iveson-Watt—BEF, Royal Artillery, 1st Anti-Aircraft Regiment; HMS *Worcester*

A. R. Jabez-Smith—BEF, 1st Queen Victoria's Rifles

Albert John Jackson—Army sergeant attached to HMS *Golden Eagle*

Evelyn Jakes—civilian, return of troops

Maj. H. N. Jarvis, TD—BEF, Royal Artillery, 53rd Medium Regiment

Alec Jay—BEF, 1st Queen Victoria's Rifles

E. Johnson—BEF, Royal Artillery

Walton Ronald William Johnson—RN, HMS *Scimitar*

Gen. Sir Charles Jones, GCB, CBE, MC—BEF, 42nd Division, 127th Brigade

George W. Jones—BEF, 1st Grenadier Guards

Dr. Adrian Kanaar—BEF, RAMC, Field Ambulance; HMS *Calcutta*

R. Kay—BEF, GHQ, Signals

Maj. E. E. Kennington—BEF, Royal Engineers, 203rd Field Park Company; HMS *Wolsey*

Professor W. E. Kershaw, CMG, VRD, MD, DSC-RNVR, HMS *Harvester*

A. P. Kerstin—BEF, RASC, 1st Division

A. King—BEF, III Corps HQ; HMS *Impulsive*

Major H. P. King-Fretts—BEF, 2nd Dorsetshire Regiment

John F. Kingshott—BEF, RAOC, First A.A. Brigade Workshop

F. W. Kitchener—BEF, Royal Artillery

Jack Kitchener—BEF, RASC; *Isle of Gurnsey*

William P. Knight—BEF, Royal Engineers, No. 1 General Base Depot

Arthur Knowles—BEF, 2nd Grenadier Guards, 12th Casualty Clearing Station

George A. Kyle—BEF, 1st Fife and Forfar Yeomanry; *Killarney*

A. E. Lambert—BEF, Royal Artillery, 5th Heavy Regiment

Col. C. R. Lane—BEF, 3rd Division, Signals

Lt.-Col. J. M. Langley—BEF, 2nd Coldstream Guards, 12th Casualty Clearing Station

A. Lavis—BEF, Royal Artillery, Anti-Tank Regiment

George Lawrence—BEF, Middlesex Regiment

John Lawrence—BEF, 42nd Division, 126th Brigade

W. G. Lawrence—BEF, Royal Artillery; HMS *Vivacious*

W. Lawson—RNVR, HMS *Codrington*, LDG Signalman

A. E. Lear—BEF, 2nd North Staffordshire Regiment; HMS *Codrington*

David Learmouth—BEF, RASC, Ammunition Company

Robert Lee—BEF, Royal Artillery, 57th Field Regiment; HMS *Worcester*

Robert W. Lee—BEF, RASC, 44th Division; *Mersey Queen*

T. J. Lee—BEF, 3rd Division, Royal Artillery, 7th Field Regiment; *Isle of Thanet*

Ron Lenthal—civilian, Tough's Boatyard, Teddington

A. E. Lewin—BEF, 2nd Middlesex Regiment

W. C. Lewington—BEF, RASC, 2nd Corps

Cyril Lewis—BEF, Royal Artillery, 139th Anti-Tank Brigade, attached to Northamptonshire Regiment

G. E. Lille—RAF, 264th Fighter Squadron

Thomas H. Lilley—BEF, Royal Engineers, 242nd Field Company

Lt.-Col. S. J. Linden-Kelly, DSO—BEF, 2nd Lancashire Fusiliers; HMS *Shikari*

Maj. A. E. Lindley, RCT—BEF, 11th Infantry Brigade; *Pangbourne*

Margaret Loat—civilian, Warrington, Lancashire, return of troops

Reginald Lockerby, TD, Dip. MA, Inst. M—BEF, RAOC, 2nd Ordnance Field Park; HMS *Venomous*

Frederick Louch—BEF, RAMC, 13th Ambulance Train

S. V. Love—BEF, RAMC, 12th Field Ambulance; *Hird*

R. J. Lovejoy—BEF, RASC, 2nd Buffs

G. E. Lucas—BEF, Royal Artillery, 2nd Anti-Aircraft Battery

D. L. Lumley—BEF, 2nd Northamptonshire Regiment; Motor Torpedo Boat

Air Vice-Marshal Michael D. Lyne, CB, AFC, MBIM, DL—RAF, 19th Fighter Squadron

George M. McClorry, MM—RNR, Whale Island

Ivan McGowan—BEF, 57th Medium Regiment, Royal Artillery; HMS *Express*

Capt. B.D.O. MacIntyre, DSC—RN, HMS *Excellent*

Capt. A. M. McKillop, DSC—RN, Block Ships, *Westcove*

W. McLean—BEF, 1st Queen's Own Cameron Highlanders; *St. Andrew*

A. A. McNair—BEF, Royal Artillery, 5th Division

H. P. Mack—RN, HMS *Gossamer, Comfort*
Brig. P.E.S. Mansergh, OBE—BEF, 3rd Division, Signals
A.N.T. Marjoram—RAF, 220th Bomber Squadron
Frederick William Marlow—BEF, 44th Division, Signals; *Royal Daffodil*
Douglas J. W. Marr—BEF; HMS *Venomous*
R. W. Marsh—BEF, Royal Engineers, 698th General Construction Company
Arthur Marshall—BEF, 2nd Corps, Internal Security Unit
J. W. Martin—RN, HMS *Saladin*
A. J. Maskell—BEF, The Buffs
R. T. Mason—BEF, Signals, attached to 2nd Medium Regiment, Royal Artillery
Lt.-Cdr. W. J. Matthews—RN, Secretary to Commander of Minesweepers, Dover
Arthur May—BEF, Royal Artillery, 3rd Medium Regiment
H. T. May—BEF, 1st Oxfordshire and Buckinghamshire Light Infantry
Pip Megrath—civilian, village near Guildford, return of troops
Kenneth W. Meiklejohn—BEF, Royal Artillery, 58th Field Regiment, and 65th Field Regiment, Chaplain; *Isle of Man*
Capt. D.B.N. Mellis, DSC—RN, HMS *Malcolm*
Harold Meredith—BEF, RASC, with Royal Engineers at Maginot Line
*Syd Metcalfe—BEF, Signals
N. F. Minter—BEF, RAMC, 4th Division, 12th Field Ambulance
Wilfrid L. Miron—BEF, 9th Sherwood Foresters
E. Montague—civilian, return of troops
Philip Moore—BEF, RASC, 50th Division, 11th Troop Carrying Company
Maj. S. T. Moore, TD—BEF, RASC, attached to 32nd Field Regiment; HMS *Oriole*, HMS *Lord Collingwood*
R. W. Morford—Merchant Navy, captain of *Hythe*
T. J. Morgan—civilian, *Gallions Reach*
Maj.-Gen. James L. Moulton, CB, DSO, OBE—Royal Marines, Staff officer, GHQ
W. Murphy—civilian, Dover, return of troops
R. A. Murray Scott, MD—BEF, RAMC, 1st Field Ambulance, 1st Guards Brigade

Arthur Myers—BEF, RASC, Mobile Workshop

F. Myers—BEF, Royal Artillery, attached to 2nd Grenadier Guards

Lt.-Col. E. R. Nanney Wynn—BEF, 3rd Division, Signals; HMS *Sandown*

John W. Neeves—RN, HMS *Calcutta*

Eddie Newbould—BEF, 1st King's Own Scottish Borderers

Philip Newman, MD—BEF, RAMC, 12th Casualty Clearing Station

R. Nicholson—BEF, GDSM Company Runner

G. F. Nixon—RN, naval shore party; *Lord Southborough*

F. Noon—BEF, Royal Artillery, 53rd Field Regiment, 126th Brigade; HMS *Whitshed*

W.C.P. Nye—BEF, 4th Royal Sussex Regiment

W. Oakes—BEF, 7th Cheshire Regiment

W. H. Osborne, C.Eng., FRI, NA—civilian, William Osborne Ltd., boatyard, Littlehampton

George Paddon—BEF, 2nd Dorset Regiment; HMS *Anthony*

Leslie R. Page—BEF, RAOC, 44th Division

T. Page—BEF, RASC, II Corps

Mary Palmer—civilian, Ramsgate, return of troops

James V. Parker—RN, 2nd Chatham Naval Barracks, beaches; HMS *Grenade*

Maj. C. G. Payne—BEF, Royal Artillery, 69th Medium Regiment; *Tynwald*

Thomas F. Payne—BEF, 4th Royal Sussex Regiment; HMS *Medway Queen*

Grace Pearson—civilian, GPO, Bournemouth, return of troops

L. A. Pell—BEF, Royal Engineers

Rear-Adm. Pelly, CB, DSO—RN, HMS *Windsor*

N. J. Pemberton—BEF, 2nd Middlesex Regiment

Brig. G.W.H. Peters—BEF, 2nd Bedfordshire and Hertfordshire Regiment

Pamela Phillimore—WRNS, naval headquarters, Dover

Lt.-Col. John W. Place—BEF, 2nd North Staffordshire Regiment

H. Playford—civilian, Naval Store House of H. M. Dockyard, Sheerness

T. J. Port—RN, HMS *Anthony*

F. J. Potticary—BEF, 1st/5th Queen's Royal Regiment; *Royal Daffodil*

J. W. Poulton—BEF, Royal Artillery, 65th Heavy Anti-Aircraft Regiment

Lt.-Cdr. H. B. Poustie, DSC—RN, HMS *Keith, St. Abbs*

Stan Priest—BEF, RAMC, III Corps; *Mona's Isle*

Kathleen M. Prince—civilian, Bournemouth, return of troops

David W. Pugh, DSO, MD, FRCP—RNVR, HMS *Whitshed*, HMS *Hebe*

M. F. Purdy—civilian, London, return of troops

Edgar G. A. Rabbets—BEF, 5th Northamptonshire Regiment

Mrs. R. L. Raft—civilian, Ramsgate, return of troops

Maj. I.F.R. Ramsay—BEF, 2nd Dorset Regiment

R.R.C. Rankin—BEF, GHQ, Signals

Maj.-Gen. R. St. G. T. Ransome, CB, CBE, MC—BEF, I Corps HQ

Col. M. A. Rea, OBE, MB—BEF, RAMC, Embarkation Medical Officer

Eric Reader—BEF, Royal Engineers, 293rd Field Park Company, III Corps; HMS *Brighton Belle*, HMS *Gracie Fields*

Edith A. Reed—ATS, BEF, GHQ, 2nd Echelon, Margate

James Reeves—BEF, 2nd Essex Regiment

A. G. Rennie—BEF, Royal Artillery, 140th Army Field Regiment; *Côte d'Argent*

Walter G. Richards—BEF, RASC, No. 2 L of C Railhead Company, based at Albert (Somme)

Gen. Sir Charles Richardson, GCB, CBE, DSO—BEF, 4th Division, Deputy Assistant Quartermaster General

D. G. Riddall—BEF, Royal Artillery, Heavy Anti-Aircraft Regiment

C. A. Riley—BEF, Royal Engineers; HMS *Codrington*

H. J. Risbridger—BEF, RASC; HMS *Icarus*

George A. Robb—RN, *Isle of Thanet*

Kenneth Roberts—BEF, RAMC, 141st Field Ambulance; HMS *Worcester*

W. Roberts, MM—BEF, 1st East Lancashire Regiment

Maj. R. C. Robinson—BEF, Royal Artillery, 85th Heavy Anti-Aircraft Regiment

H. Rogers—BEF, Royal Artillery, Signals

Alfred Rose—BEF, Royal Artillery, 63rd Medium Regiment

Capt. Stephen Roskill—RN, Dynamo Room, Dover

Tom Roslyn—BEF

P. H. Rowley—BEF, 4th Division, Signals

R. L. Rylands—BEF, HQ 12th Infantry Brigade

F. C. Sage—BEF, RASC, I Corps, Petrol Company

E. A. Salisbury—BEF, 4th Division, Signals

Dr. Ian Samuel, OBE—BEF, RAMC, 6th Field Ambulance

A. D. Saunders, BEM—RN, HMS *Jaguar*

Frank Saville—BEF, 2nd Cameronians

Maj. Ronald G. H. Savory—RASC, Ramsgate, Dunkirk beaches; *Foremost 101*

W.J.U. Sayers—BEF, Royal Sussex Regiment; HMS *Wolsey*

E.A.G. Scott—BEF, Royal Engineers

Guy Scoular, OBE, MBChB, DPH—BEF, RAMC, 2nd North Staffordshire Regiment; HMS *Codrington*

Maj. M.C.P. Scratchley—BEF, RAOC, 3rd Army Field Workshop

Lt.-Col. W. H. Scriven—BEF, RAMC; HMS *Shikari*

Robert Seviour—BEF, 2nd Dorset Regiment

Herbert G. Sexon—BEF, RAOC, 1st East Surrey Regiment

R. Shattock—BEF, Royal Artillery, 32nd Field Regiment

Reginald B. Short—BEF, Royal Artillery, 57th Field Regiment

Leslie R. Sidwell—civilian, Cotswolds, return of troops

A. E. Sleight—BEF, Royal Artillery, 60th Army Field Regiment; HMS *Salamander*

Maj. A. D. Slyfield, MSM—BEF, Royal Artillery, 20th Anti-Tank Regiment; *Hythe*

*B. Smales—BEF, headquarters clerk, Signals

Douglas H. Smith—BEF, 5th Northamptomshire Regiment

Evan T. Smith—BEF, RASC; HMS *Jaguar*

Leslie M. Smith—BEF, Royal Artillery, 58th Field Regiment; *Beagle*

Capt. George G. H. Snelgar—BEF, RASC, motor transport company

Col. D. C. Snowdon, TD—BEF, 1st Queen's Royal Regiment; *Mona's Isle*

Mrs. Gwen Sorrill—Red Cross nurse, Birmingham, return of troops

Christopher D. South—BEF, Hopkinson British Military Mission, Belgium; HMS *Worcester*

E. J. Spinks—BEF, Royal Artillery, gunner

H. Spinks—BEF, 1st King's Own Scottish Borderers

James Spirritt—BEF, RASC, 4th Division; HMS *Abel Tasman*

Kenneth Spraggs—BEF, Royal Artillery, 92nd Field Regiment

Raie Springate—civilian, Ramsgate; *Fervant*

J. S. Stacey—RNR, HMS *Brighton Belle*

John W. Stacey—BEF, Signals, No. 1 HQ Signals; HMS *Javelin*

A. Staines—RN, HMS *Hebe*

Wing Commander Robert Stanford-Tuck, DSO, DFC—RAF, 92nd Fighter Squadron

Jeanne Michez Stanley—French civilian married to BEF S/Sgt. Gordon Stanley

R. J. Stephens—BEF, Royal Artillery, 2nd Searchlight Regiment

Charles Stewart—BEF, Royal Engineers, 209th Field Company

Rowland Stimpson—civilian, Burgess Hill, return of troops

G. S. Stone—RAF, Lysander spotter plane

W. Stone—BEF, 5th Royal Sussex Regiment

H. W. Stowell, DSC, VRD—RNVR, HMS *Wolfhound*

William Stratton—BEF, RASC, troop carrier; HMS *Harvester*

Samuel Sugar—BEF, RASC, 50th Division; HMS *Grafton*

F. Summers—French Navy, *St. Cyr*; Dunkirk itself

Mrs. E. J. Sumner—civilian, Kent, return of troops

S. Sumner—BEF, Royal Fusiliers

Lt.-Col. G. S. Sutcliff, OBE, TD—BEF, 46th Division, 139th Brigade; HMS *Windsor*

John Tandy—BEF, 1st Grenadier Guards

John Tarry—Merchant Navy, *Lady Southborough*

Lt.-Cdr. Arthur C. Taylor, MM, Chevalier de l'Or—RNR, Calais

Billy Taylor—BEF, Royal Artillery, Heavy Anti-Aircraft

Gordon A. Taylor—BEF, RASC, 1st Division

L. Taylor—civilian, Local Defence Volunteer Force, Isle of Sheppey

Maj. R. C. Taylor—BEF, 1st East Surrey Regiment, Signals; *St. Andrew*

James E. Taziker—BEF, Royal Artillery, 42nd Division

Col. N.B.C. Teacher, MC—BEF, Royal Artillery, 5th Regiment Royal Horse Artillery

A. H. Tebby—BEF, 1st King's Shropshire Light Infantry

Dora Thorn—civilian, Margate, return of troops

J. P. Theobald—BEF, Royal Artillery, 58th Medium Regiment

Syd Thomas—BEF, I Corp, 102nd Provost Company

S. V. Holmes Thompson—BEF, Royal Artillery, 3rd Searchlight Regiment; *Queen of the Channel*

D. Thorogood—BEF, 2nd Coldstream Guards

W. H. Thorpe—RNR, HMS *Calvi*

H. S. Thuillier, DSO—BEF, Royal Artillery, 1st Anti-Aircraft Regiment; HMS *Shikari*

F. Tidey—BEF, 2nd Royal Norfolk Regiment

S. V. Titchener—BEF, RASC

Col. Robert P. Tong—BEF, Staff officer, GHQ

C. W. Trowbridge—BEF, Royal Artillery, 1st Medium Regiment

Joseph Tyldesley—BEF, RASC, attached to No. 2 Artillery Company GHQ

Derek Guy Vardy—BEF, Royal Artillery; HMS *Dundalk*

W. R. Voysey—BEF, 3rd Division, Signals

Maj.-Gen. D.A.L. Wade—BEF, GHQ Signals

C. Wagstaff—BEF, Royal Artillery, searchlight detachment

Dr. David M. Walker—BEF, RAMC, 102nd Casualty Clearing Station; *Prague*

George Walker—RN, HMS *Havant*

William S. Walker—BEF, Royal Artillery, 5th Medium Regiment

Fred E. Walter—BEF, 1st Queen Victoria's Rifles

Rupert Warburton—BEF, 48th Division, Provost Company

Alwyn Ward—BEF, RAOC, 9th Army Field Workshop

W. J. Warner—BEF, Royal Artillery, 60th Heavy Anti-Aircraft Regiment

Noel Watkin—BEF, Royal Artillery, 67th Field Regiment; *Prague*

J. T. Watson—BEF, RAMC, General Hospital No. 6

Maj. Alan G. Watts—BEF, 2nd Dorset Regiment

Capt. O. M. Watts—civilian, London, recruiting for Little Ships

E. C. Webb—BEF, Royal Artillery, 99th Field Regiment; HMS *Vrede*, HMS *Winchelsea*

S. G. Webb—BEF, Royal Artillery, 52nd Anti-Tank Regiment

Frank S. Westley—BEF, Signals

F.G.A. Weston—BEF, RASC; *Maid of Orleans*

George White—BEF, 7th Green Howards

Sir Meredith Whittaker—BEF, 5th Green Howards

H. Whitton—BEF, 4th Division, Signals

Miss G. E. Williams—nursing sister, hospital ship *St. David*

Maj. G. L. Williams—BEF, 3rd Division, 8th Field Ambulance

S/Sgt. W. G. Williams—BEF, RASC, 44th Division

Maj. Gordon D. Wilmot—BEF, 2nd Royal Scottish Fusiliers

George T. Wilson—BEF, King's Own Royal Regiment

S. J. Wilson—BEF, Royal Engineers

Brigadier R. C. Windsor Clive—BEF, 2nd Coldstream Guards

C. E. Wingfield—BEF, 3rd Division, Royal Engineers

Mrs. F.A.M. Wood—Public Health Nurse, Bournemouth, return of troops

C. Woodford—BEF, Infantry, The Buffs; HMS *Whitehall*

G. N. Woodhams, TD—BEF, Royal Artillery, Anti-Aircraft

N. D. Woolland—BEF, Royal Engineers

Frank Woolliscroft—BEF, RASC, 42nd Division

E. S. Wright, MM—BEF, 42nd W/T Section, Signals

Percy H. Yorke—BEF, RAMC, 149th Field Ambulance; HMS *Princess Elizabeth*

Robert M. Zakovitch—BEF, French interpreter, attached to 4th Brigade

Index